The Writer as Critic

The Writer as Critic

Essays in Literature, History and Culture

Jasbir Jain

RAWAT PUBLICATIONS
Jaipur • New Delhi • Bangalore • Hyderabad • Guwahati

ISBN 978-81-316-0417-5

Published by
Prem Rawat for **Rawat Publications**
Satyam Apts, Sector 3, Jawahar Nagar, Jaipur 302 004 (India)
Phone: 0141 265 1748 / 7006 Fax: 0141 265 1748
E-mail: info@rawatbooks.com
Website: www.rawatbooks.com

New Delhi Office
4858/24, Ansari Road, Daryaganj, New Delhi 110 002
Phone: 011 2326 3290

Also at *Bangalore, Hyderabad* and *Guwahati*

Typeset by Rawat Computers, Jaipur
Printed at Chaman Enterprises, New Delhi

in homage to

Meenakshi Mukerjee

Contents

Preface

The present collection has been a long time in the making, but now that it is together, it is a dream realised. For it has its origins in a deep-rooted conviction that we need to know our histories and understand the role of intellectuals in their various encounters with the three-pronged world—of creativity, socio-political pressures and the conflicts between the past and the present. It would be an unforgiveable arrogance to presume that the Bengal Renaissance says it all, or that we have been a passive and docile nation, or that literature today has worked only with western concepts. The debates of the intellectual world are important in the shaping of ideas and many of these writers have been intensely immersed in the debates of their times.

Any collection attempting to work across languages in the manner this has done involves at least a three-tier process—collection, selection and translation. It also raises issues of language, region and the nature of representation. Each process is challenging in its own way. And choices are at times guided by aesthetic aspects, difference (in order to avoid repeated discussions on the same issue), chronology (enabling travel through history) and the balance between the visible and the invisible. Another important question to address was—how and where did these ideas make a mark? At what point did they contribute to the stream of ideas and shift in genre formation and aesthetic values? And more significantly than all else, how do they reflect on the creative processes and their difference from the west?

I must confess that space has also been a consideration. I had to leave out a big section of Bankim Chandra's essay, which is long and detailed. The only satisfaction is that the interested reader will find his way to it. There is no representation from some languages and regions like Tamil Nadu and Punjab—I apologise for these omissions. But it was simply not possible to include work from every language and region. I was sorely tempted to include Bhartendu Harishchandra—not one of his essays, but his short play, *Andher Nagri Chaupat Raja*, which is a significant representation of political critiquing through what amounts to a farce. But I had to resist it. Forgive my sharing the difficulties of the choices I had to make. Perhaps you can forecast in this the birth of another book. Covering more than a century and a half, the essays gently nudge the scholar to engage with the issues and recognise their flow into theory and their place in the history of ideas. Amongst the several issues that are evident in these essays it is their dominant concern with the creative process. It is towards this end that the discussions on language, freedom of expression, confrontations with the socio-political situation and the nature of reality are motivated. As one reads them, one realises that they enter into philosophical debates on the concepts of life and death and time and space.

***

This work would not have been possible if the writers had not been generous enough to grant me permission to use their work. I am grateful to them for this. U.R. Ananthamurthy, Rā Gă Jādhăv, Sitakant Mahapatra, Jayanta Mahapatra, Mridula Garg—all of them. Gagan Gill graciously gave permission for both translating and including the essay by Nirmal Verma and the Vatsal Nidhi extended this permission for the inclusion of Agyeya's essays. Letters to the heirs/publishers of Ismat Chughtai, Mohan Rakesh, Jainendra Kumar Jain and Gopalkrishna Adiga have received no response. I shall be happy to apply to them in case I succeed in contacting them.

My main source of support for bringing this book to realisation has been my friend, Prof. Asaddudin, a well-known translator, who willingly took out time from his own work to translate Hali's work for this collection. And he volunteered to write the introductory note on the writer and his work, bringing his learning and reading into it. And my sister, Dr Tripti Jain, who, as you go along, you'll see has translated the essays of Rabindranath Tagore, Premchand, Sarat Chandra Chatterjee, Jainendra Kumar Jain, Nirmal Verma, Gajanan Madhav Muktibodh, Ismat Chughtai, Agyeya, Mohan Rakesh and Rahi Masoom Raza. At one glance, you can see her tremendous contribution to this volume. She has done it with great sensitivity to the idiom and the literary concepts. I cannot thank the translators enough for the help and friendship they have extended to me. All this goes to prove that learning is teamwork. I also need to thank Shobha Shinde, who helped me trace Rā Gă Jādhăv's address. I have retained the spellings used by the authors themselves where their names are concerned and a similar practice has been followed where names of magazines, journals and places are concerned, so as not to introduce differences from the original. The essays need, first of all, to be located at the point of their origin and reproductions are committed to ensuring this.

I hope this volume is successful in provoking fresh thought on Indian literary traditions and enabling fresh assessment of our critical concepts.

Jasbir Jain

Introduction

The association between creativity, criticism and the intellectual history of a country is deep, often invisible, but always valuable. We have very few attempts made at any kind of such tracing except the interpretations based on creative writing. This is so because, partly, we have tended to evaluate the past primarily through western lens, overcome as we have been by western influences and evaluations. But alongside creative writing—novels, poems and plays—there were a large number of debates engaged in by these writers on other fronts and other platforms and not all of them were political. Some of these were controversies that had blown up on aesthetics, moral issues, the nature of reality and that of the literary form, each reflecting on the nature of representation.

Several writers were seized by the question of language and its relationship to literary expression. Deeply conscious of the need to communicate with their countrymen, they felt writing in English to be increasingly a barrier. Many were bilingual or even trilingual and wrote in more than one language, at times even resorting to bilinguality within a work as both Jotirao Phule and Goverdhanram Tripathi have done. The writing in English was largely motivated by the need to communicate with the English rulers. The traffic of ideas was similarly not unidirectional. It was often oppositional and questioning as well as a movement working horizontally through translations from one language to another. Again there were many translations from one language into another. Bankim Chandra Chatterjee's novels were translated into several other Indian languages. Writers travelled and spoke on public platforms, exchanged ideas and either founded or edited journals.

One needs to ask seriously where all this exchange of ideas and generation of debate has gone? Have we absorbed them or erased them from our memory? It is not that these debates took place only toward the last two decades of the nineteenth century. Derozio and his Hindu College students were active in the 1820s. Almost every leading intellectual was in some measure a social reformer despite employment in government service or other institutions. Yet they managed to combine their two concerns of livelihood and resistance to oppression in fair measure. The struggle was three-pronged. It was not only us and the west, but also the different social hierarchies, the differences of ideology and divisions within the country that surfaced and needed to be addressed. In all this turbulence, there was a vitality and a concern for larger long term issues.

Henry Derozio, remembered as the first poet in Indian English poetry, was of Portuguese descent and conscious of his minority status. At that time, the British policies towards people of mixed blood were discriminatory. They were placed outside British law and were not eligible even for those government jobs for which other educated Indians were eligible. Debates, discussions and pamphleteering to change this situation began on a serious footing in the 1820s. Similarly, Jotiba Phule represents another marginal section. The concerns of both these writers are differently constructed, but both refer to the British rule. While Derozio, critical and apprehensive, is of the opinion that its perhaps only advantage would be the dissemination of knowledge, Phule vests his hope in it for freedom from Brahmanical tyranny, though even he complains that much provision does not exist for educating the lower castes. This internal conflict and its long history needs to be recognised not merely to trace the history/ies of Dalit concerns, writing and resistance and formation of their positions from Phule to Kancha Illiah via Ambedkar, the man who was a member of the Constituent Assembly, but also to understand the nature of caste oppression and the long term seething discontentment that divided the struggle for freedom. These two writers fall into the tradition of minority discourse.

Reading writers by locating them in their times, while at the same time, placing them in the chronicity of literary movements and aesthetic shifts allows us to see the hidden layers of our past. Neither languages nor sensibilities are a matter of indifference to culture or to a work of literature. They are intimately woven together. Our writers have time and again addressed these issues from several different perspectives—as communication with one's readership, in relationship to myth and idiom, as a reflection of the world of nature outside, as an expression of the values fostered and nurtured by tradition, and as a means of self-respect and dignity. They have looked upon culture as an inheritance with immense possibilities. While Bhartendu Harishchandra located his ideas specifically in the national scenario in his focus on language and nation, Bankim Chandra Chatterjee, O. Chandu Menon and Goverdhanram Tripathi were conscious of their responsibility of reaching the public in the languages of their regions. The issue of language remained alive even at a later point of time. We have Nirmal Verma deliberating on its significance where national pride and identity are concerned and both Ismat Chughtai and Mridula Garg, victims alike of social censure and censorship though several years apart, work with the quirks and the hidden powers of language. Chughtai playfully exposes its strength for ambiguity, while Garg examines it as a powerful medium that establishes boundaries for expression, resulting in gender discrimination and stifling original creative voices.

Similarly, India's concern for translation has a history of its own. It has been forced to look upon it as a national necessity by the fact of its multilingualism. But what is amazing is that translations have been freely made even without any central body to govern and direct the enterprise. Parallel to the bilingualism of writers are three other significant aspects of this phenomenon—the retellings and adaptations, the absorption of folk forms and the realisation of the pull of the receiving culture. It is this openness that has accommodated and given birth to languages that meet in new formations—like Hindustani. Language was not only words and their literal meaning, but a container and moulder of a whole cultural ethos. As such it flowed parallel to the shifts in the socio-political ethos. But with a translated text from a different culture the situation is somewhat different, it stirs up the intellectual atmosphere of the receiving society. The western influence which seeped in through the reading of its texts thus became both a point of debate and an issue to be addressed through creative experiments. It is not for nothing that the English have themselves often been critical of their own insularity and reluctantly yielded to an interaction with other European literatures.

Altaf Husain Hali's work of literary history, *Muqaddama She'r O Shairi,* reflects several of these issues related to language. Caught between a Persian past and the western onslaught, Hali found his own attitudes changing from unconditional admiration for his inheritance to openness to new forms, ideas and sensibilities. But moving slightly away from the Wordsworthian emphasis on emotion recollected in tranquillity, he reinforces the essential reflection of truth. It is obvious that the word *'asliyat'* carries within it certain ambiguities. It can be interpreted as 'real' at one level and as 'moral truth' at another. It is not merely self-referential and is much more than the poet's truth or felt emotions or his sincerity alone—it extends its meanings to the notion of moral truth, too. Words, for Hali, should be natural and of common speech so as not to create any distance between the poet and his audience. But what is more important than the filtering of Wordsworthian influence into his formation as a poet and his critiquing of the Persian tradition (very different from Ghalib, whose writing in its early stages was solely in Persian) is Hali's recognition of the need to respond to social change. His argument is for a living relationship with society and for a move away from purely romantic lyricism. The extract selected for this anthology projects a comprehensive view of the main issues besetting the Indian poet. It reflects a concern both with society and with language. But it is his concern for the real that is shared by Bankim Chandra, Chandu Menon and others, for Indian tradition was besieged by idealism and the pursuit of perfection.

The writers now had begun to view a new role for the intellectual, that is, themselves.

But when the nature of the real or of reality becomes a concern, it amounts to more than a debate of social issues. Somewhere along the line, the individual, his sense of identity or of alienation, and his desires as well as his romantic relationships clash with conventional frameworks. If hierarchical structures are to be challenged, then it follows that issues of morality will be debated. While Premchand directed his ideas to an involvement with the freedom movement and rural reform, conflicts between social causes and personal desire for wealth and the temptations of urbanisation, Sarat Chandra moved in a somewhat different direction. He placed the individual at the centre of his fictional world. And though some of his heroes were revolutionaries, his attention was equally given to his heroines, who are women with minds of their own. The web of personal relationships is intensely woven, and as the weaving takes place, several social conventions of social hierarchy, of family structures or role models, of marriage and of individual freedom within marriage, of love falling outside the norms and conventions of the social code are the issues that are examined and are the concerns of his major novels.

Premchand's Presidential Address, delivered to the Progressive Writers' Association in 1936, is in itself a manifesto for the new realism and a review of his own practices as a writer. There is a marked movement away from fantasy, make-belief and supernaturalism towards truth and reality—a direct bond between the word, the writer and the people. In brief, an integrated art form that appeals directly to both—intellect as well as emotion. Marking a shift from the religious traditions of withdrawal, asceticism and spiritual meditation, it shows a perceptible move towards art forms more firmly located in everyday reality. In his own work, in the context of gender, this is marked by the difference between the heroine of *Sewa Sadan*, an early novel, who has to withdraw into an ashram, and *Nirmala*, in which a young second wife is caught up in the demands of conflicting desire. Tagore, in one of his early novels known under various different titles as *Binodini*, *Aankh ki Kirkiri* and *Chokker*

Bali (The Mote in the Eye), explored the relationship of a married man with a young widow, who, after her own initial attraction, allows social morality to get the better of her.

Sarat Chandra, however, approached the subject of love, desire and sexuality at an entirely different level. He was sensitive to both men and women; any of the two could be in a situation of conflict. And behavioural norms in the eyes of society were also equally important. A man too could be labelled characterless (*Charitraheen*). Further, his women characters, once they give up their passivity, are prepared to go the whole way—lead life as a single woman, sustain a relationship outside marriage, take up a job, at times travel and, as long as they are convinced of their own moral correctness and their sense of personal dignity is not violated, even ignore social opinion. It was but natural that Sarat Chandra was involved in several controversies regarding moral values and definitions of good and bad. The essay in the present collection is in response to some of this criticism and addresses the controversy around Tagore's essay, "Sahitya Dharma", and Naresh Chandra Sengupta's response to it.

Caught between the poet Tagore on the one hand and Naresh Chandra, a lawyer, on the other, Sarat Chandra claims his right to consider morality as a contextual and a relative term, demanding a degree of freedom for personal choice and judgement. At one level, it is the nature of realism that is questioned, at another, it is the influence that literature is expected to have on society that is debated. A hidden polarity between Tagore and Naresh Chandra is the degree of rootedness that each has in the urban middle class milieu of his times. The contents of neither poetry nor fiction can be laid down according to any prescribed formula. Apparently, Sarat Chandra seeks to claim a fluid position, a non-judgemental one, but at heart, he knows that the content in literature needs to relate to its literariness—not through facts, but through psychological truths. Mindsets may be either scientific or non-scientific, but literature is neither the medium for an unnegotiated scientific fact, nor the place for an isolated distant fantasy far removed from human emotions. It is also not meant to be suffused with sentimentality and melodrama. Far removed from didacticism it can, through its location in real life conflicts, rigorously debate moral issues.

It is possible to trace a similar concern for realism in Mohan Rakesh's essay. He brings in an additional category to act as a link between the real and the ideal—the quality of imagination. With reference to Sarat Chandra and Agyeya's (also spelt as Ajneya) fiction, he distinguishes between literariness and non-literariness by referring to the reader's emotional response. It is language with its subtlety and suggestiveness, which, along with the quality of imagination, transforms non-literary philosophy into literature. Rakesh is critical of an unmediated use of ideology, philosophy and political concerns. On these counts, he finds Premchand, Jainendra Kumar and Agyeya all equally guilty. Premchand's realism is excessively inspired by idealism, Jainendra Kumar's work is dominantly placed within an intellectual mode and there are excessive inputs of abstract philosophy in Agyeya's novels. For writing to be real, it has to have characters that are lifelike, located in their situations and locales and the events integrated into their lives.

These discussions on the nature of realism move freely between eastern and western examples, assuming a certain traffic of ideas across cultures and a degree of familiarity amongst its audience. They also go on to prove beyond doubt the presumptuousness of the criticism that is frequently levied at Indian literature as being dominantly governed by realism. This is often said by many critics even with reference to many contemporary writers, because they continue to persist in interpreting realism in Marxist terminology—as socio-economic presentation and analysis—rather than an imaginative projection of psychological reality heavily layered with implied meaning. This kind of criticism does not delve deep into the way realism and the real have been interpreted in culture and literature. The shift from an anchoring in abstract spiritualism and an ascetic withdrawal to a full-fledged involvement in matters of the heart and the mind and the lived experiences of the world is clear. But this shift has been slow and painful as habits of the mind are difficult to change. And writers like Goverdhanram Tripathi, overtaken by a spirit of earnestness, get caught between their desire to reform, to send across a message and the demands of the novelistic discourse.

Jainendra Kumar Jain's essay also is a comment on the realistic content of literature, which is no longer concerned with 'flattering' society and is instead motivated to critique it, reflect its distortions of goodness and thus compel it to move forward. No longer does it indulge in merely presenting role models, but with the ways of looking for solutions. In fact, Jain admires the revolutionary spirit it invokes and the acceptability of the rebel and the outcast as a writer. Personal suffering has given them both strength and vision. Jain also explores the impact of the market forces as well as the role of power structures. For him the writer who is worthy as a writer is the one who resists them and marks his own path.

In quite a different category is Ismat Chughtai's essay—playful, defiant, autobiographical, innocent and daring, all at once. It is an account of her response to an act of social censorship, which led to a law case against her on the grounds of obscenity. The account also points to the ambiguities of language and the suggestiveness it can hold. The conclusion of this episode is not contained in the trial, but in the recording of her second meeting with the real-life character who was the subject of her story "*Lihaaf*", and that woman's delight at having been pushed out of her docility by Ismat's story to the extent of walking out of her marriage. All at once, it becomes a comment on marriage, nature of sexuality, of freedom and reciprocal relationships, as well as the support structure Ismat was able to draw from her husband in this public enactment of personal courage.

The two extracts from Rahi Masoom Raza's *Aadha Gaon* are interconnected in memory and thought. They happen to be from a fictional work laced with autobiography. They introduce two modern concepts, especially relevant to the discourses of dislocation and migration. These are the sense of belonging and the significance of location/space—ideas that have now germinated into full-fledged theoretical concepts.

But even as we move forward in history, we are not done with the past. Sitakant Mahapatra analyses in depth the idea of tradition and its multiple manifestations at the end of the twentieth century. Mahapatra is conscious of the need to depend on anthropological perceptions in order to reassess our pasts, including the colonial period. The two concepts he proceeds to examine are time and death, in both of which the Indian approach is very different from that of the west. Preoccupied with existence and eternity, history has had only a secondary importance. India has myths that work simultaneously with expanses of time in different contexts with gods and sages and are closely interwoven into memory. The boundaries between different worlds are, or at least were, almost non-existent, fluid and fluctuating. Time thus runs its own course, indifferent to historical happenings, as layers and layers of the past overlay each other. Death similarly is viewed as a new beginning. It signifies a change, not an end. After expounding on these existential concepts, Sitakant Mahapatra moves on to the constant to and fro between the cultures and arts of different sections of society—classical, folk, rural, peripatetic and indigenous. Rich in its perceptions of Indian cultures, the essay is an historical account that provokes us to look at the shifts more carefully.

A constant re-viewing of the past becomes important when earlier accounts seem to be either incomplete or exaggerated versions overshadowing the undercurrents and ignoring the side-effects. Gopalkrishna Adiga's essay, like Mahapatra's, is also such a looking back. Adiga's belief is that the nineteenth century Renaissance was incomplete and partial. European parallels do not work in the Indian context. In India, the Renaissance did not affect all aspects of forms of art and failed to establish a dialogue between them. Again, it lacked the concept of the total artist. By being limited to the educated aristocracy and the upper layers of society, it failed to reach the common man. It was also overpowered by its encounter with the west. In self-defence, writers turned to images of the glorious past and India's wealth of spiritualism, thus bypassing the claims of the present. A true renaissance needs to be more sweeping in its totality as well as in its reach.

Writer after writer turns to culture and tradition or language and nation. This constant re-examination of essential issues of identity is not without cause. Its significance lies in the fact that the reviewing is never the same and the location of the writer is also not always contemporary. As different writers discuss them, the shifts in time and perspective become abundantly clear as well as the fluidity that the above-named four categories reflect. Nirmal Verma goes on to examine the ways in which cultural pasts resist dismissal as well as being frozen in time or confined to museums. Verma explores culture's internal pasts, its location in myth, memory and language. As our intellectual thoughts are deeply rooted in language, the attempt to transfer them to another language does end up influencing them imperceptibly. Suddenly language becomes a controlling force. Whereas the thoughts articulated in one's own language have the power to stir the native imagination and inspire the people to consolidate their sense of national identity, a foreign language carries within it an underlying consciousness of its different cultural audience. Verma takes up several European thinkers, enters into philosophical discussions, offers substantiated evidence in favour of his arguments, and debates the periodisation put forward by Agyeya amongst others. Naturally, the inner framework is located in Hindi, but the outer circles expand to take in the whole country, its historical and cultural pasts and address several European thinkers of the nineteenth and twentieth centuries.

Agyeya's own essay, "Memory and Time", is simultaneously concerned with several things: memory, different concepts of time and different calendars. Placing them in the right perspective, he questions the time-lag theory, which places the west ahead of all others, anchoring its reference in the Gregorian calendar and in the development of scientific knowledge. If we use the Samvat era, then we are ahead by more than half a century, and if we cast off the western definitions of both knowledge and history, the difference between *itihaas* and *mithihaas* is not that wide. One is what is said to have happened, but eyewitness records of the distant past do not exist and the accounts have their own share of speculation; the other is believed to have happened and been absorbed through a continuity of oral traditions. Perspectives often make all the difference to what is or is not history. They tend to be selective, but once used, end up defining knowledge accordingly. Agyeya's essay provides a significant argument for setting us free from postcolonial hangovers. But, sad to say, we have so far not allowed it to shift our positions from borrowed models. The Samvatsar Lecture on "Memory and Space" is a companion piece and goes on to define nation space in the world context; further, it also locates the self firmly in the awareness of different spatial categories, going on to establish a relationship between time and space. Together, the essays are a significant contribution to epistemological structures and theory.

Henry Derozio and Jotirao Phule had, more than a hundred and fifty years ago, pointed towards the need to look after the nation's minorities. Due to a resurgence of the Dalit Movement in the 1960s, nationwide attention has been drawn towards the Dalits and there is a wealth of literature available both by and on them. Yet it is only now that serious attention has begun to be given to the aesthetics of this writing. It is true that the initial phase was more occupied in the articulation of feelings and experiences and less about literariness. It is only now that a consciousness has emerged. Sharan Kumar Limbale has a full-length book and activists such as Ramnika Gupta have provided some very insightful comments. But a major shortcoming in the work of many Dalit critics themselves is the constant comparison they make with the Black Movement and its aesthetics. Jotirao Phule in *Ghulamgiri* had also drawn a parallel with the institution of slavery, comparing it to the treatment meted out to Shudras. In its limited context, it had a certain validity. But any comparison at the level of aesthetics begins by imposing a follow-on situation. It dwarfs the development in the course it takes in this emergence from the soil. Rā Gă Jādhăv's essay appeared in one of the early collections of Dalit writing, *The Poisoned Bread* (Orient Longman, 1993), and is one essay that stays outside this comparison. Jādhăv is a *savarna*, yet the degree of empathy and understanding he displays in this essay transcends the normal limits associated with any outsider's vision. It finds a place here on account of its valuable assessment of the aesthetic development. Jādhăv begins by stating that though experiential writing is valuable, its value is limited if it is not accompanied or followed by an aesthetic consciousness. A degree of literariness alone can impart it continued value as the relationship between content and form is seen as an integrated whole and the individual in the writer as different from others.

Jādhăv proceeds to analyse Dalit writing and asks what makes it a distinctive category. The social awareness it displays is shared by most writing, but the raw reality it reflects, even though not strictly literary, is new. Some forms and modes that require greater detachment, like drama and humour, have not surfaced yet because they are forms that demand a certain degree of transcendence of the immediately felt reality. Artistic detachment calls for an intellectual intervention in the creative process, the ability to stand outside the experience and then objectively write about it. It calls for restraint in the spontaneous confessional overflow. Another requirement of aesthetics is its ability to lead the reader to introspect. Measured by such considerations, Dalit writing rises up to claim its own.

I have kept two essays right for the very end. These are Gajanan Madhav Muktibodh's extract, "The Third Moment", from *Ek Sahityik Ki Diary* and Jayanta Mahapatra's "Confrontations with a Poem". Both reflect on the creative process. Muktibodh follows a personal conversational style, travels over a period of time, enters into a dialogue with his friend and explores the mystery of writing. First the term 'objective' is explored and the whole exercise of objectifying a perception involves the mind. The problem is how does one respond to an abstraction such as beauty? What is the role of the aesthetic experience in this? Thus, in a turnabout, intense experience becomes the first moment, its separation from that immediacy becomes the second moment. Language and its welding to the content become the third and the final moment. As language is linked to its social use, it is its use that is of significance.

Jayanta Mahapatra's essay is a self-critiquing, semi-autobiographical essay, an analyses of his own creative process, in which rootedness, experience and feeling all come together in language. For him, self-reflection alone can help a writer to transfer his feelings, different emotions and perceptions into a poem, which, in its turn, can turn outward to the reader. Mahapatra's essay like Muktibodh's, is the story of two parallel journeys—one in time, the other in reflection. Poetry can never be mechanical—especially not if it is good and literary—as the meeting of emotions, thought and artistic objectivity involves a fusion that has a difficult birth. The sculpturing of thoughts so that they can retain a living relationship with language works simultaneously in several different directions. The poet, Jayanta Mahapatra feels, writes because he has to—there is no other choice before him. A physicist by profession, Mahapatra's has been, in many ways, a solitary journey inwards.

Together, these essays take us into the past and a host of related areas, which throw up evidence of the literary concepts that have been developing from the soil itself, concepts which are of value to us for a number of reasons—history, the development of genres, periodisation, aesthetic values and evaluative processes, interaction with other cultures and relatedness of our literatures across languages and regions—all flowing into a single cultural ethos.

Henry Louis Vivian Derozio

Henry Derozio (1809–31) was of an Indo-Portuguese parentage. He died at the young age of twenty-two, but during his brief adulthood, he made an immense contribution to the intellectual life of early nineteenth century India. He left his school, David Drummond's Academy, at the age of fourteen and went on to study on his own some of the major writers and thinkers of his time. For a brief spell he taught at Hindu College and inspired young students to debate questions about moral and political issues. Deeply influenced by Byron and Thomas Paine, Derozio was inclined towards rationalism and spoke openly against religious dogma and superstition. This led to his expulsion from Hindu College on the grounds that he was a bad influence on the students, who were turning into non-believers, as a consequence of which several had been withdrawn from the college by their guardians. Not to be pressurised into any kind of compromise, Derozio refused to accept the institution's polite offer that he should resign; instead, he fearlessly went on to reassert his belief, waiting for them to terminate his services. The records of this correspondence are available.

Today we remember Derozio more as a poet than as a young man who inspired his wards. Known as the first poet in Indian English writing, he wrote several patriotic poems seeped in Indian culture. His long poem, ***The Fakeer of Jungheera****, is a full-length narrative poem on widowhood and sati. He also wrote several essays which were published in the journals and magazines of his times, some under the pseudonyms of 'East Indian' and 'Juvenis'. The article included here was written in August 1829 and published in* ***The Keleidoscope*** *of September 1829. It addresses the position of the Eurasians under the Company's regime. Children of mixed parentage were looked down* *upon and were not even eligible for many of the offices for which other Indians were eligible. There was a deliberate policy to put them down.*

The essay is an important comment on the practices of colonialism and shows an early recognition of the problem by one so young. The four questions Derozio raises are related to issues of governance, race, access to knowledge and culture. An important fact to remember is that it precedes Macaulay's Minute and voices some of the fears that were later to become the objectives of the educational policy in India.

On the Colonisation of India by Europeans

The discussions on this important subject have, of late years, been very frequent and numerous, but I think the advantages and disadvantages of colonisation are still as undetermined as ever. But as the measure will certainly very soon engage the attention of the legislature, and as it will, whenever it may take place, very materially affect the condition of the natives and particularly the East Indian race, independently of partially changing the system of policy at present adopted towards this country, the subject in question cannot be too often nor too minutely examined. The following considerations at once present themselves to the mind.

1st Will colonisation endanger the British rule?
2nd Will it be beneficial or otherwise to the natives in general?
3rd Will it affect the Indo-Britons and in what manner? and
4th Will it prove the cause of the introduction of the arts and sciences of **Europe** throughout the empire?

It was observed by a former Governor General that this was an empire of *opinion,* and this observation has been widely circulated by those who have been either too idle or unwilling to substitute, for the fallacies of imagination, the dictates of truth. The most superficial observer must perceive that India is maintained in subjection only by *Military Force*—withdraw it, and the boasted opinion of the natives, instead of supporting, would immediately prove the cause of the utter subversion of the empire. It is generally known, and even confessed by our rulers, that the spirit of the natives, in the Upper Provinces in particular, is anything but peaceable. We have lately read in one of the papers that at **Lucknow**, during the late **Mohurrum**, prayers were publicly said for the destruction of the **Company's Government**!! Now, it is evident that if a large number of Europeans be allowed to settle in the country, they would form a counterpoise, in some degree, to the hostile disposition of the native subjects and in case of internal commotion or of foreign invasion, they will be found to be the only portion of the inhabitants that sincerely co-operates in the defence of British sovereignty.

On the other hand, we must reflect upon the probable effects of this measure upon the minds of the natives. At the renewal of the last charter, in 1813, Warren Hastings stated, at the bar of the House of Commons, that an intimate intercourse of Europeans with natives would lead the former to treat them so as to endanger the country by causing rebellion. This opinion has been frequently attempted to be controverted, but I think it [is], generally speaking, founded on long, intimate, and accurate observation of the real state of things, and the character and disposition of the people. It is corroborated by the observations which Bishop Heber makes upon the cruelty and oppressions which the natives suffer from the indigo planters in those provinces where they have been suffered to locate themselves; and my own inquiries convince me that the conduct of Europeans to their indigenous fellow subjects would tend to alienate them and ultimately lead to serious consequences. Besides which, I entertain strong doubts whether Europeans can settle in the country without gradually dispossessing the natives of their lands, and causing thereby incalculable misery and dissatisfaction, which, together with the inimical spirit by which I have stated they are at present actuated, would surely be anything but beneficial to the country.

Again, it will, I believe, be admitted that our race will be particularly affected by the measure—and I regret to think we may be reduced to the same, if not a worse condition than the Hindoos or Musselmans. If we anticipate the future by a reflection on the present prospects of our race, what can we expect from the colonisation of Europeans, but a state of far greater degradation than we suffer? Holding the natives in perfect contempt, would they treat us better than them? Surely not.

But in one respect the advantages of colonisation would be indubitable—and that is in the introduction of the arts and sciences of Europe and their establishment in this country. The Company indeed have never evinced a desire to improve the means of education among the natives, but there will not be wanting benevolent and public spirited individuals of all classes, who will come forward to promote the dissemination of the arts and sciences throughout the empire. Already do we see the beneficial effects produced by the introduction of the **Hindoo College**; and though some of the Hindoos educated there may *abuse* the *proficiency* they have acquired, yet I am fully persuaded that, in its remotest consequences, the greatest benefits will be derived. Education, by enlarging and enlightening their minds, would lead the way to the subversion of superstition, raise their moral and intellectual character, and ultimately produce a very sensible amelioration in their condition. But this can be done only by a paternal and fostering system on the part of the Government; they must countenance and establish similar colleges at every town in the *mofussil*—otherwise, the noblest scheme that humanity ever meditated would, like a sapless tree, wither and fall to the ground.

It is encouraging, however, to observe some degree of interest, at present, on the part of our rulers, in the education of the Hindoos; and I am convinced that every person will unite with me in wishing for the extension of this patronage to our class—which, alas! we have never yet experienced.

Upon the whole, then, we must draw the inference, that colonisation would not be beneficial, unless the British Legislature interferes and materially alters the present system of Indian policy by admitting natives and Indo-Britons to a participation of privileges on a similar footing, as far as practicable and expedient, with the Europeans. It is only by such a measure that discontent can be prevented from brooding into rebellion, and the arts and sciences, when established, can produce benefits both to the governors and governed, to Britain, and to this, at present, our oppressed and neglected native country. The basic of good government is, as Jeremy Bentham observes, 'the greatest good of the greatest number', and I heartily hope this principle the wisdom of the legislature will see fit, ere many years elapse, to adopt in every measure connected with India.

August, 1829 **S.J.**

The Keleidoscope
No. 2, September, 1829

Jotirao Govindrao Phule

Jotirao Phule (1827–90) is also known as Mahatma Phule. A writer, thinker, educationist and social revolutionary, Phule was one of those people from the margins of society who was deeply conscious of political issues and human rights. He continuously raised his voice against caste discrimination. One of his long poems is titled ***Brahmino Ki Chalaki*** *(1869) (The Wiliness of the Brahmins) and it comments on the way Brahmins, by creating an atmosphere of superstition and fear, dupe people, particularly women, in order to exploit them.*

Phule has written plays, long poems, and social and political commentaries. His very first play was written in 1855. The 'Preface' selected for this anthology was originally written in English for his political work in Marathi titled ***Ghulamgiri*** *(1873), literally meaning 'slavery'. The preface comments on the suppression of the Dalits, referred to here as Shudras and Atishudhras, and on the evils of the caste system prevalent in Hindu society. It is a powerful analysis of a social evil that has tainted our society and been both a divisionary force and a matter of national shame.*

Jotirao Phule wrote mostly in Marathi, except where he wanted to address the British. Hence, his work is not as widely known as it deserves to be. Some of his writing has now been translated into Hindi and some other Indian languages, which makes it more accessible to the non-Marathi reader. Two volumes of his work were published in Hindi in the 1990s under the title ***Mahatma Jotiba Phule Rachnavali*** *(translated and edited by Dr L.G. Mahesram* ***'Vimal Kirti'****; 2 vols; New Delhi: Radhakrishan, 1994).*

Phule also founded the Satyasodhak Society in order to involve people in the cause of social reform and change. Under its aegis, he and his wife, Savitribai Phule, established a school for female education, the first of its kind, to cater particularly to the education of women and other oppressed categories. But at no stage was his vision restricted only to the cause of the lower castes. His search for freedom and truth was in the interest of all humanity. Phule died in 1890. Ambedkar, if we recall, was born in 1891, as if the baton of struggle was being relayed from one generation to another to mature and enlarge itself into a larger struggle.

***Ghulamgiri**, with its expression of the desire for freedom, is as important a text for Indians as **The Wretched of the Earth** is for Africans, and it definitely needs to be more widely known, if for nothing else, at least in the interest of our history.*

Preface to *Ghulamgiri*

'The day that reduces a man to slavery takes from him half of his virtue.'

— Homer

'Our system of Government in India is not calculated to raise the character of those subject to it, nor is the present system of education one to do more than *over-educate the few*, leaving the mass of the people as ignorant as ever and still at the mercy of the few learned; in fact, it is an extension of the demoralising Brahmin-ridden policy, which perhaps, has more retarded the progress of civilisation and improvement in India generally than anything else.'

— Col. G.J. Haly, *On Fisheries in India*

'Many ages have elapsed since peculiar resources were afforded to the Brahmins, but the most considerate cosmopolite would hesitate to enroll them amongst the benefactors of the world. They boast of vast stores of ancient learning. They have amassed great riches and been invested with unbounded power, but to what good end? They have cherished the most degrading superstitions and practised the most shameless impostures. They have arrogated to themselves the possession and enjoyment of the rarest gifts of fortune and perpetuated the most revolting system known to the world. It is only from a diminution of their abused power that we can hope to accomplish the great work of national regeneration.'

— Mead, *Sepoy Revolt*

Recent researches have demonstrated beyond a shadow of doubt that the Brahmins were not the aborigines of India. At some remote period of antiquity, probably more than 3,000 years ago, the Aryan progenitors of the present Brahmin race descended upon the plains of Hindustan from regions lying beyond the Indus, the Hindoo Kush and other adjoining tracts. According to Dr Pritchard, the ethnologist, they were an off-shoot of the Great Indo-European race, from whom the Persian, Medes and other Iranian nations in Asia and the principal nations in Europe likewise are descended. The affinity existing between the Zend, the Persian and Sanskrit languages, as also between all the European languages, unmistakably points to a common source of origin. It appears also more than probable that the original cradle of this race being an arid, sandy and mountainous region, 'and one ill calculated to afford them the sustenance which their growing wants required, they branched off into colonies, East and West. The extreme fertility of the soil in India, its rich productions, the proverbial wealth of its people, and the other innumerable gifts which this favoured land enjoys, and which have more recently tempted the cupidity of Western nations, no doubt, attracted the Aryans, who came to India not as simple emigrants with peaceful intentions of colonisation, but as conquerors. They appear to have been a race imbued with very high notions of self, extremely cunning, arrogant and bigoted. Such self-gratulatory, pride-flattering epithets as आर्य, भूदेव (Arya, Bhudev), et cetera, with which they designated themselves, confirm us in our opinion of their primitive character, which they have preserved up to the present time, with perhaps little change for the better. The aborigines whom the Aryans subjugated, or displaced, appear to have been a hardy and brave people from the determined front which they offered to these interlopers. Such opprobrious terms as शूद्र (Shoodra) 'insignificant.' म्हारी 'the great foe', अत्यज चांडाल, et cetera, with which they designated them, undoubtedly show that originally, they offered the greatest resistance in their power to their establishing themselves in the country, and hence the great aversion and hatred in which they were held. From many customs* traditionally handed down to us as well as from the mythological legends contained in the sacred books of the Brahmins, it is evident that there had been a hard struggle for ascendancy between the two races. The wars of Dev and Daitya, or the Rakshas, about which so many fictions are found scattered over the sacred books of the Brahmins, have certainly a reference to this primeval struggle. The original inhabitants with whom these earthborn Gods, the Brahmins, fought, were not inappropriately termed Rakshas, that is, the protectors of the land. The incredible and foolish legends regarding their form and shape are no doubt mere chimeras, the fact being that these people were of superior stature and hardy make. Under such leaders as Brahma, Parashuram and others, the Brahmins waged very protracted wars against the original inhabitants. They eventually succeeded in establishing their supremacy and subjugating the aborigines to their entire control. Accounts of these conquests, enveloped with a mass of incredible fiction, are found in the books of the Brahmins. In some instances, they were compelled to emigrate, and in others, wholesale extermination was resorted to. The cruelties which the European settlers practised on the American Indians on their first settlement in the new world had certainly their parallel in India on the advent of the Aryans and their subjugation of the

---

* A most remarkable and striking corroboration of these views is to be found in the religious rites observed on some of the grand festivals, which have a reference to Bali Raja, the great king who appears to have reigned once in the hearts and affections of the Shoodras and whom the Brahmin rulers displaced. On the day of *Dushhara*, the wife and sisters of a Shoodra, when he returns from his worship of the Shumi Tree and after the distribution of its leaves, which are regarded on that day as equivalent to gold, amongst his friends, relations and acquaintances, greet him at home with a welcome: अला बला जावे और बली का राज आवे Let all troubles and misery go, and the kingdom of Bali come.' Whereas the wife and sisters of a Brahmin place on that day in the foreground of the house an image of Bali, made generally of wheaten or other flour, and when the Brahmin returns from his worship of the Shumi Tree, he takes the stalk of it, pokes with it the belly of the image and then passes into the house. This contrariety in the religious customs and usages obtaining amongst the Shoodras and the Brahmins and of which many more examples might be adduced, can be explained on no other supposition but that which I have tried to confirm and elucidate in these pages.

aborigines. The cruelties and inhuman atrocities which Parashuram committed on the Kshetrias, the people of this land, but if we are to believe even one-tenth of what the legends floated through Brahmin literature say regarding him surpass our belief and show that he was more a fiend than a God. Perhaps in the whole range of history, it is scarcely possible to meet with such another character as that of Parashuram, so selfish, infamous, cruel and inhuman. The deeds of Nero, Alaric or Machiavelli sink into insignificance before the ferocity of Parashuram. The myriads of men and defenceless children whom he butchered simply with a view to the establishment of his coreligionists on a secure and permanent basis in this land, is a fact for which generations ought to execrate his name, rather than deify it.

This, in short, is the history of Brahmin domination in India. They originally settled on the banks of the Ganges, whence they gradually spread over the whole of India. In order, however, to keep a better hold on the people, they devised that weird system of mythology, the ordination of caste, and the code of cruel and inhuman laws, to which we can find no parallel amongst other nations. They founded a system of priestcraft so galling in its tendency and operation, the like of which we can hardly find anywhere since the times of the Druids. The institution of Caste, which has been the main object of their laws, had no existence among them originally. That it was an after-creation of their deep cunning is evident from their own writings. The highest rights, the highest privileges and gifts, and everything that would make the life of a Brahmin easy, smoothgoing and happy, everything that would conserve or flatter their self-pride, were specially inculcated and enjoined, whereas the Shoodras and Atishoodras were regarded with supreme hatred and contempt, and the commonest rights of humanity were denied them. Their touch, nay, even their shadow, is deemed a pollution. They are considered as mere chattels, and their life of no more value than that of meanest reptile; for it is enjoined that if a Brahmin 'kill a cat or an ichneumon, the bird Chasha, or a frog or a dog, a lizard, an owl, a crow or a Shoodra', he is absolved of his sin by performing the चांद्रायण प्रायश्चित्त (*Chandrayan Prayaschit*), a fasting penance, perhaps for a few hours or a day and requiring not much labour or trouble. While for a Shoodra to kill a Brahmin is considered the most heinous offence he could commit, and the forfeiture of his life is the only punishment his crime is considered to merit. Happy for our Shoodra brethren of the present day our enlightened British rulers have not recognised these preposterous, inhuman and unjust penal enactments of the Brahmin legislators. They no doubt regard them more as ridiculous fooleries than as equitable laws. Indeed, no man possessing even a grain of common sense would regard them as otherwise. Anyone who feels disposed to look a little more into the laws and ordinances as embodied in the *Manava Dharma Shastra* and other works of the same class, would undoubtedly be impressed with the deep cunning underlying them all. It may not, perhaps, be out of place to cite here a few more instances in which the superiority or excellence of the Brahmins is held and enjoined on pain of Divine displeasure.

The Brahmin is styled the Lord of the Universe, even equal to the God himself. He is to be worshipped, served and respected by all.

A Brahmin can do no wrong.

Never shall the King slay a Brahmin, though he has committed all possible crimes.

To save the life of a Brahmin, any falsehood may be told. There is no sin in it.

No one is to take away anything belonging to a Brahmin.

A king, though dying with want, must not receive any tax from a Brahmin nor suffer him to be afflicted with hunger, or the whole kingdom will be afflicted with famine.

The feet of a Brahmin are holy. In his left foot reside all the तीर्थ (holy pilgrimages), and by dipping which into water, he makes it as holy as the waters at the holiest of shrines.

A Brahmin may compel a man of the servile class to perform servile duty because such a man was created by the Almighty only for the purpose of serving Brahmins.

A Shoodra, though emancipated by his master, is not released from the state of servitude, for, being born in a state which is natural to him, by whom can he be divested of his natural attributes?

Let a Brahmin not give temporal advice nor spiritual counsel to a Shoodra.

No superfluous accumulation of wealth shall be made by a Shoodra, even though he has the power to make it, since a servile man who has amassed riches becomes proud, and by his insolence or neglect, he gives pain even to Brahmins.

If a Shoodra cohabit with a Brahminee adulteress, his life is to be taken. But if a Brahmin goes even unto the lawful wife of a Shoodra, he is exempted from all corporal punishment.

It would be needless to go on multiplying instances such as these. Hundreds of similar ordinances, including many more of a worse character than these, can be found scattered over their books. But what can have been the motives and objects of such cruel and inhuman Laws? They are, I believe, apparent to all but to the infatuated, the blind and the self-interested. Anyone who wants may even read them. Their main object in fabricating these falsehoods was to dupe the minds of the ignorant and to rivet firmly on them the chains of perpetual bondage and slavery which their selfishness and cunning had forged. The severity of laws as affecting the Shoodras and the intense hatred with which they were regarded by the Brahmins can be explained on no other supposition but that there was, originally between the two, a deadly feud, arising, as we have shown above, from the advent of the latter into this land. It is surprising to think what a mass of specious fiction the interlopers invented with a view to hold the original occupiers of the soil fast in their clutches and rule securely for ages yet to come through the means of their credulity. Anyone who will consider well the whole history of Brahmin domination in India, and the thraldom under which it has retained the people even up to the present day, will agree with us in thinking that no language could be too harsh by which to characterise the selfish heartlessness and the consummate cunning of the Brahmin tyranny by which India has been so long governed. How far the Brahmins have succeeded in their endeavours to enslave the minds of the Shoodras and Atishoodras, those of them who have come to know the true state of matters know well to their cost. For generations past, they have borne these chains of slavery and bondage. Innumerable Bhut writers, with the selfsame objects as those of Manu and others of his class, added from time to time to the existing mass of legends, the idle phantasies of their own brains and palmed them off upon the ignorant masses as of Divine inspiration, or as the acts of the Deity himself. The most immoral, inhuman, unjust actions and deeds have been attributed to that being who is our Creator, Governor and Protector and who is all Holiness himself. These blasphemous writings, the products of the distempered brains of these interlopers, were received as gospel truth, for to doubt them was considered as the most unpardonable of sins. This system of slavery, to which the Brahmins reduced the lower classes, is in no respect inferior to that which obtained a few years ago in America. In the days of rigid Brahmin dominancy, so lately as that of the time of the Peshwa, my Shoodra brethren had even greater hardships and oppression practised upon them than what even the slaves in America had to suffer. To this system of selfish superstition and bigotry, we are to attribute the stagnation and all the evils under which India has been groaning for many centuries past. It will, indeed, be difficult to name a single advantage which accrued to the aborigines from the advent of this intensely selfish and tyrannical sect. The Indian Ryot (the Shoodra and Atishoodra) has been in fact a proverbial milch cow. He has passed from hand to hand. Those who successively held sway over him cared only to fatten themselves on the sweat of his brow, without caring for his welfare or condition. It was sufficient for their purposes that they held him safe in their clutches for squeezing out of him as much as they possibly could. The Brahmin had at last so contrived to entwine himself round the Shoodra in every large or small undertaking, in every domestic or public business, that the latter is by custom quite unable to transact any concern of moment without his aid.

This is even true at the present time. While the Shoodra on the other hand is so far reconciled to the Brahmin yoke that, like the American slave, he would resist any attempt that may be made for his deliverance and fight even against his benefactor. Under the guise of religion, the Brahmin has his finger in everything, big or small, which the Shoodra undertakes. Go to his house, to his field or to the court to which business may invite him, the Brahmin is there under some specious pretext or other, trying to squeeze out of him as much as his cunning and wily brain can manage. The Brahmin despoils the Shoodra not only in his capacity of a priest, but does so in a variety of other ways, having, by his superior education and cunning, monopolised all the higher places of emolument, the ingenuity of his ways is past finding out, as the reader will find on an attentive perusal of this book. In the most insignificant village as in the largest town, the Brahmin is the all in all; the be all and the end all of the Ryot. He is the master ruler. The Patel of a village, the headman, is in fact a nonentity. The Kookkarnee, the hereditary Brahmin village accountant, the notorious quarrel-monger, moulds the Patel according to his wishes. He is the temporal and spiritual advisor of the ryots, the Soucar in his necessities and the general referee in all matters. In most instances, he plans active mischief by advising opposite parties differently, so that he may feather his own nest well. If we go up higher, to the Court of a Mamlutdar, we find the same thing. The first anxiety of a Mamlutdar is to get round him, if not his own relatives, his caste men to fill the various offices under him. These actively foment quarrels and are the media of all corrupt practices prevailing generally round about these Courts. If a Shoodra or Atishoodra repairs to his Courts, the treatment which he receives is akin to what the meanest reptile gets. Instead of his case receiving a patient and careful hearing, a choice lot of abuse is showered on his devoted head and his prayer is set aside on some pretext or other. Whereas if one of his own caste men were to repair to the Court on the self-same business, he is received with all courtesy and there is hardly any time lost in getting the matter right. If we go up still higher to the Collector's and Revenue Commissioner's

Courts and to the other Departments of the Public Service, the Engineer, Educational, et cetera, the same system is carried out on a smaller or greater scale. The higher European officers generally view men and things through Brahmin spectacles and hence the deplorable ignorance they often exhibit in forming a correct estimate of them. I have tried to place before my readers in the concluding portions of this book what expedients are employed by these Brahmin officials for fleecing the Cunbee in the various departments to which business or his necessities induce him to resort. Anyone knowing intimately the workings of the different departments and the secret springs which are in motion, will unhesitatingly concur with me in saying that what I have described in the following pages is not one-hundredth part of the rogueries that are generally practised on my poor, illiterate and ignorant Shoodra brethren. Though the Brahmin of the old Peshwa school is not quite the same as the Brahmin of the present day, though the march of Western ideas and civilisation is undoubtedly telling on his superstition and bigotry, he has not as yet abandoned his time-cherished notions of superiority or the dishonesty of his ways. The Beef, the Mutton, the intoxicating beverages stronger and more fiery than the famed *som juice*, which their ancestors once relished as the veriest dainties, are fast finding innumerable votaries among them.

The Brahmin of the present time finds to some extent, like Othello, that his occupation is gone. But knowing full well this state of matters, is the Brahmin inclined to make atonement for his past selfishness? Perhaps, it would have been useless to repine over what has been suffered and what has passed away, had the present state been all that is desirable. We know perfectly well that the Brahmin will not descend from his self-raised high pedestal and meet his Cunbee and low caste brethren on an equal footing without a struggle. Even the educated Brahmin, who knows his exact position and how he has come by it, will not condescend to acknowledge the errors of his forefathers and willingly forego the long cherished false notions of his own superiority. At present, not one has had the moral courage to do what only duty demands and, as long as this state of matters continues, sect distrusting and degrading sect, the condition of the Shoodras will remain unaltered, and India will never advance in greatness or prosperity.

Perhaps a part of the blame in bringing matters to this crisis may be justly laid to the credit of the Government. Whatever may have been their motives in providing ampler funds and greater facilities for higher education and neglecting that of the masses, it will be acknowledged by all that in justice to the latter, this is not as it should be. It is an admitted fact that the greater portion of the revenues of the Indian Empire is derived from the Ryot's labour—from the sweat of his brow. The higher and richer classes contribute little or nothing to the state's exchequer. A well informed English writer states that,

'Our income is derived, not from surplus profits, but from capital; not from luxuries, but from the poorest necessaries. It is the product of sin and tears.'

That Government should expend profusely a large portion of revenue thus raised, on the education of the higher classes, for it is these only who take advantage of it, is anything but just or equitable. Their object in patronising this virtual high class education appears to be to prepare scholars 'who, it is thought, would in time vend learning without money and without price'. 'If we can inspire,' say they, 'the love of knowledge in the minds of the superior classes, the result will be a higher standard of morals in the cases of the individuals, a large amount of affection for the British Government, and an unconquerable desire to spread among their own countrymen the intellectual blessings which they have received.'

Regarding these objects of Government, the writer above alluded to states that:

> We have never heard of philosophy more benevolent and more utopian. It is proposed by men who witness the wondrous changes brought about in the Western world, purely by the agency of popular knowledge, to redress the defect of the two hundred millions of India, by giving superior education to the superior classes and to them only... . We ask the friends of Indian Universities to favour us with a single example of the

truth of their theory from the instances which have already fallen within the scope of their experience. They have educated many children of wealthy men, and have been the means of advancing very materially the worldly prospects of some of their pupils; but what contribution have these made to the great work of regenerating their fellowmen? How have they begun to act upon the masses? Have any of them formed classes, at their own homes or elsewhere, for the instruction of their less fortunate or less wise countrymen? Or have they kept their knowledge to themselves, as a personal gift, not to be soiled by contact with the ignorant vulgar? Have they in any way shown themselves anxious to advance the general interests and repay philanthropy with patriotism? Upon what grounds is it asserted that the best way to advance the moral and intellectual welfare of the people is to raise the standard of instruction among the higher classes? A glorious argument this for aristocracy were it only tenable. To show the growth of the national happiness, it would only be necessary to refer to the number of pupils at the colleges and the lists of academic degrees. Each wrangler would be accounted a national benefactor; and the existence of Deans and proctors would be associated, like the game laws and the ten pound franchise, with the best interests of the Constitution.

Perhaps the most glaring tendency of the Government system of high class education has been the virtual monopoly of all the higher offices under them by the Brahmins. If the welfare of the Ryot is at heart, if it is the duty of Government to check a host of abuses, it behoves them to narrow this monopoly day by day, so as to allow a sprinkling of the other castes to get in the public service. Perhaps some might be inclined to say that it is not feasible in the present state of education. Our only reply is that if Government look a little less after higher education and more towards the education of the masses, the former being able to take care of itself, there would be no difficulty in attaining up a body of men every way qualified and perhaps far better in morals and manners.

My object in writing the present volume is not only to tell my Shoodra brethren how they have been duped by the

Brahmins, but also to open the eyes of Government to that pernicious system of high class education which has hitherto been so persistently followed and which statesmen like Sir George Campbell, the present Lieutenant Governor of Bengal, with broad and universal sympathies, are finding to be highly mischievous and pernicious to the interests of Government. I sincerely hope that Government will ere long see the error of their ways, trust less to writers or men who look through high class spectacles and take the glory into their own hands of emancipating my Shoodra brethren from the trammels of bondage which the Brahmins have woven round them like the coils of a serpent. It is no less the duty of such of my Shoodra brethren as have received any education to place before Government the true state of their fellowmen and endeavour to the best of their power to emancipate themselves from Brahmin thralldom. Let there be schools for the Shoodras in every village, but away with all Brahmin school-masters! The Shoodras are the life and sinews of the country, and it is to them alone and not to the Brahmins that the Government must ever look to tide them over their difficulties, financial as well as political. If the hearts and minds of the Shoodras are made happy and contented, the British Government need have no fear for their loyalty in the future.

Altaf Husain Hali

Altaf Husain Hali (1837–1914), the first practitioner of theoretical criticism in Urdu, was a poet and a biographer of great renown in Urdu literature. He is a younger contemporary of Muhammad Husain Azad, the first literary historian of Urdu literature. After spending his formative years in Delhi as a disciple of Ghalib, Hali went to Lahore, where he worked at the Government Book Depot from 1870 to 1874. Hali's task at the depot was to edit and amend textbooks that had been translated from English into Urdu. As a result, he became acquainted with a variety of work in English literature and criticism and European philosophy and science. Hali describes how through this, he developed a relationship with English literature and how the prestige of eastern literature, and especially Persian literature, declined in his heart.[1] *Elsewhere, Hali mentions how translation from English into Urdu, especially under the aegis of the Aligarh Scientific Institute and Tahzeeb ul Akhlaq, transformed literary taste, with the result that the status of Persian literature fell considerably and 'the spirit of western imagining' was blown into Urdu literature.*[2] *It is only reasonable to assume that all these impressions and influences went into the making of his poetic and critical sensibility.*

Hali's ***Muqaddama She'r O Shairi****, which roughly translates as 'Introduction to Poetry and Poetics', is a long essay that appeared in 1893 as a preface to his collection of poems. This long essay, which later took the form of a book, has remained the most influential work of literary criticism in Urdu over the last century. Though Hali's thoughts in the* ***Muqaddama*** *are largely derivative, they have been put across with a force and conviction all his own, so much so that his considerable reputation as a poet seems to have been eclipsed by his stature as a critic, and as a writer of the* ***Muqaddama****.*[3]

*The **Muqaddama** is divided into three sections. In the first section, Hali discusses the role of poetry in earlier societies. In the second section, he presents his ideas derived from Milton. Poetry should have simplicity (sadgi), should spring from emotion (josh) and should be based on truth (asliyat).*[4] *In the third section, he deals with the concept of natural poetry. Natural poetry, according to him, means poetry written in accordance with nature in both words and meaning. The words should be those of common speech and the meaning should be concerned with things of this world. He gives his illustrations of natural and unnatural poetry.*

*What follows is the English translation of important excerpts from the first sixty pages of the **Muqaddama**.*

M. Asaduddin

---

1. "Hali" in Muhammad Tufail (ed.), *Naqoosh: Aap-Biti Number* (Lahore: Idara-e Faroogh-e Urdu, 1964), p. 284.
2. Hali, *Majmua-e Nazm-e Hali* (Delhi: Matba'e Murtazai, 1890), p. 2., quoted in *Hali's Musaddas: The Ebb and Flow of Islam*, translated with a critical introduction by Christopher Shackle and Javed Majeed (Delhi: Oxford University Press, 1997), p. 6.
3. For a detailed discussion of the *Muqaddama*, see Laurel Steele, "Hali's *Muqaddamah*: The Creation of a Literary Attitude in Nineteenth Century India" in *Annual of Urdu Studies*, University of Chicago, #1, 1981. pp. 1–45.
4. Laurel Steele summarises this section of the *Muqaddama* as follows: 'Simplicity means that in both words and thoughts, there should be simplicity. The thought should not be so refined and abstruse that it could not be understood by common people. The basis of poetry should be known things.... Poetry should inspire emotion (*josh*) in the heart of its listeners. The poet, when he is reciting, should keep the thoughts of his listeners in mind and his own natural emotions should be made apparent through his poetry. That poetry should be based on reality (*asliyat*) means that its subject or the idea in it should be something that is present in actuality and not made up or imaginary. The similes and allegories should also be true—that is, not fictional.' *The Annual of Urdu Studies*, Chicago, #1, 1981. p. 30.

Muqaddama She'r O Shairi

... Much has been said in praise and condemnation of poetry. Its condemnation sounds more plausible to reason than its praise. Even a poet has stated that among all the vocations, that of a poet is the most redundant in society. Plato had conceived a democratic state for Greece where people from all other arts were accommodated, excepting poets. In contemporary times, some people have compared poetry with a magic lantern—the darker the room it is in, the brighter the images. Similarly, poetry is more potent in times of darkness and ignorance.

Similar other things have been said against poetry that merit our serious attention. However, it cannot be denied that thousands of people have been born into this world whom Nature had meant for this work only and endowed with special potentials for it. Though many people have used this gift against the demands of Nature, it (poetry) cannot be declared worthless for that reason. Intellect is a valuable gift from God, but many people use it for wicked or reprehensible purposes. Similarly, valour is a divine gift, but it sometimes leads people to plunder and mayhem. Does it make any difference to the inherent worth of intellect or valour? Similarly, the worth of poetry does not diminish if anyone uses it to wrong ends.

It is an accepted fact that one cannot become a poet by effort. Only a person who has an inherent poetic talent can become a poet. The first sign of poetry is considered to be a metrical disposition. It has often been found that some couplets that are not rhythmically read by scholars of poetry are, surprisingly enough, rhythmically recited by children. It is thus obvious that poetry is not a matter of effort and endeavour, but a matter of natural propensity. Those who exploit their talents in accordance with the demands of Nature might prove to be beneficial to society.

No one can deny the impact of poetry. It certainly evokes joy, zest or sadness to a greater or lesser extent. This indicates that it can be a useful means to some purposeful end… In our country, jesters and caricaturists are considered to be practising a very lowly profession. The caricatures done during Holi through song and dance are considered harmful for society. However, in Europe, these genres have been employed for correction and there were cultural and civilisational benefits to society… .

History is replete with examples of when poets moved people profoundly through the magical effect of their poetic utterances. Often, poetry leaves such a profound impact on most people that everything that it touches, even objectionable things, seems bathed in a new light. People try to emulate those objectionable things. It is widely known about Byron that people used to eagerly buy his photographs and preserve his relics and memorabilia. They memorised his verses and tried to write verses of the same kind themselves. They wished to appear like him, wearing dresses of the same fashion and practising the same frown and pout before the mirror… .

Lord Byron's *Childe Harold's Pilgrimage* is a famous poem. One of its parts reminded Great Britain, France and Russia of their failure in freeing Greece from the suzerainty of the Turks. He remarked that the benefits that Europe, especially Great Britain and France, have derived from the intellectual tradition of Greece have remained unrequited. Even Russia, which seemed to lay great store by the Greek Orthodox Church, did not help Greece in any way. And then, to incite these three states, he exhorted the Greeks that they should not expect anything from strangers. Rather, they should rely on their own strength to free themselves from the subjugation of the Turks. This poem was published in 1812 and it became instrumental in spreading Byron's fame throughout Europe. The English were captivated by this poem. The consequence was that in France, Great Britain, Italy, Austria and Russia, this poem inflamed the imagination of the people just as fire ignites ammunition. The moment Greece rebelled against Turkey, the allied powers of Europe immediately rallied in its support. In 1827, the allied powers defeated the Turks and compelled it to free Greece. All of Europe approved of the independence of Greece... .

It is said about the famous poet from Arabia, Maimun bin Qais, who was called 'A'sha' because he was blind, that his verses had such a profound impact on people that whoever he praised in his verses was taken to be gentle and noble, and whoever he caricatured was immediately taken to be wicked and disgraced... . One can find countless examples in the age of Jahiliya in Arabia of when the poet stirred the people through his poetry to take revenge on anyone who killed a member of the tribe, or inspired the tribesmen to go into battle against another tribe for the purposes of revenge, or set the minds of the people on fire to win back a fountain or a pasture that the enemy had snatched away... .

The world has always valued poets. Kings have always patronised them and nations have inspired them. In Arabia, poets embodied the honour of the community. When a poet of a particular tribe achieved distinction, other tribes offered them compliments and they celebrated the occasion together. The women of the tribe, attired in their wedding finery, would come and sing songs of celebration... .

In the early years of Islam, before the culture of flattery made inroads into social life, poetry contained true emotions and ecstasy. People deserving of praise were praised and those deserving condemnation were denounced. When some good and wise *khalifa* or minister died, elegies (*marsiya)* were written mourning their death. Tyrants were denounced in their lifetime. Panegyrics (*qaseeda)* were written celebrating great events related to the victories and expeditions of *khalifas* and kings. Moving poetry was written on the friendly assemblies that vanished because of the crises of the time. Chaste wives pining for their husbands wrote heartrending verses and so did husbands separated from their wives. Poets drew vivid pictures of assignations in pastures, by fountain springs and in fields. They celebrated the agility and hardihood of camels in the desert in their verses, wrote about the friendship between men and their horses… . But slowly the praise and flattery required for court life effectively closed off these vital springs. There were only two spheres left where the poets could show their mettle: one, verses of praise (panegyrics) the main object of which was to flatter the praised; and two, love poetry, which fulfilled their sexual proclivities. Then, after a long period, like a bone sucked dry, there was nothing left in both these subjects, and to brighten up the assemblies of kings and courtiers, the profession of jesters and writing verses of levity (*hazal*) got a fillip. Many poets abandoned everything and took to this path. Slowly, this had its impact on the entire society. Since the beginning to the present times, there have been people in all ages and in all classes who are worthy of honour and Muslims can justifiably take pride in their works. But the ones who are commonly visible are those who have left the field of poetry fairly circumscribed for their successors, for whom they have left bad examples.

When their successors opened their eyes, they saw little else apart from *qaseedas, ghazals, masnavis,* … and *hazals*, and concluded that poetry was confined within them. But what was left in them after centuries of usage? If praise is genuine and so is love, then poets would find no dearth of subjects. As one cannot find two objects in the universe that are exactly identical, similarly, the style and substance of one's praise are different from those of another, and the workings of one person's mind are different from those of another. But when the praise is wholly specious and love becomes a matter of mere imitation, then poets are bound to go on repeating what their predecessors have said.

Now when the successors began to imitate the predecessors, they began to imitate them not only in subject matter, but also in thoughts, words, devices, styles, similes, metaphors, metres, *qafiyas* (end rhymes), *radeefs* (penultimate rhymes)—in everything. And when beating the same track, life became intolerable, they made the most vulgar kind of innovations… .

However, often the bad taste prevalent in society leads to spoilage of poetry, and when poetry is distorted, its poison may cause great harm to society. When the nation gets accustomed to false (spurious/pseudo) poetry, people get accustomed to falsehood and exaggerations. The more the falsehood or exaggeration, the greater the accolade. The poet takes recourse to greater exaggeration in order to achieve popularity and thus he moves further away from the truth. The worst kind of transformation takes place in people's taste when they are constantly exposed to false and fanciful ideas presented to them in the appealing structures of rhyme and rhythm. People stray away from truth and everyday reality and are more drawn towards strange things, the world of the supernatural and the improbable. They do not find any interest in the simple and straightforward events of history. False tales and fanciful stories appear more interesting than realistic accounts. People turn their backs on history, geography, mathematics or the sciences. Slowly, but steadily, bad morals take roots in society. And when levity *(hazal)* and parody are also added to falsehood in the concoction of poetry, then national culture is slowly eaten away, as if by termites.

The greatest harm that is caused to the nation when poetry is distorted or becomes limited in scope is that it spells disaster for its language and literature. When falsehood and hyperbole get ingrained in the poet's consciousness, its impact can be seen on the compositions of writers, on the discourses of linguists of great calibre and on the language of everyday speech because in any language, the words, idioms and turns of phrase used by the poets are considered to be the best and the most elegant part of that language. Those who want to excel in writing speeches or in the language of daily intercourse necessarily imitate the language of poets. And thus, exaggeration becomes an integral part of the literature and the language of the people. *Hazal* writing (a degenerate kind of poetry) leads to the inclusion of many vulgar and obscene words in the language… .

When the art of poetry reaches such a stage, its reform becomes almost impossible. Firstly, the poets are generally so engrossed in imitating the Ancients that they have no awareness that there can be any other way except the beaten track that they are following. And if, by chance, anyone adopts a different way, then he has to face two grave difficulties. First, to step into a new world and cross different stages to reach one's destination is by itself a challenging task. The second problem, which is even more difficult to face, is the risk of being the butt of contemporary society's ridicule. As people are strangers to this 'new light', no one can properly acknowledge the challenge involved in it or appreciate the poet's efforts... . Though it is possible that the poet, in striking a new path for himself, chooses a subject of contemporary demand and appeal, clothes it in the robe of poetry, and thus derives some appreciation and acceptance from the modernists of the time. He might receive even greater appreciation, from a certain angle, than he had expected. But this appreciation is not really for the inherent merit of his poetry, nor does he consider it as such... .

When Goldsmith (Oliver Goldsmith), right at the beginning of his career, decided not to follow the school of earlier poets whose poetry was based on falsehood, exaggeration and lustful subjects, but sought to write true and natural poetry, he faced similar difficulties. He has described this in one of his poems... . To lay the foundations of new poetry, it is necessary that some of the best samples of it be presented before the public. It is equally necessary that the real nature of poetry and the conditions that one must fulfil to become a poet should be described in some detail.

In our country, at this time, poetry is expected to fulfil just one condition—that the poet be endowed with an intrinsic metrical propensity. One who can compose verses through the imitation of some familiar metrical structures does not stand in need of anything else to call himself a poet. He already has easy access to a repertoire of hackneyed subjects, worn out similes and metaphors that have been in use for centuries. Now, if he has intrinsic metrical propensity too, he needs nothing more. But, as a matter of fact, poetry is something higher than mere versifying.

Metre (*wazn*) to a verse is what words are to a raga. Just as the raga does not owe its existence to words, similarly, poetry does not intrinsically need metrical structure. In this context, in English, there are two different words: poetry and verse. Similarly, there are two different terms, *she'r* and *nazm*, in Urdu.

Just as metre is not a condition for poetry but only for verse in English, likewise, it is not a condition for *she'r,* but should be a necessary one for *nazm*... . There is no doubt that metre enhances the merit and impact of poetry. According to a European critic, the merit of poetry does not necessarily depend on metre and, initially, it was devoid of this ornament for a long period. However, there is no denying that the addition of metre enhances its impact and makes its message more effective.

Qafiya (variations on refrain) is also as important as metre. But, as a matter of fact, it also applies to *nazm*, not to *she'r*. ... *Qafiya*, like metre, does enhance the beauty of a *she'r* and make it pleasing to the ears. However, strict adherence to the rules of *qafiya*, as practised in particular by non-Arab poets, who further added the condition of *radeef* (repetitive refrain) to it, deters poets from accomplishing their duties... . Rather than conceiving an idea and then finding the words to convey it, the poet has to think of the *qafiya* first and then find an appropriate thought amenable to the *qafiya*. This also determines the selection of words that can function as the proposed structure of the *qafiya*. For, if he does not do so, then it might happen that after arranging his thoughts in a particular order, the poet has to abandon them for lack of appropriate *qafiyas*. In sum, the poet is not free to organise his thoughts the way he likes, but is led on his way by *qafiyas*.

Poetry has been variously defined, but no definition can encompass all the characteristic features that are germane to it. From outside the canons of Urdu poetry, whatever Lord Macaulay has written about poetry may not constitute a definition, but it comes very close to what we understand by poetry today. He says, 'Poetry, as it had been practised two thousand years ago, is a kind of mimicry which is analogous to painting, sculpture and dance. The images created by painters, sculptors and dancers are somewhat more accurate than those of the poet. What are the tools of poetry? They are certainly words. And words are such entities that even if builders of the calibres of Homer or Dante use them, the listeners of their poetry cannot conceive the external forms as accurately as brush strokes or chisel may appear to them.'

A poet needs to fulfil the prerequisites of poetry. The first and foremost characteristic that distinguishes a poet from a non-poet is the power of imagination. The more powerful the imagination, the higher the poetry. The weaker the imagination, the lower the poetry. This power is not achieved through exercise, but is a gift of God. If a poet is endowed with this quality and lacks in other poetical merit, his imaginary power compensates for it. The poet lacking in this natural quality does not deserve to be celebrated as a great poet, even if he fulfils the other prerequisites of poetry. By virtue of this power, a poet transcends both time and space. Time past and time future are drawn to him by virtue of his power… .

The second requirement for achieving perfection in poetry is the study of the universe. Although the poet's faculty of imagination can achieve some results even when his universe of experience and awareness is quite limited, to achieve greatness in poetry, he must have deep knowledge of the universe and particularly that of human nature. He should closely observe the different conditions that human beings go through in life and accustom himself to putting his observations in order. He should develop insights that would enable him to look into deeper realities that are hidden from the common eye and immediately discern similitude in dissimilitudes and dissimilitudes in similitude. He must preserve this treasure in his memory… .

The third prerequisite is diction. Having got used to studying the universe, the next great requirement for a poet is the study of words, through which he is going to present his thoughts to his readers. This study is also as important as the earlier one. While composing poetry, he should select proper words and put them in the appropriate order so that the readers experience no difficulty in following its intended import. These words must be able to evoke images of thoughts before the eye that would captivate the imagination of the readers. This is no doubt a difficult requirement, but it is a necessary one. If a poet's verses do not have this quality, then he had better not write. If the poet does not have full command over the essential elements of diction and does not arrange his words in the best order with extreme care and patience, the power of his imagination will not avail him much.

Poets endowed with command over diction understand the importance of each individual word and they process them in a way that would make maximum appeal to the people. They know very well the kind of impact the inclusion or omission of a particular word would make on the narration. If there is the slightest discrepancy in the arrangement of words, they can feel it at once and realise it to be a weakness in their poetry. As an object cast in a defective mould immediately attracts the eyes, similarly a *she'r* lacking in the desired features draws the poet's immediate attention. The restrictions imposed by metre and *qafiya* compel both a perfect as well as an inferior poet to choose words that are unable to express their thoughts adequately. The difference between a perfect and an inferior poet lies in the fact that the latter gives up easily after some little search for the appropriate word and rests content with the word at hand, while the former spares no effort in finding the most appropriate word. He chooses the word available to him only after exhausting all the resources at his command. As long as the poet has not achieved perfect mastery over language, and does not show utmost patience in his quest for the most appropriate word, he cannot have a lasting impact on the minds of the people… .

People are of the opinion that a *she'r* composed spontaneously is more appealing than one that is composed through effort and reflection. The first is termed as *amad* (spontaneous) and the second one as *aurd* (laboured). In this context, some people take recourse to the simile that the juice oozing out on its own from grapes is more palatable than the essence extracted from them. We do not subscribe to this view… . Barring exceptions, poetry that is composed after much thought and reflection is always more appealing, more delicate, more enjoyable, more serious and more effective… .

As regards the meaning, Ibn Khaldun is of the opinion that 'the excellence in *belles lettres*, whether in prose or poetry, lies in the words, not in the meaning. Words have the primary position, while the meaning is secondary. The meaning is present in everyone's mind and he need not take recourse to any skill for that. What he needs is style that would allow him to express the meaning in words. To him, words are like a jar and the meaning is like the water in it. The nature of the water remains unchanged whether the container is made of gold, silver, clay, glass or shell. However, the value of the water in a gold or silver jar is more than the value of the water in a clay jar. Likewise, the meaning assumes a higher dimension in the hands of an expert, whereas it reduces in value in the hands of a non-expert.' But my humble submission to him is that if the water is brackish or muddy, and if the person drinking it is not thirsty enough, then it cannot be a pleasant experience for him to drink it, even if it is served in a gold or silver jar.

What are the subjects that should be the stuff of poetry?

As regards meaning, the poet should excel in something else that has nothing to do with words. It is not enough for the poet merely to study Nature and gather information about things. He needs to enter into the soul of those things, to know their special traits and then draw them in their true colours. For example, the poet does not see the vegetable world, flowers and fruits with the eyes of a botanist; likewise, he does not view a historical event from the perspective of a historian. He selects only those traits in objects on which the power of imagination can work and which are hidden from the eyes of ordinary people... .

Ibn Rashiq says that a poet should keep in mind the work of great poets, so that he can lay the foundation of his poetry on it. If one has no idea of the great poets of his language, even if he manages to write something because of his natural propensity, it may not attain the status of poetry and might remain at the level of inferior verse. Only when his memory is filled with the verses of superior poets and the brilliance of their poetry is imprinted on his mind should he begin to write poetry. And then the more he practises, the greater will be his poetic excellence.

Ibn Rashiq had made this comment especially in the context of Arabic poetry. It may have been pertinent about the Arabic language as it had a tradition of poetry going back to a very long time. For more than a thousand years, each age and each clan had

had its greater and smaller poets, who pushed the possibilities of the language to an extraordinary extent. There were hundreds of devices and structures present in the literature to convey any conceivable meaning. Probably, it was not necessary to create new ways of expression. But Urdu is an undeveloped language, its poetry is still in the state of infancy, its literature, if one takes a dispassionate look at it, is not more than fifty or sixty years old, its dictionary has not yet been compiled, its grammar does not yet inspire confidence, and its writers and poets of any worth can be counted on one's fingers. In such a language, if the poets content themselves with mere imitation of earlier poets, then like the Ababeel birds building their nests always on the same pattern, it will always remain swinging in the cradle of its infancy.

After this, Ibn Rashiq says, 'Some people say that after taking a comprehensive look at the verses of the masters, one should erase them from memory, as their strong presence in memory would always come in the way of using indigenous devices and styles. But when those verses will be erased from memory, an impression will be created in the mind because of internalising and absorbing them in the poet's disposition, that will enable him to create similar devices and styles as he found in the verses of the masters. In other words, without being consciously aware that a particular device had been copied from an earlier one or a particular style was the replica of an earlier author, he would go on creating them as the need arises.'

We feel that this view (of Ibn Rashiq) is worthy of greater attention than the first one. This has an even greater advantage than the one expressed by him in that as long as the verses of the masters are not totally erased from memory, the poetic disposition remains a prisoner to the same styles and structures. Those old ways that get ingrained in the mind because of reading the masters over and over again prevent the poet from innovating new styles and structures in the narrative method. Thus, no progress is made in the art of poetry.

As regards imagination, we should keep in mind that, as far as possible, it should be kept in moderation and should not be allowed to run free. When it is allowed to overwhelm the poet's disposition and dominate over the intellect, which is supposed to keep the imagination in check, it presents a danger for the poet. The power of imagination always leads to creativity and flights of fancy, but the power of intellect restrains its flight... and does not allow it to stray even one step. However mighty or high the imaginative flight, if it is subservient to the power of the intellect, it does not cause any harm to poetry. Rather, the higher the imaginative flight, the better will be the quality of the poetry. In all the great poets of the world, one finds the simultaneous presence of great imaginative flights controlled by a ruling intellect... .

So far, we have discussed the traits without which the poet cannot achieve greatness. Now, we intend to discuss the qualities that are generally found in the verses of the greatest poets of the world. Milton (John Milton, 1608–74) has described them in some cryptic terms. According to him, 'Great poetry is that which is *sadah* (simple), which is filled with *josh* (emotion/inspiration), and which is based on *asliyat* (reality/truth).'[1] A European scholar elucidates these terms in the following way:

> Simplicity does not mean the mere use of simple words. Rather, it means that the thoughts also should not be too complex or rarefied that cannot be understood by the common people. Simplicity consists in following the conventional path in matters of feelings, not straying away from the straight path of informality, and keeping the thoughts free from being abstruse... .
>
> The second[2] necessary trait, according to Milton, is that poetry should be based on reality. This means that the poet's subject matter or idea should have some basis in reality. It should not be entirely fanciful so that one feels it at one moment, and the next moment, it is not there. This holds true both in matters of thoughts and words. That is, the poet should not use similes that exist only in the world of imagination.

1. This is Hali's paraphrasing of Milton's celebrated remark that 'poetry is simple, sensuous and passionate'.
2. Hali seems to have confused the order here. In his remark with reference to Milton, *josh* figures second and *asliyat* figures third. This is Hali's paraphrasing of Milton's celebrated remark that 'poetry is simple, sensuous and passionate'.

The third trait is that poetry should be full of emotion. This does not simply mean that the poet should compose poetry when his heart is filled with emotion, or that his emotion is palpable in his description. Rather, it should inspire emotion in the hearts of the listeners. That is why it is necessary that the poet should be able to gauge their feelings and make the style of his recitation irresistible to win their hearts.

Translated by **M. Asaduddin**

Bankim Chandra Chattopadhaya

*Bankim Chandra Chattopadhaya (1838–94) is remembered mainly as a great novelist who shaped the novel in India. Like many of his contemporaries, he was concerned with the issue of language, and after a brief experiment in writing in English (**Rajmohan's Wife**, 1865), he turned to Bengali so as to reach the public. Some of his well-known novels are **Durgeshnandini**, which presented the new woman, **Vishvraksha** (The Poison Tree) and **Anandmath**, a novel in which he used 'Vande Mataram', a hymn he had written earlier. This was later to become a matter of political controversy. He also wrote some historical novels. Translated into several Indian languages, the influence of his work flowed into the fictional fabric of other Indian languages.*

*Besides fiction, Bankim Chandra also wrote on a large number of economic and political issues, on the plight of the farmers and on the new power centres that were surfacing. The questions of freedom and slavery are foremost in his writing. Editor of **Bangadarshan**, he wrote on a large number of literary issues, including forms of writing, genres and characterisation.*

*Bankim Chandra was a government employee and as such constrained in his anti-British stance. Even his restrained comments were to become an obstacle in the course of his promotion and one of the reasons that posterity remembers him with mixed feelings of admiration and approbation is the message that **Anand Math** conveys of British rule being a liberation for the Hindus from the Moghul rulers.*

The extract in this collection is from a much longer essay titled "Bengali Literature", which ostentiously takes up two books for review: **Lives of the Bengali Poets** *by Hari Mohan Mukurjya (Calcutta: New Sanskrit Press, 1869) and* **Mitra Prakas**. *No. 1 Dacca (1870), but in actuality provides a fairly detailed survey of the trends in Bengali* *writing, assessing them against the writing of the past. The essay is valuable for several reasons and two of these are the historical background he provides and his comments on the nature of realistic endings, marking a departure from the seemingly happy endings of Sanskrit drama.*

Bankim Chandra's critical acumen is sharp and analytical as he mercilessly mows down many a contemporary writer even as he selects some of them for appreciation. Towards the end, he refers to his own fictional contribution and this section may be regarded as a kind of self-review and a manifesto for his own writing. The focus is on ***Kapal Kundala****, a novel about Tantric practices, the passion of love and religious conversions, in fact a combination of the mysterious and the miraculous, but without a happy ending. The sacrificial victim escapes her slayer, but disappears all the same, upsetting both the escape from the slayer and the restoration to her lover—thus announcing the advent of realism in the midst of the miraculous.*

Bengali Literature*

Lives of the Bengali Poets. By Hari Mohan Mukurjya, Calcutta: New Sanskrit Press. 1869.

Mitra Prakas. No. 1. Dacca: 1870

The intellectual position of the Bengali among the races of India may be a prominent one at the present day, but in earlier times, it was one of the lowest. It is a Bengali writer, Babu Rajendralála Mitra, who has said that in ancient times, Bengal was the Boeotia of India. And the observation is correct. The contribution of Bengal to that ancient Indian literature which still commands the respect and attention of European scholars though small was not insignificant. The only Bengali Sanskrit poet of any eminence was Jayadeva, and he does not stand in the first rank. There is not one Bengali name that can compare with those of Kalidasa, Magha, Bharavi and Sriharsa. In other departments, the only distinguished Bengali name in the older Sanskrit literature is that of Kulluka Bhatta, the commentator on Manu. The great Bengali triumphs in the Nyaya philosophy and in law cannot be reckoned as falling within this period. The names of Raghunandana and Jagannatha belong to very recent days.

It is difficult to determine the date of the oldest Bengali writers, but probably few of their books are more than three hundred years old. Vidyapati, whose lyrics are perhaps the finest in the language, is certainly one of the first. Mukandaram Chakravartti, commonly known as Kabi Kankan, and the author of the *Chandi* poems, lived during the reign of Akbar. The *Chaitanya Charitamrita* is also one of the oldest Bengali

---

* *Bankim Rachanavali*. Ed. J.C. Bagal, (Calcutta: Sahitya Samsad, 1969) in three volumes. This work, originally written in English, is included in Vol. 3.

books. But however uncertain their exact date may be, the literary productions of Bengal naturally group themselves into five separate classes, different in spirit and to some extent successive in order of time, and if this be borne in mind, the want of exact dates need cause no difficulty in understanding the brief criticisms that follow.

The first in order are the lyric poets, at the head of whom must be placed Vidyápati. They are exclusively Vaisnavite and their songs either celebrate the amours of Krishna or the holiness of Chaitanya. They are still sung by bands of Bairágis and are popularly known by the name of *kirtan*. Their number is immense. The present writer has in his possession a collection that contains more than three thousand of these songs, and he believes that there are other collections equally voluminous. The music to which they are set is peculiar and is not ordinarily understood even by the professional musicians of Bengal. These, in fact, profess to hold *kirtan* music in utter contempt, but it nevertheless possesses a sweetness and pathos not ordinarily found in Indian music. The effect, however, is often marred by the discordant sound of the cymbals and drums by which it is accompanied. But if the music is peculiar, the language is no less so. Many of these songs are probably very modern, but others are undoubtedly the most ancient extent specimens of the Bengali language, and in these, the language is more like the Hindi of Tulsi Das than the Bengali of the present day. Doubtless, early Bengali and early Hindi differed little, if at all, from each other, and the present divergence is due to the operation of phonetic change in the same vernacular spoken by different branches of the same race, which were separated from each other by the revolution which followed the breaking up of the great empire of the Guptas of Magadha, or by others which are now lost in the silent darkness of Indian history.

It could scarcely be expected that so immense a collection as this Vaisnavite storehouse should be of uniform merit and one may well wish that nine-tenths of these songs had never been composed, but among the other one-tenth, there are gems of rare merit, which have never been surpassed in tenderness of feeling by anything in Bengali literature, and barely equalled by the best writers of the present day.

This school constitutes the literature of Chaitanyaism, while the second, we notice, represents Bengali Pauranism. The principal productions of this school are the Bengali version of the *Mahabharata* and the *Ramayana*. Their authors, Kasidas and Krittibás, were not mere translators of the great Indian epics. They did not attempt so much in one sense, yet they achieved something more. Taking the story and the matter in general from their great originals, they gave free scope to their own fancy, and in many places, established a claim to originality. We do not mean to say that they improved upon the originals, unless it were by greatly curtailing the tremendous bulk of the Sanskrit compositions, but the new matter that they added, while it detracts from the grandeur of the original conceptions of the Sanskrit poets, would, if embodied in some other form, have given them a certain position among original writers. Mukundaram Chakravartti—Kabi Kankan—though he followed no Sanskrit original, belongs to the same school and deservedly enjoys a higher reputation than either Krittibas or Kasidas. Many passages of his book are touchingly beautiful, but we cannot afford space for extracts. The language of these poets shows no traces of Hindi, but it is still very different from modern Bengali. In poetic power, they are decidedly inferior to the best of the Vaisnava poets.

The third class of writers we shall notice are those who flourished under the Nuddea Raja, Krishna Chandra. They enjoy an undeserved celebrity and are, in our opinion, a very worthless set. The best known among them is Bharat Chandra Ray, who was till lately considered the best of the Bengali poets, an opinion not yet wholly eradicated, but fast losing ground. Bharat Chandra is chiefly known by his *Vidya Sundara* and his *Annada Mangal*. Neither work has much merit, though an exception must be made in favour of the character of Hira, the flower girl, a coarse but racy and vigorous portrait, not equalled by anything of its kind in Bengali. One other great distinction, however, must be accorded to Bharat Chandra. He is the father of modern

Bengali. His versification, too, is very good and it is the model followed by many distinguished poets of the present day, as, for instance, Babu Ranga Lal Banerji. In the higher attributes of a poet, Bharat Chandra is far inferior to many who have preceded and followed him. His works are disfigured, too, by a disgusting obscenity, which unfits them for re-publication at a time when Bengali readers are not all of the rougher sex.

There is perhaps nothing more lamentable in the whole history of literature than the school of Bengali writers who followed the Nuddea poets and preceded the present generation. There is scarcely any readable work (readable even in the sense in which Bharat Chandra's poems are readable) belonging to that age—the age of the *Naba Babu Bilas* and the *Probodna Chandrika;* as for literary filth, there never was a more copious supply. Happily, the whole mass of rubbish has vanished from public recollection.

To this period belongs the well-known *kabi*, of which the wealthy Hindus of the last generation were so passionately fond, and on which they lavished immense sums of money. The *kabi* was a series of songs not often much connected with each other, sung by two opposite bands of performers. Each sought to abuse the other, and the more pungent the abuse, the greater was the triumph of the abuser and the pleasure of the listeners. The singing was generally the most execrable to which human folly has ever given the name of music, though in a few cases, the airs were sweet and elegant. The matter was often either commonplace or laboured extravagance, though among the songs of Ram Basu, Haru Thakur and Nitai Das, there are some [that are] of peculiar excellence. The following prose translation is from one of those most popular in the present day. It may be called *The Young Wife's Lament* and it will be understood only by those who know the very young Bengali wife, who has learned to love, but is too timid to speak:

> It is the spring of the year, and it is the spring of my life;
> And the lord of my life has left me for a far distant land.
> He came to me with a smile and told me he would go:
> I saw that smile, and that smile filled my eyes with tears.

I could not let him go; my heart would have made him stay;
But shame said, 'Fie ! do not, do not keep him back.'
So the sorrow of my heart is within my heart shut up.
I would have told it to him when he went to the far-off land;
But when I was about to speak, I could not.

We have preferred to give this specimen, rather than another of superior merit, because it is the most popular *kabi* among Bengalis at the present day.

There is one other writer—in a class by himself—whom we wish to notice before we proceed to consider the present state of Bengali literature. We mean Iswar Chandra Gupta. He stands between the past and the present, and singularly illustrates the literary poverty of the age in which he lived and the progress that has been made within the last few years. A dozen years have not elapsed since Iswar Chandra Gupta died, yet we speak of him as belonging to a past era, so essentially does he differ from the more prominent writers of the present day.

He was a very remarkable man. He was ignorant and uneducated. He knew no language but his own and was singularly narrow and unenlightened in his views; yet, for more than twenty years, he was the most popular author among the Bengalis. As a writer of light satiric verse, he occupies the first place and he owed his success both as a poet and as an editor to this special gift. But there his merits ended.

* * * * *

One of the most noticeable characteristics of Bengal at the present day is the large amount of literary activity to be found there in comparison with other parts of India. But while books and newspapers are daily pouring from the press, the quality of our current literature is by no means proportioned to its bulk. In fact, by far the greatest part (of) what is published is absolute rubbish. There are several modern Bengali books of which we shall have to speak in terms of high praise, but the number of these is so small in comparison with the mass of publications yearly vomited forth by the Bengali press, that they go but a little way towards redeeming the character of the whole. We can scarcely expect a better state of things from the class of men who compose the rank and file of Bengali authors and Bengali critics. Authorship in Bengal is the vocation of half-educated scribblers. The educated native has a sort of ultra-utilitarian contempt for the office and considers himself above writing in his own language. The case of criticism is worse. We can hardly hope for a healthy and vigorous Bengali literature in the utter absence of anything like intelligent criticism. The educated Bengali fails in this department almost as much as the antiquated pundit, in consequence no doubt of deficient culture.

Those who are familiar with the present writers in Bengali, will readily admit that they all, good and bad alike, may be classed under two heads, the Sanskrit and the English schools. The former represents Sanskrit scholarship and the ancient literature of the country; the latter is the fruit of Western knowledge and ideas. By far, the greater number of Bengali writers belongs to the Sanskrit school, but by far, the greater number of good writers belongs to the other.

* * * * *

It is with pleasure that we turn to the Anglicist school of writers. We have already mentioned Tekchand Thakur, the *nom de plume* of Babu Peary Chand Mitra. His best work is the *Áláler Gharer Dulál*, which may be said to be the first novel in the Bengali language. The story is extremely simple and may soon be told. Baburam Babu of Baidyabati is an old Kulin Brahman, who has amassed a large fortune by fleecing the suitors in a Court of which he was an employee. He has retired on his gains and is a zemindar and merchant. He has four children, two sons and two daughters. The eldest son, Mati Lal, is an ignorant, selfish, dissipated young fellow—spoiled from the effect of the over-indulgent treatment of his father. A Gurumahasay who had taught him Bengali, an ignorant Pujari Brahman, employed from motives of economy as Sanskrit tutor, and a retired tailor who instructed him in Persian, laboured, as might have been anticipated, with but indifferent success. The Gurumahasay, after some little time, retired from office in consequence of the playful habits of his pupil, who used to put quicklime in his daily whey, deposit burning embers in the folds of his garments, and indulge in many other like pleasantries. The Pujari resigned because he found it impossible to restrain his scholar's habit of throwing brickbats at the head of his instructor, as occasion offered. The Munshi's experience as a teacher abruptly closed on the occasion of his discovering that Mati Lal had amused himself by setting fire to his venerable beard.

Highly gratified with the progress which his son had made in Oriental learning, Baburam Babu now thought it time that he should learn English. So Mati Lal was sent to Calcutta, where he attended an English school. But he did no more good at English than at Persian and Sanskrit, and preferred to devote his time with other congenial spirits to cards, dice, cock-fighting, kite-flying and other amusements. At the same time, he took to smoking tobacco and *charas*, as well as to drinking brandy. One day he and his companions were taken up by the police for gambling in a house of ill fame. They were all convicted and imprisoned, except Mati Lal himself, who got off through the masterly way in which Miyajan Miya, an old friend of his father, proved an *alibi*. However, this occurrence put an end to Mati Lal's English studies and he at once returned home and, soon afterwards, happily married.

In the meantime, the younger brother, Ram Lal, grew up and followed a totally different path under the care of Barada Babu, an intelligent and cultivated man. He took kindly to his books, behaved well to his father and other relatives, had a courteous demeanour towards all he met, and was in fact a model of all that a boy should be. But, for some reason or the other, Baburam and his friends disapproved of this sort of thing and determined to get rid of Barada Babu. The natural way to do this was a criminal charge. So, with the assistance of Miyajan Miya, a serious charge was made against the unoffending Barada Babu, who would have paid dearly for his folly in neglecting the *amlah*. If he had not known English and so been able to put the facts clearly before the magistrate. For when the magistrate had heard so much of the evidence as he could listen to without neglecting his cigar, his newspaper and his private chits, the *sherishtadar* strongly urged a conviction, and nothing but his knowledge of English saved Barada Babu and gained him an acquittal.

About this time, Baburam Babu, who is a Kulin of high family, receives an offer of marriage likely to bring some money into his pocket, and at once closes with the proposal. Though Mati Lal's mother, a virtuous and affectionate wife, was still living, Baburam married again, and dying soon afterwards, he left two widows, one of them a mere child. Mati Lal now succeeded to the *gadi* and celebrated his father's *sraddh* in the right fashion. Henceforth, he gave himself up to pleasure, spending money like water on sensual enjoyments of all kinds. His mother remonstrates and receives a blow for her pains and is obliged to leave the house with her daughter, much to the delight of Mati Lal.

At length, as might have been expected, Mati Lal comes to grief and is sold up by his creditors. He leaves home, and having arrived in the course of his wanderings at the city of Benares, he falls in with one of the learned pundits of the place, who works his reformation. There, too, he meets his mother and sister and Barada Babu, who make it up with the repentant sinner, return home with him, and live happily ever after.

This is the simple story of *Áláler Gharer Dulál*, but the mere narrative is the least merit of the book. Its real value lies in the sketches of character and pictures of Bengali life which it contains. Most Europeans know little or nothing of natives beyond what may be learned in our Courts of Justice—places infested by a class of rascals hardly to be found elsewhere, and in which even otherwise honest and truthful men consider themselves entitled to lie, just as they consider themselves entitled to throw aside all regard for caste and for morality in the temple of Vishnu at Puri. A book like this, full of real sketches from life, is, therefore, specially valuable to them. It is true that there may be exaggeration here and there; it is true that, while the knaves are lifelike and full of character, the good characters are too much of mere abstractions. The females, too, are very faintly drawn. They are all alike, and they give very little idea of the influence which the wife within the zenana walls exercises in Indian daily life. But still the characters and pictures, such as they are, give the book a real value.

* * * * *

The next author to be considered is Mr Michael Madhusudan Datta, a most prolific writer of poems and plays. There is probably no writer whose merits are more variously estimated—some enthusiasts thinking him fit to compare with Kalidasa, while others regard him as a mere poetaster. For ourselves, we agree with neither, and while admitting his considerable merits, we are not prepared to rank him among the great poets. He has incurred much hostile criticism by his innovations in language, and by his introduction into Bengali of the use of blank verse, but his rightful place in Bengali literature is perhaps the highest.

His poetical works are the *Meghnada Badh*, the *Tilottama Sambhava*, the *Birangana* and the *Brajangana*. The two former are what in Europe would be called epic poems, and in India, *mahakavyas*. Both are written in blank verse—the first instances of the kind in Bengali. Of the two, the *Tilottama* was the earliest, but the *Meghnada Badh* is Mr Datta's greatest work. The subject is taken from the *Ramayana*, the source of inspiration to so many Indian poets. In the war with Ravana, Meghnada, the most heroic of Ravana's sons and warriors, is slain by Lakshman, Rama's brother. This is the subject, and Mr Datta owes a great deal more to Valmiki than the mere story. But, nevertheless, the poem is his own work from beginning to end. The scenes, characters, machinery and episodes are in many respects of Mr Datta's own creation. In their conception and development, Mr Datta has displayed a high order of art, and to do justice to it, or even to give a suitable idea of it, would require a much more minute examination of the poem than the space at our command will allow. To Homer and Milton, as well as to Valmiki, he is largely indebted in many ways, but he has assimilated and made his own most of the ideas which he has taken, and this poem is on the whole the most valuable work in modern Bengali literature. The characters are clearly conceived and capable of winning the reader's sympathy. The machinery, including a great deal that is supernatural, is skilfully and easily handled. The imagery is graceful and tender and terrible in turn. The play of fancy gives constant variety. The diction is richly poetic and the words so happily chosen as constantly to bring up by association ideas congruous to those which they directly express. Nor is the verse broken up into couplets complete in themselves in the Sanskrit fashion, but, abounding like Milton's in a variety of pauses, it seems to us musical and graceful, as well as a fitting vehicle for passionate feelings.

Mr Datta, however, is not faultless. He wants repose. The winds rage their loudest when there is no necessity for the lightest puff. Clouds gather and pour down a deluge, when they need do nothing of the kind; and the sea grows terrible in its wrath, when everybody feels inclined to resent its interference. All this bombast is unworthy of Mr Datta's genius and cultivated taste. Equally so is his constant repetition of the same images and phrases till they almost nauseate his readers. Nor is he altogether innocent of plagiarism. Homer and Valmiki are not infrequently put under contribution, and Milton and Kalidasa have equal reason to complain.

* * * * *

The Bengali press at the present day is very prolific, but by far the largest part of the books published are mere servile imitations of some successful author. There are imitators of Vidyasagar, imitators of Tekchand Thakur, of Hutam, of Babu Dinabandhu Mitra and of the author of *Durgesnandini,* but, perhaps, no work has formed the model for so many imitators as *Is This Civilisation*? It is a farce with a purpose, being intended chiefly to ridicule and to expose the vice of drunkenness and the other evils by which it is generally attended. The Burtolla Press and shops actually overflow with little books, containing a dozen or twenty pages each, and selling for an anna or two, all directed against the vice of drunkenness. There are farces, too, of larger bulk, one of which, called *Bujhile-Ki-Na?* or *Do You Understand?*, is very popular and often produced at private theatricals; and these, too, like the others, are mere copies of *Is This Civilization*? This little work, therefore, independently of its being in itself one of the two best farces in the language, gains additional importance from the large number of other books written after its model.

* * * * *

Among the romance writers, Babu Protap Chandra Ghose, author of *Bangadhip Parajay*, has recently been noticed at length in this review. The only other writer of this class whose works it seems necessary to notice is Babu Bankim Chandra Chatterji, whose *Durgesnandini, Kapal Kundala* and *Mrinalini* are among the most popular of Bengali books. Perhaps we cannot do better than to give a brief sketch of the story of *Kapal Kundala,* which, if not the best, is the shortest and most easily reproduced of the three. The story then runs thus:

A young Brahman named Naba Kumar, on his return from Ganga Sagar, was left by his companions on a deserted part of the coast of Hidgelee. The only inhabitant of the place was a 'Kapalika', or member of one of those strange sects which practised the wild and terrible Tantric forms of worship, whose temple is the burning *ghat,* and for whom no rite is too bloody and disgusting. From him, the young man obtained food and shelter. Having provided for his necessities, his unattractive host, with his drinking cup of human skull, went on a journey with a promise to return again. But day after day passed and no Kapalika appeared, till at length, Naba Kumar, weary of waiting, determined to find his own way, if possible, through the pathless wilderness of jungle in which the hermit's cave stood, to some region inhabited by men. But in the attempt, he utterly lost his way, and the following scene then occurs, which we quote because it is a favourite with native readers:

> He now perceived that he could not even find his way back. The deep roar of the water boomed in his ear and he recognised the voice of the ocean. Suddenly emerging from the thicket, he saw the sea spread before him. The infinite expanse of the dark waters filled him with a sublime joy. He sat down on the sandy beach. The dark foamy endless waters! Far as the eye could reach on either side, long white lines of foam flashed on the crest of the waves as they broke on the flat line of the beach, and shone against the golden sand like a garland of snow-white flowers. But over the expanse of ocean, too, a thousand waves were dancing and breaking into foam. If the wind could reach the stars and set them in motion across the background of the sky, this alone could fitly image the sight of the white foam-spots on the dark waters of the sea. The sun was about to set, and where the line of soft light fell, the water was transformed to molten gold. And in the distance, some European ships could be descried, skimming the ocean like gigantic birds with great white spreading wings.
>
> How long Naba Kumar continued to gaze at the ocean, he could not tell. Suddenly, the darkness of night came down on the bosom of the deep, and he then remembered that his way back must be found.
>
> Turning his back to the sea, he saw a magnificent vision. There stood on the sandy beach of the deep-sounding sea, dimly seen in the twilight, the figure of a woman such as he had never seen before. Her cloud-like tresses, confined by no hand, flowed down below her knee in long serpentine curls.
>
> Her face was partly hidden, but it shone like the moon through a break in the clouds. There was a mild and subdued light in her large eyes. Her expression was grave, but her face beamed on him like the moon now newly risen over the surface of the deep.

The young woman thus described in language rather more lofty than distinct turns out to be a Kapal Kundala, a girl who had been saved from the wreck of one of those Portuguese pirate ships that in old times ravaged the whole coast of Bengal in search of slaves, and who had been brought up by the Kapalika hermit in his solitary dwelling for ultimate purposes of which she knew nothing. She had imbibed from him a deep veneration for his goddess Kali, but her soul revolted from the human sacrifices which the Kapalika offered to Kali whenever occasion offered. The two returned to the hermit's cell, and it soon appeared that Naba Kumar was intended for sacrifice. His host, who was a man of vast strength, had tied him to the stake and would have at once carried out his purpose, but Kapal Kundala concealed the sacrificial knife, and when the Kapalika went to look for it, she cut the prisoner's bonds and the two took at once to flight. After a time, they reached a solitary shrine, and induced the *pujari* to marry them, Naba Kumar, it is needless to say, being deeply enamoured of his companion, and she having no objection to marriage because she had no idea what it meant. The *pujari* showed them, too, the way to Midnapore, from whence Naba Kumar's residence at Saptagram was easily reached.

This was not Naba Kumar's first marriage. He had been married once before, but while his wife was a mere child, and she having been converted with her father to the Muhammadan faith, they had left the country together, so that husband and wife had never met after the day of their marriage. A strange adventure now befell on the way back to Saptagram. Naba Kumar, having done some trifling service to a Musalman lady of great wealth and apparently high rank, she asked his name and residence and learned that he was her husband. For the lady was his wife, now Lutf-un-nissa, the favourite courtesan, whose lisp and beauty had won her power and wealth among the courtiers at Agra, where her father had risen to eminence through the favour of Akbar. As a mark of gratitude for the service rendered to her, she presented Kapal Kundala with a magnificent set of jewels, which the ignorant girl gave away in complete ignorance of their use and value to the first beggar on the road. Lutf-un-nissa was on her way back from Orissa, whither she had gone in furtherance of an intrigue to divert the succession from Prince Selim. A strange Nemesis had now overtaken her. She who boasted that she carried a heart of stone which neither prince nor courtiers could touch—she was now conquered by the poor wandering but handsome Brahman who had once been her husband. Arriving in Agra, she found Selim seated on the throne and obtained his permission to return to Bengal. She came to Saptagram, took a house, and spread her net for the affection of Naba Kumar. Finding, however, an insurmountable obstacle in his constant love for Kapal Kundala, she determined on a bold scheme for undermining it.

Kapal Kundala had now been more than a year in Naba Kumar's house. Her name, owing to its Tantric import, was changed to Mrinmayi. She herself had been to a certain extent reclaimed from the character of a child of the wilderness, but she regretted the change. Naba Kumar loved her ardently, but she did not return his feeling. Her heart was preoccupied by the great goddess, Kali, to whose service she was fanatically devoted. She would have died for Naba Kumar, if necessary, but she did not love him and she could not bear the restraints of the zenana. Setting his authority at naught, she one night stole out into the jungle to gather herbs for a female friend, who wanted them for a philtre. Approaching an old ruin, she overheard some conversation which seemed to concern herself. She was detected listening by one of the talkers who appeared to be a Brahman youth. She was seized with fear and fled. She saw she was being followed, and before she reached home and closed the door behind her, she recognised the well-known stalwart form of the Kapalika.

The Kapalika, when his victims had escaped, had given chase, but had fallen and broken his arm. While he lay helpless in bed, Bhawani had appeared to him in a dream and demanded Kapal Kundala as a sacrifice. When the use of his limbs had been recovered, he spent nights and days in searching for her, and at length, he had succeeded. But he needed assistance in bringing her to the sacrificial altar, and while watching his opportunity, he met Lutf-un-nissa disguised for purposes of her own as a Brahman youth, and it was these two whom Kapal Kundala had disturbed in their consultations. The two did not agree. Lutf-un-nissa's object was to separate Kapal Kundala from her husband, but she would not consent to violence of any kind. Finding the Kapalika resolved in his purpose, Lutf-un-nissa determined to save Kapal Kundala by telling her the facts and then to work on her feelings of gratitude. Accordingly, next day, Kapal Kundala found on her path a note from the disguised Brahman inviting a second meeting in the wood and promising important disclosures. No other Hindu wife would have kept the appointment, but she did and not unnoticed.

Kapal Kundala, when going out the night before, had been seen by Naba Kumar, who, though not yet jealous, might readily have been made so. He watched the second night and found her going out again, and to add to his torments, Lutf-un-nissa's note had dropped unperceived on the floor. He picked it up and read it, and determined to follow. But almost before he had got outside the house, the Kapalika stood before him. Disappointed in Lutf-un-nissa, the terrible devotee now sought to secure the assistance of Naba Kumar himself by working on his jealousy. He told Naba Kumar of his own fall and loss of strength, and of Bhawani's command, and called on him to assist in the sacrifice of his wife, whom at the same time he denounced as a fallen traitoress. If he wanted proof, he bade him follow, and the two plunged together into the thicket.

Kapal Kundala had met Lutf-un-nissa in the wood, and the latter, after telling her the Kapalika's story and letting her fully understand his terrible purpose, disclosed also her own identity and history, and the object she had in view. She promised Kapal Kundala riches and comfort in some foreign land, if only she would leave her husband without warning. To this, she might have consented, having no real love for her husband, but when once she had heard the will of Bhawani, nothing remained for her but to fulfil it. She left the place, and at a little distance, fell in with the Kapalika and was ready to carry out the hermit's purpose. They all went together to the place of sacrifice—the burning ghat, which is minutely described in all its horrid details, with its crowd of vultures, half-burnt human bodies, and heaps of skulls and bones in all directions. Then they prepared to worship according to the rites of the Tantriks. Naba Kumar took Kapal Kundala to the waterside to bathe her before she should be sacrificed. There, an explanation was given. He begged her to return. She declared her intention of fulfilling Bhawani's will, and while the debate between them was going on, just as he stretched out his hand to seize her and force her to return, the bank beneath her feet gave way, and she fell into the deep stream below. He leaped after her. Both for a time disappeared. The Kapalika [at] length dragged Naba Kumar to land, but Kapal Kundala was seen or heard of no more. And so the story ends, much to the disappointment of most Bengali readers, who much prefer the orthodox ending, where all live happily ever after.

Mrinalini is a book of a very different stamp and many consider it Babu Bankim Chandra Chatterji's most successful production.

But here must end our brief and imperfect sketch of Bengali literature—a literature which, with much that is feeble and base and utterly worthless, yet has within it what may encourage no small degree of hope for the future. Its character is for the most part imitative, but what literature, save that of Greece, has ever been independent and original in its youth? Once again, a voice from that holy land of beauty and truth had awakened the torpid heart and mind of Western Europe. Horace himself, the most spontaneous and genuine of all the Latin poets, entertained no higher idea of originality than to make it consist in the importation of a new form of poetry from Greece. An imitator in those days meant an imitator of Latin authors—the imitation of Greek being almost implied in the excellence of any work. And when Europe woke again from the long sleep which followed on the dissolution of the Roman Empire, it was on the translation and imitation of Greek and Latin authors that its energies were employed. Is there no imitation in Dante himself? It may seem improbable that European ideas will ever really be assimilated by the people of India—that all we can affect here is a superficial varnish of sham intelligence. But everything cannot come in a day, and there was a time when it would have seemed almost equally improbable that the little remnant of intelligence preserved in the Latin Church and the study of classical antiquity would have grown into what we now see among the Celtic and

Teutonic peoples of the East. The Bengalis may not seem to have the fibre for doing much in the way of real thought any more than of vigorous action, but it was chiefly among the supple and pliant Italians that the revival of learning in Europe began, and it is possible to imagine that the Bengalis—the Italians of Asia, as the *Spectator* has called them—are now doing a great work, by, so to speak, acclimatising European ideas and fitting them for reception hereafter by the hardier and more original races of Northern India.

O. Chandu Menon

Oyyarathu Chandu Menon (1847–99) wrote ***Indulekha*** *in Malayalam to form a bridge between the English novels he was fond of reading and the interest of his family and friends in what he read. In his Preface, he freely acknowledges the influence of the western novel, but in practice, his work reflects both Indian social concerns and storytelling methods. In 1891,* ***Indulekha*** *was translated into English by one of his patrons. Later, he was to write another novel,* ***Sharada****. The end of the nineteenth century novel reflects a concern with the idea of romance and the problems of marriage.* ***Indulekha*** *is no exception to this. The heroine, after whom the novel is titled, is representative of the new woman. She resists marriage to the man she does not love and thus steps out of the role of the docile woman.*

Employed in government service as a munsif, Chandu Menon was later to become a judge at Tellicherry. A social reformer, Menon also happened to be on the Committee of the Malabar Marriage Bill. Keenly aware of the problems of both—the practice of matriliny amongst the Nairs and that of polygamy amongst the Namboodris—he openly critiqued both of them.

The Preface to ***Indulekha*** *is important for several reasons. It works both at the personal and literary levels and tells us a great deal about Menon the man, who was fond of reading, and Menon the social being, who did not like to be cut off from his friends and family. And while the written narrative closes in the reader with the book, the oral is participatory and convivial, opening it out. The writing of an English-style novel in Malayalam implied an induction of the western model into the Malayali way of storytelling, while simultaneously absorbing several patterns of the oral narrative. One of the issues which Menon addresses, like almost all his contemporaries, is the concern with* *language: How does one reconcile the use of a foreign language with the native cultural milieu? The writer then goes on to comment on the difficulties of translating a particular cultural milieu into another culture. He experimented with translating an English novel into Malayalam and realised that the translation falsified the original. In contrast, an oral transmission was much more communicative. The issue then is placed in the larger context of nation construction.*

There is also the question of readership. The use of English builds an exclusive society, while Malayalam addresses a literate readership. Oral narratives, on the other hand, were the only way of communication with the illiterate. Thus, even though Menon's attempt is to weave the western model into an Indian narrative tradition, all along, there is an attempt to work outside any imitative model and forge a new tradition.

Preface to the First Edition of *Indulekha*

I began to read English novels extensively after I left Calicut at the end of 1886, and I then devoted all the leisure which my official duties left me to novel reading. Thereupon, I found that my circle of intimates with whom I had been accustomed to pass the time in social conversation and amusement considered itself somewhat neglected, and I accordingly endeavoured to find means by which I could conciliate its members without in any degree foregoing my novels. With this object in view, I attempted at first to convey to them in Malayalam the gist of the story contained in some of the novels I had read, but my hearers did not seem particularly interested in the versions which I gave them of two or three of these books. At last it happened that one of these individuals was greatly taken with Lord Beaconsfield's *Henrietta Temple* and the taste then acquired for listening to novels translated orally, gradually developed into a passion. The importunity of this personage in the matter was so great that I had seldom time to read a book on my own account. Occasionally, even when I was alone and studying a treatise on law, my friend (mistaking it for a novel) would come and tease me saying, 'There again, you are reading a novel to yourself. I must have it translated orally.' Thus, in one way and another, it appeared to me that by trying not to give umbrage to my associates, I had succeeded in giving considerable inconvenience at any rate to myself.

Finally, I was urged to produce a written translation of the novel by Beaconsfield which I have mentioned, and I consented. But when I had made some little progress in the work, I thought the matter over and decided that a translation thus made would be absolutely without value. I find no great difficulty in communicating to my friends, who are ignorant of English, a fairly accurate idea of an English novel by means of an oral rendering, but I think it is wholly impossible to transmit a correct impression of the story through a written translation. The reason of this is that when the translation is written, a mere string of words is presented to the mind and this alone is insufficient for the purpose. In translating orally, the true force of English expressions is, at times, maintained, but the narrative, as a whole, can be rendered intelligible only by elucidating, with the help of much commentary, the details appropriate to each incident as it is related by supplementing the pronunciation of words and by gesture and expression. If a professedly literal translation were interpolated with such details, explanation and commentary, then there is no doubt that the work, as a translation, would be completely ruined. Moreover, another obstacle is that any attempt to reproduce literally in a written translation into Malayalam the love passages with which English novels abound must necessarily be far from happy. Taking, therefore, all these circumstances into consideration, I determined to write a Malayalam novel more or less after the English fashion and gave my persecutor a promise to this effect. The compact was entered into in January last, but on one pretext and another, I delayed its fulfilment until June. Then I was no longer able to withstand the pressure brought to bear on me, but, commencing to write this volume on the 11th June, finished it on the 17th August, and thus it is that this book came into existence.

I do not know how my countrymen will be disposed to regard a work of this description. Those who do not understand English have had no opportunity of reading stories cast in this mould, and I doubt if they will relish their first experience of this kind of literature.

While I was engaged in writing this book, some of my friends, who are not conversant with English, questioned me concerning the subject I had chosen. I gave them a brief outline thereof and perceived that they did not approve of the new departure I had made. Indeed I know that one individual exclaimed, 'What is the use of taking all this trouble? If things have never taken place, what is the use of writing a story about them?' In answer to this, I could offer only one explanation—that most of the books which the world has seen are story books and that, while some of these books contain stories which, being styled histories, must be believed, the notion that the events chronicled in the rest ever actually happened, must be rejected altogether or accepted with considerable reserve. Generally speaking, however, the truth seems to be that popular appreciation of a story depends on the skill displayed in its treatment and is irrespective of the question whether the subject is one of fact or of fiction. Were it otherwise, there would be no reason why the vast majority of books should be so exclusively composed of romance. Men of intelligence, in reading books of this type, do not stop to inquire critically whether the tale is true or imaginary, but the qualities which they demand to rivet their attention are ingenious semblance of reality and elegance in the elaboration of the narration.

When a person of cultivated taste and judgement reads a clever and effectively written novel, he may feel positive from beginning to end that none of the incidents described therein ever actually occurred, but it is nevertheless certain that he experiences the same sensations that he would experience if he were satisfied that the various situations had been borrowed directly from real life. Many a grave and reverend man of learning as he passes from one stage to another in a work of fiction, admires the dexterity of the author in the construction of the plot, notwithstanding his convictions that the whole of what he reads is merely the creation of an inventive mind, and many a man of calm and temperate feelings is melted to tears or moved to laughter, as pathetic or humorous scenes are presented to his imagination. These things are of every day occurrence among persons of ordinary education and understanding, and it appears to me that works of fiction are most instrumental not only in amusing, but also in instructing mankind in general. Hence, I consider it a mistake to say that a story which is not wholly and strictly made up of facts serves no good purpose, and I think that the points which should receive particular care are style and beauty of composition.

One day while I was correcting the proofs of this book, another friend also asked me what the subject was. The only answer I gave him was that if the book was ever published, I would send him a copy and he could then see for himself. The reply he made was as follows, 'It is a good thing if the book which you are preparing treats of that branch of English learning which is called Science, but Malabar has no need of any book dealing with any other subjects,' and these words astonished me not a little.

Others again asked me while I was employed on this novel how I expected to make it a success if I described only the ordinary affairs of the modern life without introducing any element of the supernatural. My answer was this: Before the European style of oil painting began to be known and appreciated in this country, we had—painted in defiance of all possible existence—pictures of Vishnu as half man and half lion, pictures of the deity of the chase, pictures of bruteheaded monsters, pictures of the God Krishna, with his legs twisted and twined into postures in which no biped could stand and blowing a cowherd's horn, pictures of Ananthan wearing a thousand cobra-hoods, pictures of gigantic demons, and all these executed with a touch and colouring so coarse as to banish all idea of chiaroscuro, perspective and proportion. Such productions used to be highly thought of, and those who produced them used to be highly remunerated, but now they are looked upon by many with aversion. A taste has set in for pictures, whether in oil or water colours, in which shall be delineated men, beasts and things according to their true appearance, and the closer that a picture is to nature, the greater is the honour paid to the artist. Just in the same way, if stories composed of incidents true to natural life and attractively and gracefully written, are once introduced, then by degrees, the old order of books, filled with the impossible and the supernatural, will change, yielding place to the new.

I cannot, however, claim for this book of mine any such artistic merit as I have indicated and I shall be much distressed if my readers think from what I have said that I have put forward such a claim. All that I mean is that if competent persons would take the subject up and produce artistic novels, the public would find pleasure in reading them.

The language I have used in this book is the language I would ordinarily speak at home. Although I have some knowledge of Sanskrit, I have as a rule employed Sanskrit words only in the manner and to the extent in which they are employed colloquially by us Malayalis. For instance, the Sanskrit word for 'etymology' or 'critical knowledge' is '*vyulpaththi*' in the proper Sanskrit pronunciation, but in common use it became '*vilpaththi*', and I have adhered to the popular form. Many similar examples will be found, but in the case of certain words and compounds which have been absorbed into Malayalam, neither is the original pronunciation nor is the original meaning preserved, and I therefore warn my readers beforehand that I have employed such phrases only in the usual acceptation. I may also here remark that I have used the active and passive voice and transitive and intransitive verbs in the mode in which they are used in ordinary conversation, and I have made no attempt to abandon, in favour of a style modelled on pure Sanskrit prose, the diction of Malayalis conversing in Malayalam. Of my English readers, I would beg the favour of their perusing a letter which I have addressed to Mr W. Dumergue, C.S., and have had printed as an accompaniment to this volume, before they read the book itself. In that letter, I have met, so far as I was able to anticipate them, some of the objections which will be raised to certain innovations in this narrative.

In the printing of this book, Mr Kochchu Kunjen, the Superintendent of the Spectator Press, has afforded me great assistance, and I have much pleasure in acknowledging the intelligence and promptitude with which he brought to my notice from time to time, as the pages passed through the press, errors which had crept in owing to the haste in which my task was accomplished.

9th December, 1889 **Parapanangadi**

Goverdhanram Tripathi

Goverdhanram Tripathi (1855–1907), a lawyer by profession, was a writer by conviction. In his case, we have access to his four ***Scrap Books****, which were originally written in English and thus the non-Gujarati knowing reader can also read them. Like several of his contemporaries, Tripathi, too, was bilingual. The* ***Scrap Books*** *are an unusual combination of auto/biography plus diary, listing his ambitions, sketching out his dreams, analysing his physical ailments, reflecting on his relationship with his wife, and also commenting on British colonialism. They bring together the sociopolitical and the personal to reveal the amazing ways in which Indian intellectuals were concerned with national issues.*

Tripathi's four-part novel, ***Saraswati Chandra*** *(1887–1901), is still a popular and respected novel. The film version made in 1968 by Govind Saraiya starring Nutan and Manish made it widely known to non-Gujaratis. Its main appeal lies in its innocence, idealism and concern with social reform. The hero, Saraswatichandra, is a Nationalist who overcomes his reluctance to marry when he falls in love with Kumud, but this is not to be. Kumud is married off to a man set in his immoral ways. Follow a failed suicide attempt on Kumud's part, and then the death of her husband. The latter event sets her free to remarry, but instead, she chooses to dedicate her life to social work.*

The 'Prefaces' to each successive part of the novel provide evidence of Tripathi's concerns with the narrative form and his conscious questioning of the western mode. A piece of literature should have long term goals beyond the interest of and appeal to a reading public. The narrative is a medium which has a much wider catchment area than any 'abstruse or discursive matter', as the portrayal of the real world, populated by people's dreams, ideals and failures, provides space for debate, evaluation and identification. Tripathi's novel, however, is inspired by larger social goals and wishes to emphasise them by working with nationalistic causes. The 'Preface' to the fourth part is the longest of the four and sums up the journey from 1887 to 1901, from Bombay to Nadiad, a precious chunk of life when Tripathi constantly reviewed both his life and work and kept on evaluating them at every juncture to measure how far he had achieved his ideal goals. In it, he also discusses the emerging concepts of mediastin and fusion in the context of roles and cultures, offering us his own interpretation of the conflictual situation of his times.

Prefaces to *Saraswati Chandra*

Part I
Preface

Novels have in these days become a universal luxury and, in competing for public interest, have succeeded to an extent almost unrivalled. The very natural result has been that the bulk of fiction in the West has ceased to aspire beyond an artistic display of such of the sentimental and emotional idiosyncrasies of mankind as happen to tickle the fancy of the ordinary reader. It is however certain—and the higher class of novelists never fails to recognise and claim—that the functions of the novel are more numerous, higher and more sacred than the mere pandering to the taste of the novel-reading public.

The writer of these pages admits that the origin of his undertaking was in the first instance neither so ordinary nor so ambitious. Like all who live and look around, he had his memoranda of what may be called the substrata of this, our world of human affairs. When he first desired to give an objective existence to all that was so sketched out in his mind's book, he intended to give it the form of essays. Second thoughts discovered that the reading class in Gujarat was, for various reasons, difficult to reach through abstruse or discursive matter, and that illustrations of real or ideal life would be the best medium, best in the sense of being attractive and impressive for communication like those which the writer has to make. Hence, the present contribution.

The conviction has also grown upon him that reality in flesh and blood under the guise of fiction can supply the ordinary reader with subtler moulds and finer casts for the formation of his inner self than abstract discussions and that this is especially so with a people who must be made, and not simply left, to read.

It remains to note that by inducing reality into fiction, it is not meant to convey any personal allusion whatever in any part or even a line of the book. The actualities of life or locality are referred to only and strictly so far as they belong to any of the varied conditions of life amongst our people. And even these are on occasions ideal. The ideal and the actual are in some places inseparable.

Bombay,
April 1887

G.M.T.

Epigraph to Part II

Blessed is he who has found his work in the world and does it, making his claim to wages a zero

'... The ideal which governs me in the care and development of my wife and children will supply me with a sample for an incomparably vast but kindred ideal for the well-being of my countrymen, by a training of their physical and mental and moral constitutions, so that they may be fitter to take care of themselves and to look after their concerns, than what they may be made by any events and results that a group of patriotic individuals may ever hope to bring out. To qualify myself for the attainment of this ideal is the first object of my studies. To attain the ideal and secure its practical end for my country by study of books and of life, by thinking, discovering and inventing means and methods and materials, and by taking such actions as may be necessary in practice for giving a practical shape and turn to the realisation of the ideal, is the next and last object of my studies and work as reader, observer, thinker, writer and preacher, or, as a man of action, if time, means and exigencies call me to taking the wheel on my shoulders. *To create a new and living force among my countrymen by training them into a higher life in this way, is the mission of my life, so long and so far as I may be able to live.*'

— Private ***Scrap Book*** of **Goverdhanram Tripathi**

Part III
Preface

With the third volume, this narrative enters upon a different phase of its career. It still continues to be a mosaic or even blending of the actual and the ideal aspects of our life in these days, but the latter, henceforth, begin to acquire a distinct predominance over the former. It is eleven years since the first volume was published, and the progress of the reading classes during the interval has been equal to the writer's aspiration to interest them in the principal problems of the day.

This and the succeeding volume will bring this tale to a close. The labours of the writer will be sufficiently rewarded if his book will have stimulated, among the various classes of our society, an abiding interest in some of the great questions that make the young and the old in the country thrill with interchanging hopes and fears in all the varied matters which make up our life, and if it can enable them to follow with patience the solution which society is evolving upwards along a slow, but sure, gradient in relation to each of these pressing questions.

Each one of these problems is complicated and difficult, and the writer of a novel cannot be expected to do it the justice which a scientific or philosophical essayist can struggle for. An artist—and a novelist is no more—can only hope to give that simplicity to problems which the passive reader craves for, to bring out for his gaze the fascinations of their lights and shades so as to recreate and not tax his eyes, and yet to hope that, humble as this province of the writer is, he may enable the reader to rise a stage higher than where he was. At the same time, it is no object of the writer to do so with that partisan spirit which may fairly find room in polemical essays, where he who has formed his convictions must strive to force them upon the erring world. To the artist, the world is not so much a mass of errors as a prospect of beauty, even where it errs, and he can simply propose to draw upon the resources of his own soul to enlarge the vistas which he is picturing, only with a view to add to the beauty, and not to the logic, of his work. As the Athenian believed, his beauty carries a silent logic more potent than reason and her quarrelsome ways.

What these problems are is a matter best left to the text itself. In the preface, one can only attempt to introduce. Well, we are at present undergoing strange transitions in matters domestic, social, religious, political and what not. What with the laden atmosphere of our domestic difficulties, what with the currents of our social ideals and forces, what with the many-tongued voices of the religions which a multiform and party-coloured nation is singing into our ears, what with the constant upheavals of new and jarring worlds of political entities and nonentities rising within one's view whether he locates himself in one of the native states or in any place in British India, one, standing in the midst of all this, is simply tempted to wish, like Cowper, 'for a lodge in some vast wilderness', or for a transmigration back into the body of some quiet and retired Rishi of antiquity.

This universal jar and noise casts a gloomy shadow over many a wistful eye and disconcerts many a well-built hope. We shall leave it to other fields of learning to settle with conviction whether the world in India will survive this deluge of conflict or not, and we may be sure that even in discussing that, men will differ and fall to quarrelling. The only place where we may safely look for a peaceful picture in spite of all transient facts is art and poetry. In the several volumes of this tale, the landing-places of our relief are sought to be pictured. We, no doubt, start even here with the jar and noise that surrounds us, and we hope to travel a good deal in the midst of these regions. But Progress and Harmony at home, in society, in religion, and with Government, both in and outside British India, peer overhead in the long run in spite of all this bewildering confusion: at least that is the postulate fundamental to our perspective. To look at these two cherubs of beauty and hope as they look at us, is at least a vision of glory and happiness, and what is vision today may be reality tomorrow.

True it is that the realisation of this vision of the future taxes our patience and we may never live to see it. Well may one grumble with the poet:

When will the hundred summers die
And thought and time be born again,
And, newer knowledge drawing nigh,
Bring truth that sways the soul of men?
Here all things in their place remain,
As all were ordered, ages since.
Come, care and pleasure, hope and pain,
And bring the fated fairy prince.

But after all, we may also have the privilege of seeing with him

Faint shadows, vapours lightly curl'd
Faint murmurs from the meadows come,
Like hints and echoes of the world
To spirits folded in the womb.*

The vision is not altogether a dream. Transient hours will come and go. But the student of permanent elements and constant factors will be able to trace the birth and growth of an inward homogeneity in what is heterogeneous in the inception, and to hail the slow, but sure, triumph of Progress on lines which may not satisfy either theoretical, revolutionary and precipitate visionaries and reformers, or those who on the other hand wish to give an eternal rigidity to the today, whether of belief or of power, and to dam out the influx of a sure and different tomorrow, for the lines of that Progress will certainly be such—*gradual and harmonized resultants* of numerous currents of life and facts as are still not dreamt of in our Horatio's philosophy. Such will be the *modus operandi* of the elements that do and shall vivify individuals, societies and governments with new forms of life, and our visions may be realised according to the extent that they harmonise with this progress. Indian society and religions, orthodoxy and reform, visionaries and practical people, Indians and Englishmen, and even Government and states and subjects—all on Indian soil—must yield to this irresistible process of reciprocal assimilation, at least as an inevitable duty in the working of the much talked of unity of all. And our vision is that none of them, whether of Eastern or Western

* Tennyson's *Sleeping Palace.*

boast, will be able to resist yielding to this process in this way and to this end, more or less, sooner or later.

Dear reader, more were better left to the text.

Bombay, 1898. G.M.T.

Part IV
Preface

The last volume of *Saraswati Chandra* is here offered to the public. It endeavours to complete the programme laid down in the preface to the third volume. In that preface, it was suggested that the varied conflicts of life and thought at present visible all over India may one day end in reciprocal assimilation and harmony of the warring elements.

This process of assimilation, while it may not be able to surprise us with any sudden advent of peace, will make its presence felt sooner or later by floating on our horizon ideas and sentiments as foreign to our past experience as possibly Columbus and his ships may be imagined to have been to the minds of the anxious aborigines of old America as they watched his approach towards their shores. This may sound like an exaggerated note of alarm or an idle conceit at first sight; cooler thoughts will, however, bring home the conviction that our present state of transition must one day end the effervescence of its lighter elements. That stage over, India must have her day of peace and comfort, and the only question is what kind of day that will be.

There seems to be a sort of presumption in proposing to answer such a question, and a presumption it might be if this book were of the nature of a historical disquisition or a scientific forecast. The writer of a novel may, however, well be allowed to indulge in dreams of future days according to his own lights, even where the forecast of any future at all must fall short of the exacting tests of scientific or philosophical critics.

It is in such a dreamland or Manorajya that the design of the present volume is laid. It is on account of this feature of the volume that it is given the title of the Manorajya of Sarasvati or the Dreamland of the Minerva of our Indian Atheneum. And the writer's justification for this part of his performance is not that his dreams are prophetic, but that he may, by allowing the reader to have a clairvoyant view of them, help his countrymen in groping their way out of darkness into some kind of light. It will be some gain if, by that procedure, he can show and signal a 'line clear' for those that may be wishing to know their place in the programme for hastening the hour of peace.

This object the writer has attempted to attain partly by speaking in the language of myths, legends and traditions familiar to his countrymen. There is, in his opinion, a deep and almost scientific evolutional allegory consistently running throughout the plot of the great and prolific *Mahabharata* and he has devoted a long and, perhaps, tedious chapter in this work to the exposition of this feature of that venerable epic. He is aware that in doing so, he has obviously sacrificed well-known canons of modern art, but considering the use made of this allegory in the latter part of the volume, the critic will probably be disposed to agree with his views as to the necessity of that course and the appositeness of this otherwise irrelevant-looking matter.

This groundwork of that epic has so much in common with some of the leading ideas worked out by modern social and political speculations that it has been found possible to translate the latter into the terms of the former supplemented by other similar materials drawn from our ancient literature and modern popular beliefs even where the beliefs are, to all appearances, superstitious. It is expected that such a use of these materials will enable the ordinary Indian mind to grasp and appreciate Western ideas and ideals to some extent and to some useful purpose.

The existence of such common ideas and their possible influence on the people of this country will arouse a varied interest.

If there is a vast distance between modern India on the one hand and modern Europe and America on the other as regards their modes of thought and life, a similar distance can also be traced in several important points between ancient and modern India itself. It is usual to speak as if the present generation of Indians were witnessing the Fusion of two great civilisations in the contact of the West with the East. If one can admit that India herself has exhibited more than one phase of civilisation, and that the phases presented by her in her ancient days were far different things from the phase she now presents, it will be more accurate to say that we were not only hemmed in between the two civilisations of modern East and West, but that the awakenings of the far different ancient Indian Civilisation are also upon us as a third element of the fusion. If this last element differed in essential points from modern Western civilisation, it also agreed with it (as the abovementioned common ideas will attest) in recognising some very vital principles of thought and life as being of the essence of progress and Civilisation, as, for instance, when the Aitareya Brahmana defined the Satya Yuga as the Age of Action or Progress and the Kali Yuga as the Age of Sleep or Stagnation. One of the objects aimed at in this volume is so to lift the veil from this part of our literature and history as to show some of the lines of our ancient thought and life along with those of the West in modern times and to bring their converging points into prominence. For that may enable our readers, as representing a part of modern India, to realise what elements are likely to have a preponderating influence in the fusion of the three great civilisations brought by Providence to bear upon the life of our nation and combined by that same power to shape her destiny by their confluence.

What is popularly called our stage of transition has consisted more or less of a condition in which the communities, professing to be under the influence of the one or the other of these civilisations, have been started by the near approach and close contact of the rival civilisations, and have at times received one or the other of them with curiosity, suspicion and distrust. The part played by the ordinary Indian mind during this stage has been shown in the first three volumes of this work. The present volume is mainly taken up with the part that is being played and will be played in that drama by a class of Indians which has been directly evolved by the actual contact and growing relations of these civilisations themselves. This is the class which is composed of educated natives. By reason of these very circumstances and others connected with its genesis and development, this class is expected to take upon itself special and active functions in bringing about a happy fusion of the elements which have brought it into being and which constitute the special sphere of its usefulness. It is proposed in this volume to present, on the surface of mythical allegories and doctrinal language dear to Indian hearts, a faint but visible etching of the lines along which, by the performance of these functions by this class, assimilation and harmony may be expected to issue in the country out of the temporary phantoms of that religious, social and political unrest and conflict, which, in the course of this fusion, apparently disturb the mental peace of so many races in modern India, not excluding our English brethren. It is possible to fancy ourselves having a peep at a situation of peace, cooperation and harmonious progress for all these, and if we can even conceive the feasibility of such a peep, we may also hope that what is only such a fiction today may become a fact tomorrow.

This hope is not without its foundation so long as educated Indians are assisted in maturing the robustness of their communal body in order that they may be enabled to perform their legitimate functions with independence. Theirs is the position of the mediastin between the rulers on the one side and the masses of their own countrymen on the other, as also between the masses and the diverse classes of their countrymen themselves. They are a median organism in this way between various other sets of complicated and contradictory organisms, each of which is sufficiently charged with its own latent, but powerful and impatient, energies. These energies are by no means an evanescent factor in the case, but have in each case been stored up by the long and persistent action of civilisations, which are bound to make the severest struggle for self-preservation. It has fallen to the lot of the educated classes to serve as organic sheaths and conductors between the multiform sets of organisms forming the repositories of these energies. The many sided strain now put upon those classes, and likely to grow in quality and quantity while performing these functions, requires that they should find proportionate strength and support from all those who contribute to the strain and will benefit by the capacity of this class to meet it.

The method of developing and maturing, in this mediastin class, a right and beneficent capacity, not only for meeting this strain, but also for performing their difficult functions, is a problem in whose solution all India—including its English population—is deeply and directly interested. The extent to which those at the helm of the State will be equal to the task of pursuing this method with foresight, sympathy and even sacrifice will also be the measure of their own reward in the long run. But any such method, if method itself be not altogether abjured by them, must in any case involve a concession of the necessary and sufficient amount of free scope for independent action to the median organism, and must thereby afford a valid ground for the hope that some of the fictions here offered of what in part are only our hero's visions today, may indeed become facts in some more practical fashion tomorrow.

The existence and the soundness of this hope are assumed in this volume. It is also assumed that educated natives, while grasping at all available extraneous assistance with all their might, will also enter manfully into a struggle on their own behalf to bear their manifold strains and to perform their functions as much with patience and fellow-feeling as with intrepidity, perseverance and wisdom. This volume attempts to present a perspective in which the description of this struggle will connect the reader with contemporaneous actualities, while his introduction into the dreamland of the attainment of the final fusion of the heterogeneous elements will open upon him distant but happier vistas of the past and future of his countrymen. Whether the various characters which fill this perspective are drawn with sufficient art and neatness is a question best left to the critic.

Nadiad,
27th August, 1901 G.M.T.

Rabindranath Tagore

Rabindranath Tagore (1861–1941), known as Gurudev and referred to by his contemporaries as 'The Poet', is a towering scholar of his age. Born in a Brahmo Samaj family, he was the youngest of thirteen surviving children. Several of his siblings were also writers or artists, but none else rose to similar heights of fame. Tagore was awarded the Nobel Prize in 1913 and, at that moment, his collection, ***Gitanjali****, rose to fame. A person of many talents, he was a man with a vision. Writer—poet, lyricist, playwright, novelist—he was also a painter and a musician. His lyrics and his music—Rabindra Sangeet—find a home both in India and Bangla Desh and in every Bengali home, no matter where it is.*

Tagore was intended for the legal profession. But distracted by literature, he gave up his studies midway and returned home from England without a degree. This was in some ways a defining moment in his life. Later, his own discontentment with the education system led him to establish Shantiniketan, an educational centre that was based on a more open system aimed at an all-round education, including other arts—a system not bound by rigid divisions and separations between disciplines as was ordinarily the case.

The essay included here is somewhat unusual. It looks closely at the novel as history. Some of the writers Tagore discusses here are Walter Scott and Bankim Chandra. If we read the essay closely, we can see his debate veering towards a more modernist stand and one should read it along with Premchand's essay on the one hand and Agyeya's essay on time referring to 'itihaas' and 'mithihaas' on the other. Fact, imagination and social relevance of the past to the present can all be seen coming together in the fiction of history. Should a novel based on history be well-researched or is it a mere fictional representation? How do we distinguish between fact and truth?

Today, when we realise that the present day historical novel has travelled a long way, this debate becomes more significant than ever before. There was a national impulse to review history, one which needs to be explored. As the writer tosses different approaches into the air, we, as readers, have to accept the challenge.

The Historical Novel

Where has that period of infancy of human society gone, when natural and unnatural, real and imaginary, lived as children of one family, laughing and sharing all with each other, and had grown up together to become good human beings? Who could ever dream that there would be such a schism in the family?

There was a time when *Ramayana* and *Mahabharata* were considered history, but modern history is now reluctant to acknowledge the relationship. It asserts that the family connection has been damaged by the fact of their marriage to poetry, and it is extremely difficult to revive the relationship, and *Mahabharata* and *Ramayana* should now be accepted as poetry.

Poetry avers: 'Friend History, there is plenty which is speculative in you, and many truths are hidden in me. Therefore, we should restore the relationship that existed between us.'

History contests this with the answer: 'No, it is better to divide our areas and mark our boundaries.' And this task of delimiting the jurisdiction of the two has already been initiated by an official called Knowledge. He is determined to draw a clear and specific line between the realm of Truth and the kingdom of Imagination.

The break-up of the family of literature is clear from the manner in which the historical novel has been hauled up for violating the divisions between History and Fiction.

This sort of complaint has been made not only in our own country; Navin Babu and Bankim Babu* are not the only ones held accountable for this, even that pioneer of the historical novel

* Navin Chandra and Bankim Chandra Chatterjee are famous Bengali authors.

and the ideal of all writers of historical novels, Sir Walter Scott, has not been spared.

Freeman, the well-known historian, is very critical of the manner in which history has been distorted in Sir Walter Scott's novels. He asserts that those who do not know anything about the Crusades should not read Scott's *Ivanhoe*. We agree that we should learn the truth about the Crusades, but it is also essential that we know the intrinsic truths about human nature enshrined in Scott's *Ivanhoe*. In fact, the desire to know them is so strong that many of us cannot resist the temptation to read the book, even though we know that it contains many historical distortions.

It is relevant to consider the question whether Scott could have written *Ivanhoe* keeping all the historical facts in place as well as keeping faith with the eternal literary values. It may be difficult to assert whether he could or not, but it is evident that he has not done so. Maybe, he did not do it deliberately. Perhaps, he did not know those facts about the Crusades that Freeman knows. At that time, it may have been difficult to research and analyse facts of history. I am sure my opponents will rebut this by arguing that when Scott decided to write about the Crusades, he should have researched the facts fully and only then written the novel.

But where will all this investigation end? Is it possible for us to say definitely that we have discovered all the facts about the Crusades? How can we be sure that what we know today may not be dethroned from the pedestal of historicity by some newly discovered facts? If writers of historical novels, who write on the basis of these facts today, are criticised by historians tomorrow for twisting facts, then how will they defend themselves?

Our opponents will now say that let whosoever wishes to write novels do so, but he should not write historical novels. Though this issue has not yet been raised in our country, such views are being voiced in English literature. Sir Francis Palgrave asserts that, on the one hand, the historical novel is the enemy of history and, on the other hand, it is also an enemy of fiction. This implies that novelists distort history for the sake of the story, and the distorted history, in turn, destroys the story. In this manner, both the families with which the story is connected—History and Fiction, the in-laws and the biological parents—suffer.

Then why do historical poetry and novel find place in literature? It is this that I shall try to explain to you in this essay.

Our books on rhetorics define poetry as a poetical sentence full of *rasa*. A more brief and yet apt definition, I have yet to come across elsewhere. We do not have any way of explaining what *rasa* is, but one who has the capacity to savour and to enjoy needs no definition, and one who lacks this power has no need to know it.

They mention nine different types of *rasa*; there are also several undefined but mixed *rasa*s that have not been mentioned. One of these undefined *rasa*s can be called historical *rasa*, and it is this which is the life and soul of all epics.

The joys and sorrows of a great man are not insignificant for him, and even important events pale before them. If the life of one great man or a few such individuals, with all the ups and down, is narrated in a novel, then it makes the novel more engrossing for us. The boundaries of our own pleasures and pain are circumscribed. All the interests and excitement of our lives are centred round our near and dear ones. We can share the happiness, anguish and grief of Nagendra, Suryamukhi and Kundnandini in *Vishvraksha*, as the focal point of all this is Nagendra's family, and we have no problem in accepting Nagendra as the man next door.

But there are some individuals whose joy and pain is tied up with certain larger events, which form the backdrop of their lives. Their own personal drama, with all happiness and grief, is enacted to the sound of music played by the hand of Destiny, and is intertwined with the rise and fall of empires and the thunder of Time and Fate. Their personal problems form a part of a larger, intricate pattern etched by some larger and unseen forces.

We cannot see Time as it marches alongside man. And when a man of destiny is in our midst, we cannot see him in the larger context. Though the opportunity is there, yet we fail to see great men in their proper background and in all their proper honour and dignity. If we want to see them as a part of a larger scheme of things, then we have to distance ourselves from them and establish them in the past, and then view them as a part of the great drama in which they played meaningful roles.

The real flavour of history lies in the fact that it helps us to rise above our ordinary personal problems, and enables us to be free of the deadening routine of our daily grind, watch the unfolding of the great dramatic events through the lives of great people moving along the highways of life, and albeit briefly, helps us to step out of our own small world. This is the real savouring of history.

It is not that one cannot create such events purely from imagination, but something which is naturally distant to us and beyond our experience, if it can in any way be related to some real event, then it becomes easier for the readers to believe it. The purpose is to generate the right flavour—the *rasa*—and to create the appropriate ambience and the writer does not hesitate to select whatever raw material he needs, in whatever quantity he wants, from history.

The intrinsic truth in Shakespeare's *Antony and Cleopatra* is well tested and universally accepted. Many unknown and unsung but capable men have messed up their lives by getting entangled in the web of a woman's love. The world is littered with the wrecks of such lives of little significance. But here, the poet has taken the tale of passion of a man and a woman and put it at the centre of a larger historical event, and he has made it great. After the tragedy of love, comes the tragedy of the nation. The conflict of love is inextricably bound to the preparations for a destructive war in Rome. On the one hand, searing love and passion dominate the luxurious palaces of Cleopatra and, on the other hand, war drums are being sounded on the distant shores, drowning the music of love. The poet has interwoven the romantic and the tragic *rasa* with the historical and, through this device, has succeeded in creating an atmosphere of touching greatness, which lingers in our memories.

If the historian, Manson, were to examine this play of Shakespeare for historical authenticity, then he is sure to find many anachronisms and there is plenty that may not be historically true, but the manner in which Shakespeare has bewitched his readers and woven a fine texture by combining history with imagination cannot be demolished by any newly discovered facts of history.

Earlier also, in a review, I had written: 'A special *rasa* is created by mixing history with fiction. Novelists love this particular flavour. They are not unduly concerned about truth. If anyone does not like the flavour of the novel and seeks authentic history, then he is like a man, who, not having liked the taste of a dish, seeks to identify the flavour of the various spices used in creating the particular blend. Some use whole spices and others grind the various spices to a paste. Those who use whole spices, let them, and those who grind them, we have no quarrel also with them, for the intention here is to generate a particular flavour or taste. Spices are merely the means to an end. This means that the writer is free to adhere to historical facts or to twist them. His real purpose is achieved when he succeeds in weaving the semblance of true history—the historical *rasa*.'

If someone depicts Ram Chandra as low and Ravan as a sadhu, will it not be wrong? Surely, it will be wrong, but it will not only be a wrong against history, it will also be a slur on poetry. When a truth, universally known and acknowledged, is twisted, it leaves a bad taste. It is like a blow on the head for the reader, and a single such blow is enough to floor him!

Not only this, even if a lie is accepted as the truth by the people, and if literature intervenes, by citing history and truth, to set the record straight, then also it will be the fault of literature. Just imagine that it is established that the alcohol loving and immoral Yadu clan was Greek in origin, and the freedom-loving, flute-playing Sri Krishna was a cowherd in Greece; if it is established that he was as fair as his brother, Baldev, and it is proved that the homeless Arjun had eloped with Subhadra, who was a princess of some state in Asia Minor, and that Dwarka was an island off Greece; if it is established that the Pandavas had won their kingdom with the help of the Greek Sri Krishna, a strategist par excellence, an outstanding warrior, and that his political acumen, diplomatic skills and martial supremacy, and his total commitment to the ideology of action and duty, had so intrigued and bedazzled the Indians that he was acknowledged as an avatar here. But all this, even if proved historically, will not demolish Ved Vyasa's *Mahabharata* and no other poet will dare to turn dark into fair.

I have said all this in a general manner. But the question whether Navin Babu and Bankim Babu have really distorted history or not in their novels and poems can only be considered while critically reviewing their specific books.

What should our duty be in such a situation? Should we read history or should we read *Ivanhoe*? The answer to this question is very simple. We should read both. History for the truth and *Ivanhoe* for pleasure. If we deprive ourselves of the pleasure of poetry by being particular about what we read, so as not to acquire the wrong sort of knowledge, then we are sure to end up by denying ourselves all enjoyment and pleasure.

Whatever historical distortions there may be in fiction, we can always modify that by reading history. A person who reads only poetry or prose and does not get an opportunity to read history is unlucky. But a man who reads only history and will not read literature is definitely dimwitted.*

Yatsyadanuchitam vastu nayakaya rassasya va;
Visodhim tat paityajaymanytha va prakalayat.

From this we learn that even in ancient times, it was not considered wrong to make changes in history for poetry, drama or romance so as to create an atmosphere for the appropriate *rasa,* and even in those times, this issue was given careful and serious thought.

Translated from Hindi by **Tripti Jain**

* Our ancient texts on rhetoric assert that whatever is improper in history, or is unsuitable to the hero or the flavour, should either be dropped or changed.

Sarat Chandra Chatterjee

Sarat Chandra Chatterjee (1876–1938) is a much widely-read novelist in India, whose popularity goes much beyond his time. Several of his novels have been made into films, thus generating a secondary level of audience. Yet, it is not that his work is one of light romances; his novels discuss serious social problems and issues of equality and freedom. ***Pali Samaj, Brahmin Ki Beti*** *and* ***Shesh Prashan*** *take up various questions related to women and their victimisation by social practices.* ***Path Ke Davedar*** *concerns itself with the revolutionary movement and religious issues.* ***Devdas*** *and* ***Parineeta*** *debate the innocence and madness of love.* ***Devdas*** *has almost become on unconscious representation of the nation's unfulfilled aspirations and an inability to act. The novel has a fresh film adaptation surfacing for every generation. Recently, another film version, titled* ***Dev D****, converted the narrative into a postmodern story of a lost soul, this time outside the romantic aura of the earlier versions and outside Bengal. Sarat Chandra's novel,* ***Charitraheen,*** *also considers the definitions of goodness and morality.*

Sarat Chandra was a rebel with a cause and his narrative style was absorbing. But he remained a controversial figure. The Bengali journals of his time reflect many such debates and his novel, ***Shesh Prashan****, was criticised for its bold moral projections as much as for the portrayal of an independent woman. Vishnu Prabhakar, the well-known Hindi writer, has written a fascinating biography titled* ***Aawara Masiha*** *(Vagabond Saviour), which reflects upon Sarat Chandra's vagrant ways and direct from-the-heart moral values, reflecting his non-dogmatic intellectual make-up.*

What is not so well known about Sarat Chandra are his literary comments and his essays, wherein one can see the ongoing debates and oppositional stances of Tagore and Sarat Chandra. The essay in the present collection is one such and its inclusion here seeks to introduce the non-Bengali knowing reader with this lesser known aspect of the novelist's work and to emphasise the need for us to know something outside the text in order to fathom the mysteries of creative art. The living controversies and the professed concerns of the writer comment alike on the age and its intellectual concerns.

The Tradition and Virtue of Literature*

The world famous poet, Rabindranath Tagore, explained the essential attributes of literature in the Shravan issue of the magazine, *Vichitra,* and in the next number, Dr Naresh Chandra Sengupta, underlined the limitations of these qualities, and in all humility, dubbed the illustrations, arguments and metaphors advanced by the poet as a piece of humorous writing.

The difference of views between the two revolves around the question of grace, dignity and honour, or otherwise, of modern literature.

My position in this confrontation, due to no fault of mine, has become rather precarious. Shri Sajnikant, a member of the group opposing Naresh Chandra, has expressed views similar to mine in his "Saturday's Letter" in a very emphatic and genuine manner. I cannot disown these views in any way, howsoevermuch I may want to. I have, in this way, been virtually thrown into the lion's den.

Then, there is the problem of my followers, for, over the passage of time, I have also been able to collect a number of fans and they are now urging me to proclaim my opinion on the whole issue, as they think that I am no less than the others.

I tell them, even if I declare what my opinion is, I am still not sure which camp I belong to; and then, there is Naresh Babu to contend with. He is not only a well-known scholar, but is also a famous lawyer. He has turned the Poet's considered opinion and views into a piece of humour with his arguments. If I get caught in the web of his logic and reasoning, I may not survive even for a

---

* From Saratchandra Chattopadhya. *Swadesh Aur Sahitya*. Translated by Mahadev Saha. Benaras: Hindi Pracharak Pustakalaya, 1954.

moment. The Poet has at least reached a stage where he is acknowledged and accepted, and is in a position to set his own norms and determine his own standards. On the other hand, I may not be able to decide any norms or standards and would keep hanging in the vacuum like a firefly.

My fans sneer that I am a coward. I assure them that this surely is not true.

Then they dare me to prove myself. I assert that it is not as simple as all that!

Is there anything more ambiguous than the creation and articulation of a *rasa*—the real savour of any piece of writing? It can only be established through a piece of humorous writing. But right now, I do not have the time for that.

This is my opinion. I am not aware of the view that the other party holds, but can well imagine it!

The beloved characters of the Poet are now besieging him: 'Sir, now we are lost and you must defend us. You must take up cudgels on our behalf. No, no, bow and arrows will not do! You must use a club! And throw it with a flourish in the direction of the most modern literary group. Target? There is no need to aim it at anyone in particular! There are many of them there.'

The club of the Poet's has fallen from the skies right into the midst of the group. There may not have been any beneficial fallout of this hit, but plenty of dust has been raised in the form of words. Naresh Chandra has been jolted from his slumber rather rudely, and has been asking repeatedly in humble yet angry tones, who the target of this attack was! He also insists on being told the purpose behind this attack and insists on knowing why he has been targeted.

But the questions raised by him are unwarranted. The Poet spends thirteen months out of a year abroad, then how does he know the myths and traditions of India, or even the multifaceted genius of Bengali writers? He has neither the time and patience nor the inclination to read Indian myths and to comprehend them, and has other and better things to do. His impressions are based on whatever little he has read and it is on the basis of that knowledge that he now asserts that modern Bengali literature lacks both dignity and influence. Now, one can hear the sound of footsteps on Chitpur Road!*

The Poet's opinion of modern writers has surprised and pained not only Naresh Chandra, but is a matter of deep regret even for me.

What can be more conclusive evidence than the praise of one's admirers? Thus, he is convinced that realism in modern literature has come to mean the depiction of the man-woman sexual union alone. There is no sense of shame or modesty or grace, beauty, or even warmth in this depiction. It is pure and simple Freudian psychoanalysis. Had he asked any writer, he would have been informed that this is not true; they are all aware that depicting the truth alone does not make literature. There are many real but abominable events in the world, which can never be made the basis of any literature.

The Poet has suddenly come to know that there are several varieties of flowers that find no mention in poetry, although they are equal in all respects to the acacia flowers. Why? Precisely because they are edible and found useful in the kitchen. He has also given the example of the crocodiles of the Ganga, but he has not bothered to ponder over the plight of the swan, which also lives in the Ganga next to the crocodile and is the carrier of Saraswati, the goddess of learning, and which has been practically eaten out of existence by man. There are many examples of seeds and fruits that are edible and yet have been used in poetical metaphors, and no poet has despised them.

Naresh Chandra has reminded him of all this and pointed out that many flowers, vegetables and fruits are eaten and yet used in poetic metaphors. I do not know what the Poet will say in answer to this, but his admirers may probably say that it is wrong to eat these flowers and vegetables, and those who do eat them do so out of dislike for realistic literature.

It is futile to add to the size of this article by going on about these things. These arguments serve no purpose and are of no use to anyone. But by putting together all such irrelevant examples,

* Rabindranath Tagore's residence.

the Poet seems to be asserting that there should be no doubt about his views being right and whatever the others say being wrong.

I do not say that there is no cause to be concerned about modern Bengali literature, or that this sort of attitude on Rabindranath's part is sudden. He may not remember, but a few years back, he had told me that a boy of twelve or thirteen from his school had written a story about a fallen woman.

I recall another event from my childhood. My younger brother suddenly decided to become a poet. Having discovered that it was not very easy to write about serious matters in Bengali, he decided to write a poem in English. Whether he wrote it or copied it from elsewhere, I do not know, but I still remember the poem:

A lion killed a mouse.
And carried it into his house,
Then cried his mother,
And therefore cried his sister.

As far as rhyming and the idea contained therein, the poem is above reproach, but its logic raised a storm. Whose mother? The lion's or the mouse's? Thinking over it for some moments, my wife said: 'No, no, not theirs! This is a reference to the poet's mother!' Were she to hear the story of the fallen woman, my wife would probably say that those who manage the school should be ashamed of themselves. So much for the modern writer! On the other hand, there seems to be no dearth of young and budding poets writing devotional poetry. All of them, whether writing lyrics or poems, write the same thing: 'It is your music that permeates the strings of my heart!' 'I see your divine beauty in each line of the stanza.' 'My heart beats to the fall of divine footsteps.' et cetera...et cetera.

I quote an example. The following lyric appeared in the 'Bhadon' issue of the magazine, *Ketaki*:

''तुम्हारे गाने के कोष में तुम्हें पहचान लूंगा,
हृदय से सुन लूंगा तुम्हारे पैरो की रून झुन।
देख लूंगा तुम्हें बैशाख की आंधी में
और तुम्हारे श्रावणधारा को अपने अंग से लगा लूंगा।।
तुम्हारे आघात चिह्न है मेरे अन्तः मन में

मेरे रूदन में छिपी तुम्हारी देव वाणी।
भूल से भी तुम्हें भूलना नहीं सम्भव,
कैसे छुपाऊँ तुम्हारे आघात की पीड़ा?
बिखरी है वह हर ओर मेरे
तुम्हारे सब सुख दुख घिर आये है मेरे ह्रदय में।
तुम्हें मैं वहीं खोजूगा और पहचान लूंगा।
और सुनूगा अपने ह्रदय में तुम्हारे नुपुर की रून झुन।।*

I will look for you in your song,
And in my heart hear the
Music of your anklets!
In the storms of the summer
I will seek you
And embrace you in the pouring rains.
My heart bears the
anguish of the pain of your separation
Your divine voice echoes
In my sobs.
How can I forget you
For you are everywhere.
You are in my heart,
And there will I look for you
And in my heart
Hear the music of your anklets!

(Translation mine)

In its lyricism, the depth of its emotions and the anguish of separation, this lyric is as irreproachable as the poem quoted earlier. I asked the editor of *Ketaki* how old was the poet who had written it. His proud answer was: 'About fifteen or sixteen.'

---

* *Tumhare gaane ke kosh mein tumhe pehchan loonga*
Hriday se sun loonga tumhare pairon ki run-jhun
Dekh loonga tumhe vaisakh ki aandhi mein
Aur tumhare shrawandhara ko apne ang se laga loonga.
Tumhare aaghat chinh hain mera antahman mein
Mere rudan mein chhupi tumhari dev vani.
Bhool se bhi tumhe bhoolna nahin sambhav
Kaise chupaoon tumhare aaghat ki peeda?
Bikhri hai woh har ore mere
Tumhare sab sukh dukh ghir aayen mere hriday mein
Tumhe mein wahin khojoon aur pehchan loonga
Aur sunoonga apne hriday mein tumhare nupur ki run-jhun

I sighed and thought to myself, 'O old man, when the young have become such devoted worshippers of Krishna that they have forsaken all in his love, what is the purpose of your life?'

You cannot create literature through imitation—neither good nor bad. Literature is born of deeply felt emotions, intermingled with genuine happiness and sorrow, embellished with beautiful language and tempered by experience. *Gitanjali,* which the Poet wrote in his advanced years, is as great poetry as is his *Chitranganda,* which he wrote when he was young. Good literature must spring from authentic and genuine experience and emotions. A mere collection of beautiful words does not create literature. It is futile to write about fallen women because it is in fashion. It is equally senseless to imitate *Gitanjali*. It does not add to the literary wealth of the country in any way.

I have already asserted that I will not be able to criticise the concept of *rasa* for I do not know what it is. I also cannot define the difference between a man of taste and one who has none. It is beyond me to understand exactly the Poet's craving for knowledge and his spiritual hunger and how it can be satiated. But one thing that I do know is that poetry and fiction are not the same thing, and modern fiction is definitely very different from modern poetry. Whatever is the subject matter of *Sonaratri (The Golden Boat)* it cannot do for *Chokker Bali (The Mote in the Eye)*. There may not be any need to refer to flowers in *Sonaratri*, but Binodini's kitchen needs them for she uses them to flavour her dishes! One can write a poem on a flying horse or empty open spaces, but surely not a novel. Here you need the power of the four legs of a horse and one cannot depend on a horse that spreads its wings and flies away in the skies.

The Poet, in his essay titled "The Duties of Literature", writes:

> The Medieval Age in Europe was the age of military power. One who had said that the earth revolved round the sun was silenced. They had forgotten that science is supreme in its own sphere. It is beyond the control of religion. Today the situation is exactly the reverse. Science is strong and is no longer willing

to acknowledge its limitations. Its influence has extended far and wide, and permeates all areas of life. New ideas do not hesitate to assert themselves and need no permission to go wherever they want. Man, by nature, is not scientifically inclined. His true nature is to seek the truth without bias or partiality. This natural scepticism is gradually overwhelming literature also.

This statement of the Poet has many implications. Therefore, I want to test some of them. It may be that the Poet is naturally indifferent to science, but I fail to understand what exactly he means by 'the area of science'. If science refers only to a psychological analysis of sex, knowledge of biology, or of the female body or of female disorders, then I would also oppose its unrestricted entry into literature. Not only because it is undesirable, but also because it is irrational and irrelevant. However significant the truth of the earth revolving round the sun may be, it is of very little consequence to literature. The well-arranged and systematised rational processes that have produced this truth may not be necessary in poetry, but the novel surely cannot do without them. Science is not an impartial enquiry alone; it is a rational cause and effect process. Four and four make eight, or subtracting four from eight leaves four—this is science. Why should one be afraid of this attitude? But this does not mean that there is no obscenity in literature. I have already said that even if it is scientific, teaching minerology in the form of a story is not literature. I also do not accept that a sex manual in the form of a novel is literature. And none of the most modern writers of Bengal say it is.

A religious text may be written by rejecting science; even a spiritual poem can be composed. It is also possible to write fairy tales. But it is not the best way to write a novel. A young prince goes looking for a beautiful princess, crossing a difficult terrain. He does not have the sharp instincts of a detective, but he is a lover of beauty. This is all that I can take. I agree that there is no dearth of people who enjoy a romance. But surely there are many who think differently. And if they say: 'Prince, it is not the youth and beauty of the Princess you admire. You are also not concerned about half the kingdom that you may inherit. You are great! This girl is no beggar maid, but a princess, and that alone is important for you. There is no need to drag psychology into it! But Prince, you do not openly assert what is in your heart and it is therefore difficult to enjoy this story fully.' Then, who can silence these people?

Many such examples can be found in the writings of the late Surendra Nath Bhattacharya. I do not mean any disrespect to the late author, but am merely quoting him as an example of a non-scientific mindset—and he has many admirers in Bengal. I have myself seen a man at the corner grocery shop, reading aloud from a book, surrounded by a crowd listening to him raptly with tears in their eyes. Goddess Kali appears in a dream to an upright young devotee and tells him of a treasure under a tree. He digs up seven pitchers full of gold coins and becomes rich. The boy dies, but there is nothing to fear. A sanyasi with matted hair and an aura of power surrounding him suddenly appears on the cremation ground, and the boy rises from the pyre with a cry of 'Father!' on his lips. The crowd of listeners is shedding copious tears. They are enjoying themselves thoroughly, but no one asks the question: 'How?' For them, the fact that the poor boy has become wealthy is sufficient. The fact that he has risen from the dead is important. For this assuages our hunger of perception as also the craving of our soul. It is indescribable!

What is there to quarrel about in this? But if I am not able to do this? I may not be able to turn my poor hero into a rich man with the blessings of the Goddess, and I may be forced to cremate the dead boy as I may fail to find a sanyasi with matted hair to bring him back to life. I am sure my readers would burn my books. But what else can I do? I would request Brahma with folded hands that some of my others books also be burnt, for I may tolerate that, but it is beyond me to satisfy the demands of such readers… .

But why? Precisely because writing poetry and writing a novel are two totally different arts. Even their attributes are not the same. Their boundaries are also not the same, and the difference between the demands of a man's intelligence and the cravings of his soul is so deep and vast that nothing would make any sense if all scientific principles restraining imagination were to be abandoned.

Naresh Chandra rejects the example of the stone and the lotus, which the Poet has given as illogical. He says it is surely not a logician's paradigm, but asserts that it is a piece of humour. In my opinion, even if this were true, it is so convoluted that I have not been able to understand it. Is the stone more worthy than the lotus? Or is the sparrow better than a car? It is very difficult to say. What the Poet has written about the man-woman sexual union in his article, "The Virtues of Literature", in my opinion, is true even of fiction. He probably means to say that it is a reality, but of the two different aspects it has—one physical and the other mental, one animal and the other spiritual—the real question is which of the two should be highlighted and made an embellishment in literature. This should be the core question. Naresh Chandra asserts that specific limits should be laid down. But is there any clear and specific boundary that can be drawn? Everything depends on the education, inclination and capacity of the writer. What is beautiful in the hands of one, may become crude and ugly in the hands of another. Instead of debating on decency and obscenity, honour and dishonour, all of us who are serving literature should appreciate the Poet's suggestions in all humility. Sex is the basis of the flavour of all literature and the Poet doesn't reject this truth. Even then, the essence of what he says is that this subject should form a part of the deep and inarticulated aspect of literature. If the foundation is well laid, the edifice will be strong and the architect can work on it with a free hand. The tree survives if its root is well grounded and protected, and only then can it flower and bear fruit. But whether this is happening in modern literature or not is another question. Quoting extensively from Rabindranath, Naresh Chandra writes:

> All bodily functions are not unmentionable. All leading writers, from Bankim Chandra to Rabindranath, have given the kiss a prominent place in their writings. Even embraces are being written about.

But let alone embraces, I cannot even write about a kiss unless it is absolutely essential. I normally avoid using the word. I am aware that men and women kiss each other. It is accepted, I know. I don't say it is bad, but still, I cannot make myself write about it. In our society, such things are not talked about openly. Perhaps, my upbringing is such that I fight shy of writing about these things in the frank manner they are written about by European writers. Yet, I think that even with this inhibition, I have written many love stories and have had no problems. Poetry is one thing and writing stories another. Whatever he may have written in his poems such as *Hridaya Yumana, Stan, Vijayini, Chitrangada* and others, it seems that the Poet has not been able to overcome his inhibitions in the same manner that I have not been able to ignore mine. Perhaps, he has been hurt by a couple of critical remarks regarding his inhibitions. It is surely a matter of regret to be charged with importing things from abroad. The language of literature is different in different countries, but the Poet knows that the distinction between indigenous and foreign does not always apply to all literatures. And he knows it better than others or he would not have been acknowledged as a poet par excellence by the whole world. The Poet's creativity is endless, like the ocean. There is enough evidence to support this view. Yet, I feel it is not only impertinent, but also unjust, to take what suits your opinion from the same ocean of creativity to mock him.

The Poet has said, 'If one were to ask the people of the countries on the other side of Indian Ocean, that is Europe, why this uproar in your literature? The answer one gets is that this turmoil is not for the betterment of literature, but for the sake of a turmoil. We have been swamped by market forces. When I ask the same question this side, then the answer I get is that though there may not be any sign of the market, yet there is enough uproar, and this is the strength of modern literature.'

Who has given this answer to the Poet, I do not know, but whosoever he maybe, I cannot praise him.

Naresh Chandra asserts, 'It is not that there have been no attempts to establish a market here. This sort of upheaval has been seen even earlier in the history of literature. The writings of

Rousseau and Voltaire helped in creating the French Revolution. And can we remain untouched by things happening in the West in this age where ideas know no boundaries? Whatever market there is in the West, my right to buy whatever I want from it is in no way less than any other citizen of the East.'

I do not know of anyone else who has stated his point of view so emphatically and fearlessly about modern literature.

Among the various functions of literature is the duty of nation building and helping in the country's all-round development and growth. It does not matter whether this idea is Western or Eastern. It is also not important whether it is indigenous or foreign. What is significant is whether it is beneficial for the language and the nation or not. If the good sense of a writer tells him borrowing one thing from one language into another will be beneficial for society, then there is none who should stop him. Despite disagreement, any attempt to stop something by force can be disastrous. But I am rather hesitant about reminding the Poet of this very ordinary truth. I know that this discussion has become rather unwarranted, but I am convinced that whatever needs to be said must be said, and there is no other way to it.

I will not add to the size of this article, but must say a couple of things and appeal directly to the Poet. The language at the end of his essay, "Sahitya Dharma", ("The Duties of Literature") is as sharp as the punning is cruel. No one may deny that he has the right to insult, but it seems that modern Bengal has also accepted that the real way of serving literature is to resort to mud slinging. Perhaps, someone might have blundered at some time, but is it right to inflict such a heavy punishment on all modern writers for that mistake?

The Poet has written, 'The literature of this country can at least rue the failure of science to influence our behaviour, our intellectual processes, and that it has not been given any opportunity to have any entry into our social system.'

If this alone is the truth, then it is unfortunate for India. Maybe science has not been given an entry, or maybe it did not exist here at all. But does he insist that merely because something did not exist here, it should never be permitted to come in?

In the next line, he writes, 'In what way and in whose name will we try to suppress this borrowed shamelessness in Bengali literature?'

There is no need to decry anything. It is unjust to use any sort of pressure. But is it not wrong and unjust to accept the opinion of a follower as the Gospel truth?

Naresh Chandra has given a fitting reply to Rabindranath's "Sahitya Dharma". Perhaps he feels that the Poet has also targeted him along with others. What is the basis of this belief, I cannot say; I have not read all his books. I have read only what has been published in the magazines and have not been able to form any consistent opinion about him. At times, I have had the feeling that he has violated the accepted norms of depicting the love between a man and a woman. But here also, I do not assert that my opinion is infallible. I am aware that there are many who are unhappy with Naresh Chandra. But I do not insist that he writes in the style of a wrestler planning a strategy for his match. I have not met him personally. And I don't think I have even seen him. But there are few writers in Bengali who can match his scholarship, knowledge, command over language, and the skill to use words with magnificent artistry and express his opinions independently and fearlessly. It is the duty of the Poet, as the universally acknowledged doyen of Bengali literature, to read all his books. He should clearly and explicitly point out where the limits of decency have been violated and the norms of morality ignored. But there is also the possibility that it is not Naresh Chandra who has been targeted by the Poet; he may be alluding to some other person. Then, I suggest that he should read all the books of that person. I remember an incident which occurred the other day. I have written many books, yet have not managed to please all. I have made some enemies. I have made many mistakes, but one mistake I have not made. I have never retaliated whenever I have been attacked. Maybe this is because I am a man of peace, or maybe I am incapable of attacking anyone. I have also never attacked anyone. The Poet may recall his own statements in the days to come. There has always been a section of people who like this type of literature. I am now getting old and death is fast approaching. I will not be able to abuse people. The other day a Rai Sahib deputy heaped abuses on me through the columns of the magazine, *Manasi,* for writing *Path Ke Davedaar*. He declares that I have ridiculed Sonagaachi in my book, and it had not escaped his experienced eye. Whatever it is, our days are now over. A new group of devotees has now taken over the task of serving literature. I bless them with all my heart, and I will continue doing so in whatever time that I have.

But since some time, I have seen that a severe attack has been mounted against the modern writers. There is neither any forgiveness for them, nor any patience, and nor is there any desire to mend fences by making a friendly overture to them. There is only the determination to hurt them with harsh and cruel words. There is only the pitiless wish to humiliate and demolish them before one and all. This difference of opinion, which has created such a sharp conflict in the temple of literature between the different groups of worshippers, has neither grace, nor does it benefit anyone. It is unfortunate that the Poet is annoyed with me and may not believe me, but I am telling him the truth when I say that all devotees of Bengali literature revere him as the Guru, and even those who may oppose his views are as devoted to him as those who are egging him on with cries of Bengali literature being in danger.

(*Bangabani* 1334, Ashvin issue)
Translated from Hindi by **Tripti Jain**

Premchand

Premchand (1880–1936), a well-known Hindi writer, was a contemporary of both Tagore and Sarat Chandra. One is amazed both at the quantity of work and the legacy he has left us. Premchand's given name was Dhanpat Rai, Premchand being a pseudonym he adopted for literary purposes. He wrote initially in Urdu, but later began to write in Hindi. Greatly inspired by Gandhian ideas, several of his novels focus on village reform and the movement of educated youth towards rural areas. He resisted the tradition of superstition and the miraculous and went on to introduce social realism in his writing, placing it right in the midst of caste issues, problems of widowhood, temptations of urbanisation, evils of the zamindari system and the contrary claims of the joint family, thus making literature meaningful and relevant for the man in the street.

Premchand has earned for himself an enviable position in the history of Indian literature. Several of his novels and short stories have been made into films and television serials. This is so because his characters are human and realistic, and their relationship with the social context is psychologically explored as they reach us across time.

The essay included here is the Presidential Address delivered by Premchand at the first session of the Pragratisheel Lekhan Sangh (Progressive Writers' Association) in 1936. The address was originally delivered in Hindi and has been translated for this volume. Referring to the conference, Premchand is conscious of the historicity of the move to reinforce the forces of social change and of the forward-looking concern with political and social matters. For the average Indian, literature emerges out of a social need and is a search for a direction as well as a place for debate and exchange of ideas. The development of a literary language was the first major concern, but language for him is 'a means, not an end' to the creation of a literature that searches for and expresses some truth. Like Bankim Chandra, Chandu Menon and others before him, Premchand also resists the continuation of the miraculous and the fantastic and moves toward serious human experiences connecting with each other. He emphasises the need for progressive thinking to be connected with action, if any social change is to be effected.

The article that follows marks an historic moment in Indian writing as a host of writers from different languages were associated with the Progressive Writers' Movement, which initiated them into experimenting with new themes and forms.

The Intent of Literature*

Gentlemen,

This conference is a memorable occasion in the history of our literature. In most of our assemblies and conferences, discussions have usually centred on language and its usage. So much so that the aim of whatever literature exists in Urdu and Hindi was to create language, rather than influence ideas and opinions. This was also a very important task. How can a language acquire the power to articulate views and emotions until it attains a permanent status? We must be grateful to these pioneers—the ones who cleared the path—and created the Hindustani language, and if we do not acknowledge our debt to them, it would be the height of ingratitude.

Language is a means, not an end in itself. Our language has now attained the form, and we must move ahead and consider the ways and means to achieve the objective for which this whole process of creation was initiated. The same language in which *Baital Pachisi* and *Bagh-o-Bahar* were taken to be great literary achievements in its formative years, has now become strong enough to be used to analyse issues of religion and science, and this conference is a clear acknowledgement of this truth.

Language is both colloquial as well as literary. Colloquial language existed even during the times of Mir Amman and Lallo Lal, but the language they created and nurtured was literary language, and that is literature. We use colloquial language to communicate with the people around us—to express our feelings to them. A writer does precisely the same through his writings. True, his audience is large and, if what he says is authentic, then

* Presidential Address to the Progressive Writers' Association, 1936.

his writings will live for ages and continue to influence minds for ages to come.

But I do not mean to say that whatever is written is all literature. Literature is that creation which contains an element of truth and which is written in mature, polished and beautiful language and which has the quality of touching the heart and affecting the mind. And this quality in literature is produced when it expresses the reality and experiences of life. Stories of the supernatural, ghosts and the tragedies of love may have affected us at one time, but now they do not interest us much. It is also true that a sensitive writer can depict the reality of life even through love stories of princes and tales of supernatural, and create beauty, but this is also a confirmation of the fact that literature can be effective only when it mirrors life as it is. Then you can fit it in whatever frame you like. The story of the sparrow or the tale of the flower and the *bulbul* can also be an appropriate setting for it.

Literature has been defined in many different ways, but to my mind, the best definition of literature is the phrase, 'criticism of life'. It may be in the form of an essay, a story or even a poem, but it must seek to analyse and criticise our life.

The era that we have recently lived through had no connection with life. Our writers would create an imaginary world and embellish it with supernatural events. There were stories of wonder and imagination, like *Chandra Kanta Santiti*. The aim of these stories was plain entertainment and to satisfy our hankering for something not within our ken; that literature had any connection to life was beyond imagination. A story is a story and life is life. Both were taken to be contrary. The poet was also very individualistic. The ideal of love was to satisfy lust, and that of beauty to soothe the eyes. And poets were busy exhibiting their talents and imagination in expressing these romantic emotions. A new arrangement of words in rhyme, a new flight of fancy, was enough to draw a round of applause and it did not matter how removed it all might have been from the ground reality. Poets were involved in the depiction of love and separation, hope and despair, and all this was sufficient for the audience to gasp in appreciation. We are all fully aware of how popular this form of poetry is even today.

There is no doubt that poetry and literature must seek to accelerate our experience, but human experience is not confined only to love between man and woman. Can a literature which is only confined to romantic emotions and all other feelings that spring from these emotions, such as the pangs of separation and despair, and which seeks to distance itself from the world and all its problems satisfy our emotional and intellectual needs? The emotions of love are a part of human life, but a society or an era cannot take pride in the fact that a large part of its literature is concerned only with this.

The state of affairs in the poetry of both Hindi and Urdu was the same. It was difficult for writers to ignore the predilections of the people for a particular type of fiction. Who doesn't want appreciation and fame? The poets earned their living through their writings. And who else appreciated poetry except for the nobility and the rich? There were no opportunities for the poets to face the realities of life and be affected by them, and there was so much of intellectual degradation that there was hardly any intellectual life left anywhere.

We cannot blame only the writers of that time. Literature is a reflection of its age. It expresses the emotions and the ideas that pulsate in the hearts of the people. During a time of decline, people either take to the sensual or turn to spiritualism and renunciation. When literature is imbued with the idea of the mortality of the world, and each word is a cry of despair at the adversities of the times and an echo of sensual emotions, then one should accept that society has been caught in a web of insensibility and decline, that it no longer has any spirit or capacity to struggle, and that it has closed its eyes to higher goals and lost its ability to see and comprehend the world.

But our literary tastes are changing very fast. Literature is no longer a means of entertainment; it has other aims besides entertainment. It is no longer a recital of love and separation of the heroine and the hero, it also ponders over the problems of life and seeks to solve them. It does not pursue strange and wondrous events to thrill and excite, nor does it delve into alliterative rhymes; it is interested in issues that affect society and the individual. It is now judged on the intensity of the experiences that it depicts and which create and lend momentum to our feelings and ideas.

Ethics and literature have the same objective—the only difference is in the method in which each preaches. Ethics appeals to one's mind and reason on the basis of arguments and logic, and literature has made the mind and emotions its chosen area. Whatever we see around us or experience in real life, that experience and pain stimulate our imagination into creative activity. The sharper the sensibility of a poet or a writer, the higher the quality and attractiveness of his creativity. A literature that does not awaken a fine sensibility in us and does not give us any spiritual and mental solace, fails to stimulate our capacities and cannot appeal to us. A literature that does not make us determined to overpower the difficulties around us is of no use to us and does not deserve to be called literature.

Earlier, religion was the guiding force in society. The basis of the spiritual and moral development of man was religious in nature, and he used the method of fear or reward, and the issues of sin and purity dominated his thoughts.

Now literature has taken over this responsibility and its method is the love of beauty. It endeavours to stimulate this love of beauty in man. There is no man who is not moved by beauty. The more developed and active this trait is in a writer, the more effective his writings; his sensibilities are so stimulated by the exquisiteness of nature around him that all that is ugly and crude and devoid of humaneness becomes intolerable for him. He attacks it with all the power of his words and emotions. Or we can say that he weaves the fabric of humaneness, divinity and civilisation. Whosoever is oppressed, exploited and deprived, whether it is an individual or a group, it is the duty of the writer to support them and to plead their cause. His court is the society and it is in this court that he presents their case, and after he has awakened society's sense of justice as also its love of beauty, he feels that he has been successful in his endeavour.

The litterateur, however, does not make proper or improper claims on behalf of his clients like other advocates; he does not exaggerate and does not fabricate things. He is aware that these devices will have no effect on the court of society. Any change of heart of this court is possible only when the writer himself does not turn away from the truth, or else the court will have no faith in him and will decide against him. The writer writes a story, but keeps reality in sight; he sculpts, but takes care to make it lifelike and expressive; he scrutinises human nature with a keen eye and studies psychology and tries to make his characters, in all conditions and circumstances, behave like real human beings made of flesh and bone. He succeeds in understanding those subtle situations of life that are very difficult for man to reach precisely because he is a man.

In modern literature, the trend towards realism is increasing, and now the story does not violate the boundaries of possibility and experienced reality. The fact that all the characters resemble real people psychologically does not satisfy us; we seek reassurance in the facts that they are real people and that the writer has chronicled real events in their lives, for we do not believe in persons created by our imagination; they do not impress us by their acts or their thoughts. We want to be sure that whatever has been created by the writer is based on real experience and that he is speaking through his characters.

That is why some literary critics have called literature the psychological life of the writer.

The same event or situation does not have the same effect on all. Each person has a different attitude and point of view. The skill of the writer lies in that the reader should agree with whatever point of view or attitude is being projected by the writer. His success lies in this. Besides, we also expect the writer to stimulate us with the vastness of his ideas and his multifaceted knowledge, help us in extending the horizons of our minds, that his understanding should be subtle, deep and penetrative, that his writings should give us both spiritual pleasure and strength.

Every man wants to better the condition he is in. Whatever weakness we have clings to us like a disease. As physical health is natural and illness its reverse, in the same manner, mental and moral health is also natural and we are not happy when there is a moral and intellectual decline. As a patient is always on the look-out for a doctor who can heal him, in the same way, we are always seeking ways and means to discard our frailties and become better human beings. That is why we look for ascetics and mendicants, seek solace in prayers and the company of the wise, the learned and the old, and listen to discourses and also read literature.

All our infirmities can be traced to our bad desires as also a denial of love. Where there is a genuine love for beauty, where love pervades everything, how can there be frailties? Love is the ethereal food for our souls, and if we are deprived of this food or if we get contaminated food, we are bound to fall ill. The artist creates a feeling for beauty and the warmth of love in us. His one sentence, one word or one gesture overwhelms us and seems to illuminate our very beings. But until an artist is himself intoxicated by love of beauty and his own soul is permeated with its radiance, how can he lead us?

Now the question is, what is beauty? Apparently, the question seems irrelevant, for there should be no doubt in our mind about what beauty is. We have seen the sun rise and the sun set, seen the red of dawn and of twilight, smelt fragrant blossoms, heard the dulcet twitter of the birds, the soft murmur of fast-flowing rivers, seen swirling waterfalls—this is beauty.

Why do we feel happy when we see all this around us? Because there is a fine mixture of colour and sound. A fine blending of the various musical notes of different instruments makes music attractive and captivating. Our very creation is the result of a fine balance of different elements—that is why our souls seek the same fine harmony all around us. Literature is the expression of the spiritual balance of the artist, and this balance fosters beauty and does not destroy it. It strengthens the feelings of loyalty, truth, compassion, fairness and affection within us; where such emotions exist, there is life and strength. Where they are absent, there is dissension, opposition and selfishness—as well as enmity, spite and death. This dissension and malice are anti-nature, just as disease is a symptom of an anti-nature diet and lifestyle. Where there is balance, agreement and conformity with nature, selfishness and narrow mindedness can never survive. When our souls are nurtured in a free and natural atmosphere, then the worms of meanness die a natural death in the free atmosphere of freedom. These mental and emotional diseases occur when we detach ourselves from nature and limit our own selves. Literature makes our lives natural and free. In other words, it is literature which gives mental strength and refinement, which is the essence of humanness. That is the main design of literature.

The very name *Pragati Sheel Lekhak Sangh* (Progressive Writers' Association) is a misnomer in my opinion. A writer or an artist is progressive by nature. Had he not been progressive, he would not have been a writer. He is assailed by a feeling of deprivation, both within him and also without. He yearns to remedy the situation. He fails to find around him the happiness and freedom that he seeks for the individual and society. He is pained by the prevailing social and intellectual conditions. He wants to demolish them and make the world a better place in which to live and in which to die. It is this pain and yearning that keeps his mind and heart active. He is pained at the thought that a society should be fettered to outdated traditions and suffer in the process. Why couldn't things be arranged in such a manner that poverty and enslavement are eliminated? The greater the intensity of his pain, the more powerful his writings and the more realistic his portrayal. His ability as a writer lies in the manner in which he arranges and portrays his experiences. Perhaps it was thought necessary to emphasise this quality of being progressive, for every writer does not interpret the word in the same manner. Conditions that one group may understand to be progressive, another may take to be a clear indication of decline—this is because no writer wants his art and ability to be used for any vested interest or purpose. For him, his art is a manifestation of his emotions, whatever the impact these ideas may have on the individual or society.

Progress, to me, is that situation which generates in us the resolution and the will to act, which makes us aware of our pain, which helps us to identify the various internal and external reasons that have led to this condition of desolation and decline, and which impels us to try and overcome them.

The poetic sentiments that impress upon us the destructibility of the world around us are meaningless for us and may only make us sadder. The love stories that fill most of the pages of our magazines are insignificant if they do not create life and energy in us. If we have narrated the love story of two young people and it has had no effect on us, or even if it has had an impact, it has only been to make us cry over the pain of their separation, then how has it enhanced our sensibilities? Such stories may have had an emotional impact earlier, but they are of no significance in the present context. The time for this melodramatic art is past. At present, the need is for art that gives the message of action. We have to agree with Hazrat Iqbal says when he says:

Ramze hayat joi juzdar tapish nayaab,
Darkuljum aaramidin nangast aabe joora,
Ba aashiyan na nashinam ze lazzate parvaaz,
Gahe bashakhe gulam gahe baral be juyum.

(If you are seeking the secret of life, then you will not find it in anything except struggle—it is a matter of shame for the river to go to the sea to rest. Sitting in the nest to rest gives me no pleasure, but twitting from flower to flower does, as does the flutter on the river edge.)

Thus, for us to emphasise egotism or to give importance to our own personal point of way may lead us to carelessness, insensibility and decline, and such an art is not useful to us either personally or socially.

I do not hesitate in asserting that I measure art on the scales of utility like all other things. Undoubtedly, the aim of art is to affirm the existence of beauty and this is the key to our spiritual discernment, but there is no intellectual or spiritual happiness that does not have its own utilitarian angle. Contentment is in itself an object of utility and, from this point of view, the same thing can give us pleasure as also pain. The flush of early dawn is beautiful, but if the sky is overcast with the same reddish colour during the monsoons, then it will not give us any pleasure, for at that time, we would be happy only with the presence of dark, billowing clouds in the skies. Flowers give us happiness for we expect them to give us fruit. Our harmony with nature gives us spiritual bliss for this harmony enhances and embellishes our lives. Growth and progress is the essential law of nature and the sensibilities, perceptions and ideas that give us happiness are the ones that help us in this growth and development. The artist, by using his art to create beauty, makes the conditions appropriate for development.

But beauty also, like other things, is not absolute in its essence—it is relative as well. What constitutes a thing of pleasure for one man maybe a cause of pain for another. A rich man may enjoy great comfort as he sits in his secluded lush garden listening to the birds sing, but another may take all these things as detested objects of luxury.

Fraternity and equality, civilisation and amity, have existed since the beginning of society and have been the golden dream of idealists. Religious preachers have through religious, moral and spiritual bonds made persistent but unsuccessful efforts to turn this dream into reality. Mahatma Buddha, Jesus Christ, Hazrat Mohammed—prophets and preachers of all religions—have tried to erect an edifice of equality on the foundation of ethics, but none was successful; the cruel reality of high and low still persists in society and has never been more visible as it is today.

There is a saying that it is foolish to test one already tested. If we seek to attain the higher goal of social equality by clinging to religion and ethics, then we are bound to fail. Should we then abandon this ideal as the creation of a fevered mind? Then there will be no ideal left for the elevation and fulfilment of man. It would be much better that man should cease to exist. We have nurtured this ideal since the beginning of civilisation, for the attainment of which man has made untold sacrifices, for the fulfilment of which religions have been founded; the history of mankind is the history of the attainment of this ideal, and we must keep moving forward by accepting it as the supreme goal, as a transcendental truth. We have to establish a new system where equality has acquired a more tangible form and does not depend on moral restraints alone. Our literature must keep this ideal in mind.

We must change the norms of beauty. So far, this has been based on standards of wealth and luxury. Our artists wanted to hang on to the train of the rich and, as his very existence depended on their applause, used his skills and artistry to explain their pleasure and pain, hope and despair, competition and rivalry. His sights were fixed only on their *havelis* and palaces. The hovels and ruins of the poor did not merit his attention. He considered them outside the pale of humanity. Even if he did mention them, it was to ridicule them and to make fun of their rustic dress and ways. Their bad pronunciation or wrong turn of phrase constituted a permanent butt of his humour. That the poor man was also a human being, he also had a heart and desires—this was beyond the imagination of art.

Art was, and is even now, a limited concept of beauty, of a stilted arrangement of words and management of mind and sentiments. There are no ideals, no high principles of life. Avoiding all such ideals as devotion, ascetism, spirituality or renunciation of the world was the best thing an artist could imagine. To such an artist, this is the highest goal of life. His point of view is not yet comprehensive enough that he should be able to see beauty in the very struggle for survival. He doesn't accept that there can be beauty even in nudity or fasting. For him, beauty is a beautiful woman—not a poor woman who, after lulling her children to sleep at the edge of the field, is sweating it out in the field. He has made up his mind that beauty lies in painted lips, rosy cheeks and well-shaped brows, so how can there be beauty in tangled hair, dry lips and faded cheeks?

The fault lies in a narrow point of view. If only his view of beauty were to become more discerning, then he would also be able to see that there is cold-heartedness behind the painted lips and cheeks, and that there are tears of sacrifice, devotion and acceptance of pain behind the faded lips and cheeks. True, there is no delicacy or tenderness or affectation.

Our art is obsessed by love of youth and doesn't realise that youth doesn't mean reciting poems with a hand on your heart, or bewailing the indifference of the beloved, or even pondering over her beauty and affectations. Youth stands for idealism, courage, the will to face problems head on and for sacrifice. The young must agree with Iqbal:

Az daste junoon-e-man Gabreel Zabun saide,
Yazdan bakmand aawar-e-himmat-e-mardana.

(Gabreel is not a fit game for my powerful hands; O, the courage of man —why don't you entangle God in your noose?)

or

Chun mauj-saj-e-sajood bazudam ze sail be parvaast,
Guman mabar ke dari bahar saahil-e jo yom.

(The boat of my life is indifferent to the flow of the waves; don't think that I seek the shore in this sea.)

And this situation will arise when our sense of beauty will become more comprehensive and it will encompass the whole world. It will not be confined to any particular class and its flights of fancy will not be confined to the boundary walls of one garden, but will soar high into the space that embraces the whole world. Then alone will we reject bad taste and be eager to strike at its very roots. Then we will not tolerate a system in which thousands are enslaved to a few oppressors, and will not be happy by creating a world on paper alone, but insist on erecting an order that will not be opposed to beauty, discernment, self-respect and humanism.

The aim of the writer is not only to grace soirées and entertain—do not devalue him to that extent. He is also not the reality that follows patriotism and politics; he is the truth that shows them the path with a torch in hand.

We often complain that there is no place for writers in society, meaning thereby writers in India. Writers are respected members of civilised countries and important ministers and other rich persons are proud of knowing them, but India is still living in the medieval ages. If the writer has elected to be the petitioner of the rich and is ignorant of the movements, agitations and revolutions that are taking place in society and is busy in making, laughing and weeping in a world of his own, then there is no injustice if there is no place for him. When there is no other restriction on becoming a writer except that of talent, as you don't need education to become a *mahatma,* it is enough to have spiritual leaning, and *mahatmas* are now a penny a dozen, in the same manner there are writers galore.

There is no doubt that a writer is born and not made, but if one can enrich this inborn gift by education and discernment, then surely he would serve the cause of literature in a better way. Aristotle and other scholars have laid down very strict rules for aspiring writers and have drawn up principles and laws for their intellectual, moral, spiritual education and development, but at present, a natural inclination to be a writer is considered sufficient to become a writer in Hindi, and he doesn't need any other preparation. He may know nothing of politics, sociology or psychology, yet he is a writer.

Keeping in mind the ideal presented to a writer today, the knowledge of these subjects is essential for him, and literature is no longer confined to egotism or individualism, but has become psychological and social. Now, it doesn't look at the individual apart from society, but takes him to be a part of society. Not because he should dominate the society or make it an instrument for the fulfilment of his own selfish interests, as if there were a traditional enmity between him and society, but because his very existence is dependent on the existence of society and he has no worth apart from society.

Those of us who have the best of education and have the best intellectual abilities, have a greater responsibility to society. Would we venerate a man, rich with intellectual ability, who has acquired the highest education with the money of society and then uses his ability for his own selfish motives? No writer would ever like using society for his personal ends. It is the duty of the intellectually rich man that he should place the interests of society above his own personal ends and make the best use of his knowledge and ability to give the utmost benefit to society. Whatever areas of literature he may enter, he should have specialised knowledge of that particular genre, as also be generally aware about all other aspects of literature.

If we read the reports of international literary conferences, we will find that there is no classical, social, historical and psychological question that is not discussed there. And when we discover how limited our own knowledge is, then we feel ashamed. We think that a superficial understanding and a quick pen is enough for a writer. But this very idea is responsible for our literary decline. We will have to raise the standard of our literature so that it can be more advantageous for society and attain that status in society which it deserves, and it may analyse and criticise all aspects of life, and we should no longer be content by borrowing from the literature of other languages, but should be able to enhance that wealth.

We should select subjects that we like and find interesting and master them thoroughly. It may be a difficult task because of economic constraints, but our ideals should always be high. We may not be able to climb to the top, but we can at least go up the mountain halfway, and that is so much better than crawling on the earth. If we can radiate our inner selves with the glow of life and adhere to the principle of service, then there is no difficulty in the world that we will not be able to overcome.

There is no place for those who love wealth and luxury in the temple of literature. Those devotees are needed here who have made service the be-all and end-all of life and are motivated by love and are moved by the sufferings of others. If we serve society with an open heart, then respect, prestige and fame will be ours. Then why should we worry about prestige and fame and why should we be unhappy if we do not get them? The spiritual bliss which we get from serving others is a reward in itself, then why should we want to assert our importance and seek to direct them? Why should we desire to have a more comfortable life than others? Why do we wish to be counted among the wealthy? We are the standard bearers of society and our aim should be simple living and a lofty vision. One who is a real artist can never be selfish. He doesn't need to be ostentatious; in fact, he detests all affectations. He agrees with Iqbal:

Murdam auadam aagoola rayooram ke mara,
Meetwa kershtav yek jame julale deegran.

(I am free, yet so humble that even the dregs of the cup of another can kill me.)

Our Association has initiated a similar programme. It doesn't like literature being associated only with fun and frolic and partying. It wants to make literature the vanguard of action and creativity. It has no quarrel with language. If our ideals are high, our language naturally becomes simple. The beauty of expression and ideas can be indifferent to external adornment. A writer looking to the rich adopts the style of the wealthy; one who belongs to the masses will use the language of the common man. Our aim is to create such an atmosphere in the country, which encourages the development of good literature. We want that such associations should be set up in all literary centres, and there should be regular discussion on creative tendencies, articles read, discussion and criticism indulged in. Only then can we establish such an environment. That alone will usher in a new era in literature.

We want to establish such associations in every province, for every language, so that we can send our message to every language. It would be wrong to think that this is some new plan of ours. No, those who serve literature are brimming with feelings of service to society. Nature and circumstances have already sown the seeds of this idea in every Indian language and they are already germinating in many places.

We writers lack the will to work. This is a bitter truth, but we cannot overlook it. The ideal that we had accepted so far did not require any action on our part; its very lack of exertion was its quality, because action often brings bias and prejudice with it. If a man is religious and is proud of his religiosity, then it would be better that, instead of being religious, he should believe in the policy of eat, drink and be merry. Such an independent spirit may have a claim on the mercy of God, but one who is arrogant about his religiosity may have no such expectations.

As long as literature was considered a means of entertainment, to sing lullabies, or to make people shed tears, literature had no need for action. Literature was like an obsessed being, whose pain was suffered by others.

But we do not consider literature as a means of enjoyment and luxury alone. Real literature for us is one which consists of high philosophy, a desire for independence, the essence of beauty, the instinct for creativity, and which is illuminated by the realities of life—one which can generate a momentum in our lives, make us restless and generate in us the will to fight; it should not put us to sleep, for to sleep any more now is a sign of death.

Translated from Hindi by **Tripti Jain**

Jainendra Kumar Jain

Jainendra Kumar Jain (1905–88) is a reputed Hindi novelist whose work is appreciated for its social analysis and handling of bold themes. It is not easy to forget his ***Tyagpatra****, which in itself is only a slim novel.* ***Tyagpatra*** *is powerful not because it deals with the life of a woman who cherishes dreams of freedom and love and, through an involuntary violation of social conventions, is turned into an outcast both from her husband's family and her parental home. Pushed into an extreme position of isolation, she begins living with a man. Later, when her nephew becomes independent and manages to trace her, he comes to take her back, but now she refuses. It is here that the novel touches a new peak when the nephew, who is a judge, tenders his resignation on account of the social and personal guilt he feels.*

Jain's other novels such as ***Sukhda*** *and* ***Sunita*** *are also thought provoking and deal with the social conditions that are deterrent to feminist freedom.*

Born in Aligarh, Jain was later a student of Benaras Hindu University. He participated in the Non-Cooperation Movement. His creative work brought him many honours, including the Sahitya Akademi Fellowship in 1979, and before that, the Padma Bhushan in 1971.

In the essay included here, his concern is with Hindi literature, which for years has been elitist, but suddenly the 'writer' has been dislocated from this distanced and respected position. It is the changed relationship between literature and society and the shift in their expectations from each other that are of importance. One of the changes is a closer relationship between the two, resulting in greater realism. Literature has stepped down from its lofty and idealistic position to hold a mirror to society. This does not imply a singleness of purpose. Society also needs to pursue ideals and be inspired by them in order to provide stability and balance to it. Thus, on one hand, we have literature upholding idealism and values, on the other, reflecting the real, critiquing dogmas and orthodoxy and advocating social change. The 'writer' as such is neither a distant person to be placed on a secure pedestal, nor an outcast from society, but one who also has to grow in the role of an intellectual leader within the society as one of them.

Delivered as a talk, the essay was followed by a discussion, which is also included here as part of the exposition.

Literature and Society

Most of the newly emerging forces in Hindi Literature do not have any social standing. Till some time back, our literature was elitist. The makers of literature were respected members of society. But things are no longer the same. Today, people who hardly have any place in society are also writers. This raises the question of what are the mutual expectations of society and literature from each other? What is their relationship?

Literature is becoming highly realistic these days. Earlier, it was more involved with society. It depicted conduct that had social approbation and faithfully condemned impropriety. The same literature now portrays the opposition and revolt of the common man against those very socially accepted and approved norms. Thus, it may be asserted that if literature was like a mirror, reflecting society as it was, now it has become something which, while it depicts the realities of society, is not much bothered about flattering it and is more concerned about striking a blow at it, and in this way, compels it to move forward. It also inspires society. It doesn't only give, but also encourages action. It does not contain only our past, but also embodies our convictions and desires.

Today, one who is a rebel against society, has rejected its norms and constraints, has marked out an independent path for himself, is an outcast and deserves to be punished, is, at the same time, not considered incapable of being a writer. Contrarily, it has often been observed that those who have been rejected and condemned by society have produced outstanding literature with their singleminded devotion, have received social acclaim and become highly respected icons of society. The brightest of stars on the literary skies are the ones who have suffered humiliation earlier, but later on were honoured and feted by the same society. On the path of their progress, they ignored the contempt of society and were also indifferent to the social approbation showered on them. Their discerning minds had created an ideal which they pursued with unwavering devotion. It was for society to disregard them or to revere them. But they nurtured the flame in their heart, did not let it die out and stoked it continuously. True, in the beginning, they were kept poor by society. It called them uncivilised, took them to be irresponsible, hurt them and even ridiculed them—all this is true. But they went ahead, traversing the high road of progress, with friendship for all in their hearts, ignoring the recriminations heaped on them, and ultimately, society realised that they were blessed with some divine power and that it was society that needed to reset its own goals.

Such people were first reproached and then respected. One can see that this is true of the lives of all great men. Their relationship with society is not one of subjugation, but of leadership. Society laughs at them, but later on seeks to emulate them so that its own future may be illuminated.

Rather than a difference in time, we have identified a distinction in the nature of literature. But even on the basis of difference in quality, two types of literature are found in society—one which is essential for social stability, the other which makes society progressive.

Literature of both categories is essential. But if we want to assert that any one type of literature is more essential, more vital, more enduring and more fulfilling, then it has to be literature which meets dangers head on and keeps society on the move, even if it is by cracking the whip. Such literature is idealistic, forward looking, and even fresh, but such literature is not easily accepted.

Two distinct elements appear to be at work in society. Members of society can be considered representatives of either of these two elements. One is a receiver and the other is a propagator. One is bereft of any personality, the other has a strong individuality. One looks outside for motivations and direction; the other feels that he is motivated by something which is within him. One is submissive, while the other is dynamic.

Social living, or a social being, is a mixture of these two elements, each trait existing in a small proportion. On one hand is the village *bania,* who has been sitting in his grocery shop since the days of his forefathers, busy accumulating wealth and property and increasing his family. On the other is the one who is unconcerned about home and hearth—makes his home wherever he finds shelter, does not like to think of marriage and is happy leading a peripatetic life. These two types, one bound to a business and stationary, the other dynamic and mercurial—both types of lives and individuals are found in literature. Neither of the two is inappropriate or forbidden.

Society, however, unlike literature, does not nurture desires and is therefore not as liberal and significant as literature. The commercial element is given greater respect in society and enjoys greater powers. Thus, society is largely indifferent and disrespectful to members of the other group. This implies that it is dominated by the market; the mendicant is irrelevant to the market. The businessman will capture power, the recluse will survive only on the money of the businessman. If the mendicant does not accept the benevolence shown by the businessman, then the businessman sets up courts and prisons for him.

These are the conditions prevailing in society. But the same society celebrates the very same mendicant in its ideals and literature. For the businessman, the ideal of the recluse is very attractive. If the mendicant does not create any problems, then the trader is even willing to set him up as a deity in his own home, seeking to ensure a more comfortable life for himself in the worlds to come, but were his own grandchildren to utter even a word about traversing the path of the mendicant, then all hell would break loose.

What should literature, which embraces both elements, expect from a society which has a unidimensional way of life? What should the relation between the two be? There is no straight answer to the question. The only answer can be that its relationship with society would be determined by the expectation that the writer has from society.

Coins, guineas and gold—all things made of metal—are a solid reality. People whose imagination does not go beyond the reality of this fact, or even below it, if such people were to write, then the relationship of their writings with society would be one of acceptance, obedience and conformity.

It may also be that their literature may apparently abuse society, but this criticism would be in the manner of what an irritated and annoyed wife says about her husband. This criticism means that they really seek the grace and attention of society. Those who want money, they live for money and write sweet or spicy things as an offering to society. Who does not know that if sweets sell, so does the tangy and spicy *chaat*? The relation of such writers to society is like that of a shopkeeper, who treats one and all as a customer, or like a wife, who is aware that she has no life without her husband. Such literature, howsoever full of sarcasm and bitterness, is supported and approved by society. It is very entertaining, but contains little truth. There is more of a plot, but very little analysis, plenty of artificiality, but hardly any depth. But the bulk of literature in society is of this category for the number of people with small incomes is larger in any society.

The number of mendicants, however, is small. Mendicants who are not trading their mendicancy—what is their relation to society? They are the well wishers of society. They do not know how to abuse society, but they can be indifferent to the trading that goes on in society. They do not seek the approval of society to live. They write for the benefit of society and consider it their duty to write. They write for they want to honour truth (meaning the truth which is established within them—not outside). It may be asserted that they do not write for the numerous people loitering around in the market of the society. Their link to society (it can be said on their behalf) is one of goodwill for all, and of a pursuit of the truth. The attitude of society towards them is of indifference, reproach and reprobation, but ultimately, of respect and veneration.

The real creators of good literature, in this manner, are those who have traversed a road that they themselves have marked out. They did not hanker for the approbation of others. They presented themselves to society as they were. Society may consider them important today, but as the moral sensibility of society develops at a very slow pace, it is therefore also compelled to think of them as immoral and brazen. Undoubtedly, the radiance of their goodness brings about a change in social attitudes. Yet, there can be no sudden change in social sensibilities and they are often not developed enough to encompass all shades of excellence. That is why Christ is worshipped by two-thirds of the world, yet the same world could not refrain from crucifying Him. What was Christ's relation with the world? He was a deliverer, a preceptor and a devotee. What did the world do? It crucified Him, thus removing the obstruction in the system. And what is the relation that the same world has with him? The world says, 'He was a God, He was divine.'

A writer (meaning the other kind of writer) lives more in the future than in the present. He seeks the welfare of the world, rather than to flatter it. That is why society is compelled not to understand him, to ignore him, or at the most, to worship him—to be scared of him. The world, because it cannot comprehend him, cannot love him. It is the misfortune of such a writer, or it may be his good fortune, that he is like a beacon! He does not want to please the world, does not seek to flatter it—he seeks its happiness, but why should the world want its own well-being? It wants its own happiness.

Most writers provide entertainment to the world. Such literature is addictive. Almost eighty per cent prose is of this type—licentious and addictive—intoxicating to an extent and also deceptive. Writers of this category of literature are accepted by society. They are the entertainers of society, friendly to the lifestyle that society has. They are neither concerned, nor have the time to perceive and to embrace the deep anguish hidden in the depths of the heart of society.

There is another category of people which accepts that society will deride them for they are not inclined to indulge society in any way and are unwilling to provide the means of intemperance. They do not look to what society wants, but look to the illness it suffers from. They are humble, but also extremely hard. They want to create a present which has the radiance of their dreams. Their connection to society is not one of acceptance; it is also not of rejection—as though they are disinterested.

In this manner, there is a literature which is created to entertain society. The other literature is created to provide leadership to society. Society enjoys the first type of literature for it makes society happy, for it derives great pleasure from it. It finds the other type of literature insipid; it seems to be too difficult and indigestible in the beginning, but later on, society comes to accept it as a medicine. In the same manner, there are writers in society who appear to be wealthy and also writers who seem to be aloof and despised by society.

This has been the relation between society and literature since the beginning of time. And I don't think that this relationship will ever change.

Questions and Answers

Q. *What should the relation between society and literature be?*

Ans. Literature walks ahead of the social system. It does not reflect only the present. It also projects the potentialities of the future. It is a precursor and, therefore, it is natural for it to assume the leadership of society. But one thing is at least clear and that is the pace of social development is slow and ideas move at a faster pace. There is always a gulf between those who think and society, and this is unavoidable. There is another thing. The thinker, living in a world of imagination, becomes more imaginative rather than a performer, he can live in a world of illusion rather than one of reality. Therefore, society feels it is dangerous to follow him. For this reason, society mostly gets excitement from literature, not leadership. The bulk of literature belongs to this category. It amuses people and is a source of entertainment for them. Society is happy with this literature. But it is never benevolent to literature that is innovative and enthusiastic. Literature is nurtured by emotions and society is fostered by commerce. There is a mutual give and take between the two, but there is also a continuous conflict between the representatives of literature and society, who, on the one side, are too deeply literary and keep dreaming, or, on the other side, who have become extremely opportunistic, materialistic and businesslike.

Q. *Is it impossible to achieve national and social progress without literature?*

Ans. Let me ask: Is our growth dependent on our high ideals? Is it possible to progress without high ideals? What else is literature? We seek to reach the infinite with our finite beings, we feel our limitlessness within our own circumscribed beings—it is these very moments which create literature. Now, what is progress? Progress of society, national development—what is this? I take this enrichment of personality to be development. The development of society is that it should be healthy and affectionate and devoted to all. The development of a nation implies that it should itself be independent and dedicated to universal welfare. I don't accept arrogance as progress. A large empire is not the symbol of the growth of a nation. Untiring selfless commitment to service and the vitality of its people are the characteristics of a nation's development. Literature is nothing apart from all these things. I would like to emphasise that a library is not literature. If literature means something, it means the sum total of all those emotions and desires which endeavour to create a balance between aggregation and individualism. In this manner, all progress, whether of the individual or of the social group, is possible only through literature—because literature is the name of that road to progress.

Gajanan Madhav Muktibodh

Gajanan Muktibodh (1911–65) is a respected name in the field of poetry. Besides being a poet, he was also a prolific essayist and political critic. He was assistant editor of **Naya Khun** *and later of* **Vasudha** *and a major contributor to the Experimentalism of the times (Prayogvaad), the distinction of his work lying also in literary criticism. Deeply influenced by both Marxist and Existentialist ideas and thought, Muktibodh brought out several collections of poetry and was included in the anthology,* **Tar Saptak** *(which in itself is a landmark in Hindi literature). For a brief period he did some dialogue writing for films, including that of* **Satah Se Uthata Aadmi**. *Muktibodh shares with Adiga the belief that the Renaissance was an incomplete movement and, somewhere, it put a halt to the Bhakti movement.*

The long extract translated here is formed of several excerpts from one section of **Ek Sahityik Ki Diary**. *(Some parts have been skipped.) This was first serialised in* **Naya Khun** *and, later, when Muktibodh shifted to* **Vasudha**, *the serialisation continued there during the years, 1957–61. It was published in book form in 1964.* **Ek Sahityik Ki Diary** *makes fascinating reading and it transfers one to an entirely different world—of creativity, self-reflection, self-analysis and intellectual friendship and has a little out of the way, strolling, meditative style.*

This section is titled "Teesra Kshana" ("Third Moment") and is written in the form of a narrative interspersed with dialogue carried on at lengthy intervals of time with his friend, Keshav, as well as with himself. And it looks at a past which took place twenty years ago, one belonging to his boyhood and shared with Keshav. All along, depths are emphasised, depths which we are unable to fathom, of the penetrating eyes, of the mysterious womb of the earth, of the complex human mind, and of the mystery within one.

The thoughts, questions and discussions go on to focus on the concepts of beauty, philosophy, the self and the other, the personal and reflexive. As each persists with his views, the discussion heightens into an argument until it comes to rest on the creative process, which is analysed as one marked by three moments—first, intense experience; second, when it is separated, transformed into a mental experience and lifted up into a fantasy; and the third, the expression through language—from the subjective to the objective concretisation.

***Ek Sahityik Ki Diary** is part memoir, part travel, part inner monologue and part external dialogue—an absorbing combination of genres as philosophy and literature work together on the borders of psychology. The essay ranks with some of the best pieces on the nature of creativity.*

The Third Moment*

Teesra Kshana

This happened some twenty years ago. My friend Keshav and I often went for walks in the forest. We would climb mountains and cross rivers. Keshav was, like me, a boy of fifteen. But to me, he seemed very mysterious. His problem was rather strange. And in my heart, I was terrified of that mystery.

Very early on, Keshav had explained to me what Ida, Pingla and Sushmna were. I was scared of the Kundalini Chakra**. He had told me many other things in detail about the Hathyogis.

Keshav's head was very large at the back and long and wide in the front. He had an ordinary forehead with thick eyebrows and deep, black eyes, like two wells, framed in glass and enclosed within the lashes. They appeared to be bottomless. I had the feeling that that there was another pair of eyes beneath this pair. His bushy eyebrows met at the top of his nose. Sometimes, he got a barber to shave this hair, but it grew again. Under these eyes, his face was long and pale, and he always wore a lazy, irritated and weary expression.

He was of medium height and had no interest in games. He was good at maths. That was why Keshav had become necessary for me, for my middle and matric exams.

Yet, I was not enthusiastic about Keshav, though I felt that he had greater affection for me. He was the son of a respected friend of my father's and a frequent visitor to our home.

There was only one thing common between us. He was a great wanderer. I also was very fond of walking. We would both

---

* Extracts from *Ek Sahitayik Ki Diary* (A Writer's Diary). Hindi, New Delhi: Bhartiya Jnanpith, 1964.

** Lunar, solar and the balancing factor where psychic energies are concerned.

ramble about, morning and evening, and when on a holiday, we often spent the whole day walking.

His long face, however, still continued to be pale and sallow, though he was actually healthier than me and physically much stronger. But his complexion had a yellow hue. His deep dark eyes on that faded pale face, with thick brows, thick hair and a round stubborn chin all seemed very mysterious to me. He did not have the playfulness of a child and would go about with me, silent and motionless, like a statue of stone.

I had the feeling that there was an ancient lake in the womb of the earth. There were *ghats* with frightening and horrible idols and old temples with cavern-like chambers, full of mystery and terror on its banks. They had all been interred by history. Layer upon layer of earth, fold upon fold, and rock upon rock had all piled up and the whole scene was buried under this and had vanished. In its place, new foreign trees of eucalyptus had been planted. Bungalows had been built. Beauties in flashy clothes roamed the place. And my friend Keshav lived in one of these bungalows, who, in some earlier birth, must have drunk from this lake and must have roamed about in this area.

The mind of a man is a deep puzzle—and the first inkling of this I had was from Keshav—not because Keshav was not open and frank with me. There was nothing in his life which needed to be kept a secret. He was very compassionate, serious and patient and was capable of facing problems easily, and also very forgiving. He was languid, calm, lazy, matter of fact, but innately affectionate. His biggest fault was that he had no childlike qualities or faults. I always felt that his rational attitude was more appropriate for an old man.

When we were in high school, Keshav often took me into the forests. We would visit Bharathari's cave, Machindranath's *samadhi* and many other isolated holy places. The river Kshipra flowed, deep, fierce and ponderous, near Mangalnath. We would look for new sites along its banks. We spent many pleasant and unpleasant evenings on the banks of the Kshipra. We took in the forest land through our breaths and gathered the earth to our chests.

I had never seen Keshav practise Yoga and had no knowledge of what it was. Yet, he would often talk about Yoga and explain the importance of the nervous system to me. It was he who highlighted the significance of the Shatchakra—the six *chakras* of Hathyoga—to me. But the darkness of my mind was not dispelled by the light he had thrown on Yoga. His exposition on Yoga, however, affected me and they seemed to me mysterious and scary. I had the sensation that I was walking into the deep darkness of caverns and could hear the piteous cries of a woman coming from within these caves.

I told him of this image in my mind. This attracted him all the more to me. He took greater care of me. Gradually, I also came closer to him. It had become difficult for me to do anything without seeking his advice.

I would often tell him what I thought and felt—whether the feelings were good or bad, worthy of being revealed or not. We had come to believe that to disregard a fact or to hide it or relegate it to the back of our minds was not only wrong, but often led to many problems.

I must say one thing. I would often become very emotional while expressing my views or ideas. I had the feeling that the mind is mysterious. It is dark, and in this darkness, there are steps, and these steps are wet, and the l west step is under water. This deep dark water is frightening. And out there, there is someone in those black waters. Perhaps, it is me. And this bottomless and pitch-black water is pierced by a broad ray of moonlight, bright and shining, and my eyes are glittering like blue stones, which are lit from within!

The echoes from within my mind attracted him. Gradually, he became more interested in me. When I would tell him what was in my mind, he would steadily look at me with his intense eyes from under his bushy eyebrows. Ordinary things, which were characteristics of our society, were the main topics of our conversation. Though his knowledge was limited, yet our conversations covered a wide range of subjects. I still remember that he was the first one to tell me that Gandhism stresses the emotional act in such a manner that the tendency of intellectual enquiry has been suppressed. He was of the opinion that Gandhism disregards the whole rational process of intellectual inquiry, analysis and conclusion. He had explained this to me at the time when the Satyagraha Movement of 1930–31 had come to an end, and the inclination to enter the legislatures was gathering momentum. We were studying in the first year at a local intermediate college at that time. It was then that we had first heard about the Soviet five-year plans.

Then we joined the degree college in another town. I did not know that Keshav had also joined the same college. I had not even tried to find out where Keshav was. The fact was that I was not particularly fond of him. I didn't like such intense and serious persons. Yes, I respected and admired him, and he was very fond of me. I was compelled to like him. Perhaps he was aware of this. But he never said anything about what his feelings were in this connection.

Once, when we were in the fourth year, he took me to the college canteen. I was the one who kept talking. In fact, what could he say, for he did not know the art of conversation! I had got the highest marks in Philosophy. I was happily explaining what answers I had given. Then, we moved on to a pond, which was about half a mile away, and sat on its embankment. He was silent. I had started talking about psychoanalysis. When he got bored with my non-stop chattering, he started throwing pebbles into the water. Waves rose to the surface in a circle with sounds of dup-dup.

The evening hung on the water. The twilight hesitated to enter the water, which shimmered in the reddish reflection of the attire of the setting sun. And I was ecstatic about the colourful and young evening.

We got up, walked about and then stood under a peepul tree. Suddenly, I was frightened. I don't know why, but one thought scared me. As we stood under the tree, the evening deepened into darkness around us. In an agitated and strange tone, I said: 'Evening! This colourful evening! It seems to have overwhelmed me. It has a magical quality and its delicate, bewitching power scares me! I am frightened of the power within me!' I shivered as I said this.

By this time, the dark of the evening had deepened further. Trees seemed to turn into mysterious pillars of blackness. Silence pervaded everything. And then, a pale yellow wave erupted from within this silence. The moonlight shimmered on the rotundas of the college building, hung on the high branches of the trees, spreading its silvery whiteness all around.

Keshav suddenly put his flaccid hand on my shoulder and said, 'Do you remember you had once asked me to define beauty?'

Without paying much attention to what he was saying, I answered rather indifferently, 'Yes.'

'You are experiencing beauty now.'

I didn't know what I was experiencing. I can only say that I was in the grip of an indescribable excitement. There was a mysterious force within me and it seemed to have overpowered me. I could feel its presence all around—had felt its presence many times. But now it seemed to have gripped me from within. What I was, he had become. Someone vast, exceptional, different from me, some other.

Suddenly, I thought of the inner emptiness of this stone-hearted friend of mine. How distant he was from me, how different, how distinct—in an undesirable manner.

He was talking to me in a rather pompous way, 'When man tends to identify himself with some object, or a scene, or even an emotion, he experiences beauty. Subject and object, a thing and its appearance, the distinction between these two separate entities is obliterated, and the subject and object establish a harmonious relationship, and a feeling of beauty is born!'

I paid scant attention to what he was saying. Someone who had not been touched by beauty, like my friend Keshav, to define beauty! Even if the definition was correct, so what? And, if it was wrong, then what? It hardly made any difference!

Days passed. We two friends, coming from the same village, but with different temperaments, different qualities and different attitudes! Though we were often bored with each other, yet we were often together. We discussed various things. My tongue would wag! Keshav seemed like a lock, which hung on a bolt, open and yet untouched. Anyone could go into the house, steal whatever he fancied, and then put the lock back on the hook of the bolt on his way out. There was no need for a key. The lock was broken and the key didn't work.

Suddenly, a key did work on this lock! It was a holiday. The sun was resting under the trees, and I was bored at home. I saw a face in the distance, cycling down, shining in the heat of the sun!

By this time, I had written many poems. Here is a victim walking into my trap, I smugly thought to myself. There was excitement on Keshav's face, something strange, something new that I could not place. I had been too busy writing poems and had had no time to pay him any attention. I was on my own high!

Had I not started talking then, the silence would have thickened and darkened and lengthened. Therefore, I began, 'What brings you here?'

Keshav bent his neck to one side. His hair fell on his forehead. I felt he wanted to relax. But he said, 'I have thought a lot about what an aesthetic experience is. And today, I have also written something on it—I want you to hear it.'

Something seemed to shrivel within me. I was myself wanting to recite my own poems, and here was Keshav wanting me to hear what he had written. My whole afternoon would be wasted. *Chi*!!

'Why don't we talk about it?' I suggested.

'Sure, but you would have to be disciplined about it,' he said with a smile.

His smile hurt me. Am I a drivelling idiot? This fool seems to have studied my nature thoroughly! I must have been boring him. It is not right to give him another opportunity to understand me so deeply. I keep yapping like a fool and this gentleman makes a mental note of all my weaknesses!

I tried very hard to sound convincing, 'We will discuss things with full propriety.'

He said, 'I had told you that when the "self" and the "other", the reflexive aspect and the objective aspect, become one, then a compatibility between the two is established.'

His ideas were profound and his face so serious that I had to suppress my laughter. First, I did not like his choice of words.

This much I knew that the basis of all philosophy is the concept of the relationship between the object and the subject—the premise of the personal and reflexive, and their mutual relationship. Or, one could say it is the basis of epistemology. It is on the foundation of epistemology that the whole edifice of hypothesis has been erected. From this point of view, I had no need to laugh at his language. His argument may have been controversial, but certainly not laughable. Yet, I laughed because his words had given me a glimpse of his queer personality. The same heavy, inert, cold, stony personality!

His brows contracted slightly. He looked at me with some surprise, his face pale and insipid, as if trying to gauge my attitude.

I said, 'I don't understand matters of similarity and oneness of shape and form. In fact, I cannot identify with any object. I do not refute the issue of resemblance, but I cannot accept it as a tenet.'

'Why?' he asked.

'One, I don't exactly understand the term "objective aspect". In Hindi, what is external to the mind is taken to be an object—this is what I think. But, I say, even if an element of mind can be an object, there is no sense in talking about the similarity or harmony of such an object because it is a part of the mind. Yes, I can imagine an attitude of indifference to this component of the mind, not of similarity.'

My deliberate and soft tone and words convinced him that I was not trying to scoff at him, but really making an effort to understand what he was trying to explain, and making an effort to overcome the difficulties that I was encountering in the process.

After all, he was my friend and was intelligent and sharp. He gave me a slight smile and said, 'You are talking like a writer. But not everyone is a writer. There are viewers, readers and listeners. They are, therefore you are, and therefore they are! They are not for you, you are because of them. If the reader or the listener begins with the talk of identification or similarity, then you should not be surprised.'

'Then?' I asked.

'Then, would you analyse and investigate beauty from the point of view of the writer or a viewer, or would you appraise and describe beauty by your own aesthetic experience? Answer this question,' he asserted.

I was ensnared. I could have said that I'll follow both methods. But I thought it best to be honest and said, 'I would prefer to examine and define beauty as a writer. Not because I want to put the writer on a very high pedestal, but because that way I would be standing firm on the solid rock of my personal experience.'

First, he knitted his brows, and then relaxed them and remarked, 'Quite right, but then there are those who are not writers; they also all must be standing on the firm basis of their own experience and would rather base their views on that experience alone. Therefore, there is no need to scoff at them and it would be wrong to do so.'

He went on, 'A lot depends on the point you begin your analysis from. If you begin as a reader, a listener or a viewer, then your intellectual journey would follow a different path. If you think as a writer, then the whole issue would assume a different form. From whichever point you begin, the issue of discussion would be an interpretation of beauty, but as the path taken would be different, the dissimilarity of the road traversed is bound to make the thought processes different.

'It is not necessarily true that the two journeys would inevitably be contradictory because they are mutually different. Difference can be complementary as well as contradictory.

'If we talk about facts only, even then, the difference in the manner in which we emphasise different points may lead to divergence in analysis.

'But the most significant thing is the manner in which the question is presented. It represents the road your thought processes will travel. If this journey is not to be made a synonym of a trip into the barren desert, then the question must be presented in a proper perspective. If it is explained in a faulty manner, then the road ahead is bound to be bad.'

He gave me a keen glance. Perhaps he wanted to ascertain that I was listening to him seriously. Probably he thought me to be very impulsive, easily excitable and restless. But I was cool and collected. The only thought in my mind was that Keshav thought that I did not know how to present the problem correctly. And I was offended by this attitude of his. I was aware of this feeling of his, for he had often reiterated this. In fact, he thought himself to be intellectually superior to me. His coldness, which had created a distance between us, the manner in which we respected this distance, and our continuous proximity despite this distance and in contrast to the irritation I felt for him—I often thought that all these things had rather complicated my relations with Keshav. The threads were badly entangled. I could neither accept him fully, nor could I dismiss him from my life. This was the situation I was in. As this situation had existed for a long time, I had got used to it. Yet, my annoyance would often come through, and then he would have a wicked gleam in his eyes, and I would have a feeling that he was playing a subtle game with me. At that time, I hated him with all my heart!!

Somehow I overcame my irritation and was successful in regaining my mental balance; I wanted to show him that I was listening to him attentively. I thought it best to let myself drown in the flow of his arguments and reasoning for this was the only way I could preserve my self-esteem. Though outwardly, I appeared very cool and collected, yet my mind was not on what was being said.

I have seen many who appear very calm and tranquil, deep and serious. But I was now convinced that they are empty-headed. Their outward seriousness and energy is a facade for the emptiness that is within. Look at me. For instance, I pretended to be listening very seriously to what he was telling me but I was listening only to the sound and not the words that were being uttered.

But I was restless. His ideas found their way into my mind in the same way a gust of wind blows into a room from outside. The flow of his voice continued like the natural flow of a stream. I could only identify a few waves. I was like this. Then why should not I be indifferent to myself?

The thought upset me. In this state of perplexity, I said, 'Let me get some tea. I'll be back in a few minutes.' I went in and in about fifteen minutes came back with a tea tray. Suddenly, I heard:

'Different people have different creative processes, and these creative tendencies take on different forms at different times. Then, the creative process for different genres is also different.'

Placing the tea tray on the table, I answered in all seriousness, 'Give me some time to think about it. What do you say? What you are asserting is really significant.'

He agreed. A burden seemed to be taken off my mind. I had got rid of him. This made me a little happy.

Glancing at me, he remarked, 'I want that views about literature should be based on a real analysis of literature. As we proceed from induction to deduction in science—collecting facts, appraising then, marking similarities and then establishing a rationale—in the same manner, why should we not proceed from induction towards deduction in literature? Why should the field of induction be limited to Hindi literature alone? When we teach what a novel is, we should cover the entire spectrum of novels in all countries and then establish certain generalisations about what a novel is, and what is the art of novel writing, and what are its main elements... in the same way, the reasoning of what is beauty in literature should also not be limited only to Hindi poetry and fiction. If we extend our range, then we would discover that our definition of beauty will be free of all ambiguity, as also of diffusion and exaggeration. I have strong suspicions that the present definition of beauty (shall we call it an explanation?) is based only on the characteristics of poetry, and that also only autobiographical poetry. The overt and covert aim of these definitions is to defend the existing poetic sensibility... but these definitions are being made in such a manner, with so much of flourish and flamboyance, as if they are the universal manifestations of the supreme truth. There is no need for this pose or posture. It is an unscientific point of view. If one must investigate the beauty of literature, then one should not confine oneself to the study of poetry and that also, only contemporary poetry. And if one has to explain it in this manner, then all postures must be abandoned. I detest it.'

My role in this long monologue was that of a listener. However, I did not want to play this insignificant role and wanted to hit back, to retaliate. I felt that he wanted to discuss beauty in a scholarly manner. I had no desire to go on with this discussion… why cast pearls before swine?

I tried to change the topic. 'How are things?'

He made no answer. What could he say!

We got up and started walking. I said, 'Let me walk some distance with you.'

The evening was deepening. The white flowers in my garden glowed like bright lamps in the dark. The scent of the forest pervaded the air around us. The dusk was weaving its magical spell on all things. There was a temple in our compound. He said, 'Come, let's sit here.'

The sheer loveliness of the surroundings overwhelmed me. My very being was happy and there was a new passion in my heart, a subtle intoxication. A feeling of pure physical pleasure obsessed me. An untrammelled energy, a surge of power brought a gleam to my eyes.

But my friend sat there—calm, motionless, as if carved of stone. And here was I, overpowered by the waves of passion and wonderment, which seemed to engulf my very being.

He began again, in a very cold tone and halting manner. I felt as if a lump of ice was being rubbed on my skin. It was then that I heard a familiar name in the flow of sound and was startled, 'What?'

'Yesterday, we decided to get married this summer.'

I asked him in amazement, 'What?… Who with?'

'Katie.'

'Katie who?'

He made no answer, but an image flashed in my mind.

I was never so surprised. Can Keshav do this? Impossible! Then, all my investigations and observations about him have been proved wrong—at one stroke! Good that I was to be proved wrong!

My face was suffused with pleasure. And in a light tone, I said, 'No wonder you were talking about harmony and affinity! Why, Sir!!'

His answer was rather neat!

'Only a man who is neutral can talk about affinity! Do you get it?' he asked rather seriously. His voice was full of a new energy. But I failed to understand the meaning of what he had said. In fact, I was so happy that I embraced him. He blushed and seemed flustered. Overcome by shyness. In these circumstances, how could I understand what he meant?

Time passed. He was not successful in life. A man like him could not be very successful in this age of free-for-all!

Our faces reflected the dryness and despair that life had dealt us. Withdrawn from the world, in the darkness of loneliness, the two of us were living in two different corners of the world.

Despite this, whenever I asked him for money, he sent it immediately. And he also wrote that I should not hesitate in asking him for money whenever I needed it. Five years passed and neither did I write to him, nor did I ask him for money. I had no information about him and he also did not get in touch with me.

It is like steam rising from a pond, spiral after spiral of steam rising high and moving upwards, and taking on the shape of a man and moving closer to you, engulfing you. How would you feel? I would surely be scared! What about you?

When I was informed that Keshav was arriving in town, I had the same scary feeling. I felt that a swirling wave of steam had taken on the shape of a man and was gradually moving closer to me. I was terrified.

I was in a fix whether to go to the railway station to receive him or try to improve upon the ugliness of my home. But when my goodhearted wife assured me that she would see to that, I was a little relieved. Had Keshav wanted to come here, he should have informed me well in time—it would have been more comfortable for us. When times are bad, even a guest seems like an enemy, particularly one who has known one in earlier, much better, more prosperous and well-appointed conditions.

There was a remarkable change in Keshav. His hair had turned grey and his face was marked with deep wrinkles. He looked haggard. But he was healthy and had a good physique, with well-developed muscles. It was clear that he must have been exercising vigorously in these last six-seven years. He had taken up swimming. He had never been impatient, but he was more energetic than before. His cool seriousness had not diminished, but now he was more voluble. I felt that he had faced up to his circumstances with great strength and confidence. He laughed a great deal and even cut jokes. I also felt that he had read extensively. All the while, I had a sneaking feeling of having been left behind and that he had moved far ahead of me.

When the two of us sat down for dinner, I was stunned to see his fair, healthy and well-built body from within his vest. I was not happy. An old fair wheatish face and a fair body! He looked handsome! Sure, there were worry lines on his face—they were very deep. But were they worry lines? Or lines produced by deep thought? I could not decide.

During dinner, he said something very funny. With a morsel of food in his hand, he looked at me and remarked, 'There is one big difference between you and me. Ideas agitate me and prod me into action. You immediately turn ideas into sensations and sensations into images. There are two different developments in you. If your poems seem too complex to some, you should not be discouraged… I read your poems very carefully.'

I asked him rather hesitantly, 'Do you like my poems?'

'They need some editing. But I am not one of these who sacrifice content for the form.'

We were silent for a long time. The distance between two human points lengthened. After one moment, a small point developed in the middle, at equidistance from the two ends. A miniscule line emerged from the point on one side. On the other side also, another simple, straight line developed. These two lines advanced and formed a link between the two human points—joining us.

I said with a sudden enthusiasm, 'In my opinion, the important thing is that art has three moments. And if there is even the smallest inner weakness in them—it may be of a weak intellectual analysis or of sensibility—the writing is definitely affected by it.'

He thought over what I had said for some time. I was also silent. Then he said, 'Please elucidate your meaning.'

I answered, 'The first moment is the moment of intense experience. The second is when this experience separates itself from its painful and agonising roots and turns itself into a fantasy, which seems to take form before one's eyes. And the third and final moment is the one of giving this fantasy the garb of words. The flow of the words within this process is the flow of our total persona and life. And the fantasy is continuously developing and changing within this flow. In this manner, as it is being embodied in words, it takes on a new form, abandoning many elements of its original form. It undergoes such a change that it is difficult to say that it is the same form which has evolved from its original root. Whatever is created during this process of giving a word-form to the fantasy—leading to its continuous development—that is the third and final moment of art. The first moment is undoubtedly the moment of experience. There can be no flow or momentum without that. The first moment is essential to strike the first blow, which marks the initiation of the process of intellectual self-expression. It decides its direction and also its constituents, determines its manifestation. The significant thing is that this experience merges with other intellectual factors and transforms itself during its projection. As soon as this experience detaches itself from its painful roots, it transcends the purely impersonal and acquires a new emotional purpose. It is this emotional content which lends it its colour and form. Despite this, the fantasy cannot be the image of lived experience. During the process of its transformation from personal into impersonal, it has taken on something new, which liberates it from its original experience. Fantasy is born out of experience, but has its own independent existence, which is capable of development. It is independent because it is born out of experience.

'This is the second moment of art,' I continued. 'But during the process of acquiring a word form, the fantasy is diffused and merges with the process and flows along. When it blends into this eternal flow—all the colours of the fantasy, its persona and all its consciousness—all interweave and flow along with this surge and create an image which is the product of the fantasy of this second moment, not its reflection. Therefore, its persona is different, independent and distinct from the original. This is the third and final moment of art. Without these three moments, no art is possible. And the rules of the development of each one of these moments are distinct.'

I went on, 'If you want the answer to the question what is beauty, or what is the experience of beauty, and in what way is it different from the actual experience, then you will have to study the psychology of all three significant moments. Without such an analysis, you will not be able to find the solution to this question... .'

I stopped here. I was breathless. I glanced at him as I waited for him to respond. But he made no answer.

The day passed. We reviewed our lives, and under the influence of this retrospection, who knows what we told each other!!

Next day, when we were about to go to bed, he said, 'The three moments of art! A good hypothesis! It has to be considered.'

He emphasised, 'One thing is sure. The knowledge of beauty is related to the process of creation. There can be no experience of beauty without the creative process.'

He continued, 'Any viewing of natural or female beauty is entirely individualistic and cannot be really considered an experience of beauty.'

I intervened. 'Actually, beauty is born when, with the help of the creative imagination, the actual experience is extended. Imagination has a role to play between the actual experience of the artist and the fantasy which emerges from the sensibilities generated by this experience. This role is creative. The same imagination lifts the personal experience from its individually-felt anguish as it deepens it and also elevates it.' I was very keen to hear his answer.

He remarked, 'Within these moments of art, why does it become representative? Why does the artist feel that what he has to say is significant for all? I ask you, why?'

'This happens because the situation-free individual perspective merges with the situation-related sensibility which this perspective has generated, and this intermingling elevates the whole experience.

'The fantasy, therefore, contains both empirical knowledge and an informed sensibility based on this knowledge. That is the reason the writer/creator feels that his experience is significant and valuable for all. This means that the conflict between undergoing an experience and being a mere spectator is submerged, and pushes the creative process forward as each takes on qualities found in the other. The awareness of the spectator and the sensibility of the one who has actually experienced, mingle and encourage the tendency to rise above itself. In this manner, the particular in the creative process seems to reflect the general interest. In other words, the situation-related dark colours of experience are refined by the situation-free form of the eye and become representative of a larger and shared experience. This is what I think. Empirical knowledge and the sensibility generated by it are so inherent in the fantasy that is created in the second moment of art that the writer feels impelled to articulate them.

'... . This is where the third moment begins. Now, this is interesting. Listen to me carefully.

'A new struggle begins at this point. As soon as the writer begins expressing it in words, the colours of the fantasy begin to melt and flow continuously. In this process of manifestation, the fantasy undergoes a change. Why does this happen?

For some time, there was silence. He couldn't say more. Having posed a question, he could not give the answer. He threw me a glance. I took up the thread and said:

'It happens that during the process of giving the fantasy a word form, many new elements join the fantasy and keep continuously modifying it. You must understand that this fantasy is the product of an experience, but is still only a reflection of experience. Apparently, there is an emotional purpose inherent in the fantasy, and it is this purpose which gives the fantasy a direction. This purpose which is within the fantasy is its very core, its heart.

'The fantasy cannot remain static as it acquires this purpose and direction. It is not a lifeless picture. It is a dynamic process because of this purpose and the direction of this goal. It acquires this dynamism from the moment it comes into being, at the last point of the first moment of art. The fantasy, which, at the beginning, is a hazy vision, turns into a well-ordered sequence of various images. And each one of these images form a cluster round a vital point and move forward in an organised manner.

'What is meaningful is that as soon as the fantasy is being articulated into words, the emotional purpose, or, let's say, the anguish underlying it, initiates the process of amalgamating the various experiences which support, nurture and protect it. The secret core of the fantasy, in which is inherent its purpose, its pain, as also its direction, desires to be supported, nurtured and protected by the various real experiences as it is being articulated. The images, moods and voices of these real experiences merge with the core of the fantasy and flow along with the surging fantasy, making it more effective and meaningful...

'... When the fantasy is being rendered into a word form, various images, moods and sounds created by these experiences flow into it, and the artist is compelled to regulate and control the emotional flow, so only those sounds, feelings and images come into the poem which support the core, and in this process, some other supportive experiences of a similar design and pattern flow in and are integrated within the flow of the fantasy.

'The significant thing is that in the third moment of art, the core of the fantasy, as it is integrated with various moods and sounds generated by different experiences, undergoes such drastic changes that the writer looks at it in a new light. I mean that the anguish inherent in the fantasy is now expanded and takes on the form of a perspective. This perspective changes the design of the fantasy as it is being turned into words. It is no longer the old pain, but has a new form. Many new mental images have joined it.

'As long as it has the original power and momentum, it will go on acquiring new elements. But when this momentum ceases, then the flow will also stop and the purpose will come to an end.

At this point, the poem should be complete. But if it is not, then this means that there is some flow in the perception of the pain, or the direction is not right, or the very purpose was weak—this will have to be accepted.'

Here I stopped. I could not say anything more.

It was very late. Darkness had deepened on the roads, despite the street lights. Loneliness was all pervasive. The wind blew in gusts and the mind was restless. My friend was silent. Why?

This is life. An idea doesn't come to you merely because someone has given it a voice, or you have yourself expressed it. My friend has now left me. He has gone far away, without telling me his opinion. We had some good times together.

Many days later, I received his letter. It was no letter, but a thesis! Only at the end had he written, 'Regards to Bhabhi and love to children', et cetera. I did not read the letter, but put it away in a drawer so that I might read it at leisure. But even when I had the time, I could not read it. In between, I got a reminder from him. I put that also in the drawer.

In fact, my home had been invaded by illness those days. Life had compelled me to learn those very things which went against my nature. And during this difficult period of learning those lessons, I also fell ill.

And then one night, when the groans around me had fallen silent and the lamp in the niche in the wall spread its benign light all around, I lay thinking about life with a restless mind. I was depressed and felt as if my life was being crushed by my failure.

Lost in my own thoughts, I recalled some international events. Being a journalist, I often noted down new ideas. I opened the drawer looking for some paper and my eyes fell on both the letter that my friend had written and the reminder he had sent. His thoughts warmed my heart. I read his letter a number of times. It had been written by a cool and collected mind. To me, it seemed like the essence of roses. I don't need to say that the letter was very long, running into twenty-five pages. Small, beautiful, well-formed letters and paragraphs where they were needed, such was the letter—or was it the mother of all letters, I could not say.

Days passed, and now the answer to the reply I had sent him… Keshav had written it with great aplomb…

'… It is true that the fantasy begins changing during the process of being rendered into words. How does this happen?

'In my opinion there are two factors behind it. Both are interconnected.

'The third moment of art is of great significance and perfection. It is at this juncture that the fantasy assumes the form of literary, artistic expression.

'It is here that the dedication to the word begins. A word has its own sensibilities, comprising images as well as sounds. The artist seeks to give expression to the forms, shapes and colours of his mind, and therefore he is continuously matching the sounds of his own emotions, his words and the nuances of their meanings.

'This has two consequences: (i) The attempt to match the nuances of the words to the resonance of the emotions creates a situation where many emotional factors abandon their original power and take on new contexts and forms. Many poets go to the extent of sacrificing the emotional content of their words for the sake of linguistic splendour and purity. And we often find that in this process of giving it a word form, some parts of the fantasy itself get edited out or shorn off. (ii) On the other hand, the important thing is that in this process of acquiring a word form, the articulation itself enriches the fantasy, seeking to make it fuller and perfect. Seeking to manifest itself, the fantasy uses words with similar sounds—and expressions. Language is a living tradition. Words have their own vibrations. These vibrations create new thought processes as they are being articulated. These thought processes are close to the fantasy and extend the world of the fantasy, giving greater force to the power it already has. They contain varied experiences, old as also new, lived and acquired. The significance of the world of fantasy is enhanced and it takes on a new perspective as well. With this new perspective, the fantasy glows with greater splendour. The fantasy has now become truly universal.

'Why does this happen? Language is a social asset. The words have traditional meanings. These meanings are associated with experiences of life. The fantasy evokes the nuances inherent in the words. The fantasy has to fit the framework created by the essential power of the fantasy. The nuances of the words diffuse the basic colours of the fantasy, change its shape and also reduce its original depth by editing out the personal context. Many poets delete those very elements of the ideas that need to be articulated for the sake of maintaining the purity and incandescence of the language.

'On the other hand, the words that have been articulated by the fantasy create new fringe meanings and images. These thoughts are closer to the fantasy and comprise several old and new experiences, which extend the significance of the fantasy, and during this process of expression, the thought and fantasy act and react on each other. This whole process of action and reaction further extends the boundaries of the fantasy and lends a new perspective to the experience. The essential purpose inherent in the fantasy and the direction of fantasy are also expanded.

'In other words, the third moment is very consequential and creative. The artist receives new images which enhance and enrich the old fantasy and make it more universal. This universality is produced by the vibrations of the hidden meanings of the words that are articulated. Behind the rhythm of the words lies a whole tradition of universal and shared social experiences. Thus, the traditions of expression not only edit the original fantasy, but also enrich it with new concepts and give it greater momentum, as also expand the horizons of its significance.

'That is why the poet undergoes new experiences as he seeks to articulate his ideas. On one hand, his mind is busy with expressing the original fantasy, and on the other hand, his very existence is being enriched because of this absorption. He has new experiences. One experience reveals several layers of truth, and one confrontation leads to another, and the process goes on.

'Behind this psychological process lie the strength of language and its continuous growth. Language revises the fantasy and also helps in the development and fulfilment of the fantasy.

'The poet's fantasy embellishes the language, adds new imports, and creates new images. In this way, the poet creates language. And the poet who envisages language and nurtures it is undoubtedly a great poet.

'In this way, the real conflict lies in the third moment of art—the conflict between language and concept. The mutual interaction, as also the conflict between these two, is extremely complicated and induces changes in both. The two are continuously being modified. This conflict is very significant, and creative also. Language in the form of a tradition stretches the colours of the fantasy, but also keeps altering it. The fantasy seeks to retain its originality, and also to express its own individual colours, exerts pressure on language, gives its words and phrases new meanings, the ability to impart new suggestions, interpretations, and also gives it a new expression. There is this significant contest in the third moment of art.

'The artist, thus, feels that whatever he had to say, he has not been able to express it, give it full expression, and has said much that he was not aware that he would say!! Don't you have this feeling?'

I have given a few excerpts from Keshav's letter here. The letter gave me some pain, also happiness. Pain because, during this period, my life had become rather complicated, and happy, because Keshav had taken my concept much further. I think Keshav must have been testing and retesting these ideas.

Undoubtedly, Keshav is an interesting man. But the most important thing is that he is my friend. Sure, I have to begin some new assignment with him. It would be of great help to me.

Ismat Chughtai

Ismat Chughtai (1911–91) is one writer whose work has made waves across different mediums of art and across different ideological platforms, whether feminist, political or those of freedom of expression. Chughtai has often been in the midst of controversies as she has moved ahead of her times not only in her attitudes and writing, but also in continued resistance to social conventions.

Born in Badayun in Uttar Pradesh, Chughtai spent much of her childhood in Jodhpur. One of nine siblings, her writing reflects the feeling of crowding and oppression in large families, especially her novel, ***Terhi Lakeer*** *(The Crooked Line). She reflects with ruthless honesty on the callous attitude that women are likely to develop towards their bodies and their progeny due to repeated pregnancies. Unlike her sisters, Ismat resisted an early marriage and pressed her desire for continuing her studies and went on to take a degree in teachers' training. It was in Aligarh that she came into contact with several leading writers and came under the influence of Rashid Jehan. In 1936, Ismat also attended the Progressive Writers' Meet, an event that further fanned her fiery spirit.*

Ismat Chughtai has published several collections of short stories, handling bold themes with honesty and ease. But it is her work in films that extended her range in other directions. She won the Filmfare Best Story Award for the film, ***Garam Hawa****, along with Kaifi Azmi. She went on to play other roles—as director, actor, script writer—for many a film.*

The passage selected for this collection is from her autobiography, ***Kagzi Hain Pairahan****, and recounts her experience of the court trial on charges of obscenity, which, of all times, took place in the early days of her marriage. Saadat Hasan Manto was also hauled up at the same* *time on similar charges. The trial took them from Bombay to Lahore in those pre-partition days. In the present anthology, it is being used to highlight several things—the unwritten censorship that controls writing, the need for a writer to resist such control, the personal war that has to be waged, and the role of reality and authenticity essential to its portrayal. Another important fact is the awareness that a writer has to be, is and needs be ahead of her times in order to probe the depth of human experience of which the body is as much a part as the mind. The reader, I am sure, will not miss out on the remarkable sense of humour, which comes from a genuine experience of freedom.*

To Those Married Women*

'Un bahatayon ke naam
Jinke badan
Bemohabbat riyakar sejon
Per saj-saj
Ke ukta gaye hain.'

Faiz Ahmed Faiz

To those married women
Whose bodies
Are weary of adorning the
Loveless beds of deceit.

It was four in the evening, or maybe half past, when there was a sharp ring at the front door. The servant opened the door, but retreated in fear.

'Who is it?'

'Police!' Whenever there is a theft in the neighbourhood, it is the servant who is the first to be questioned.

'Police?' Shahid sat up with a start.

'Yes, sir.' The servant was trembling. 'But sir, I haven't done anything. I swear, sir.'

'What is it?' Shahid asked, going up to the door.

'There is a summons.'

'Summons? But… all right, give it to me.'

'Sorry, I can't give it to you.'

'But… what summons? And for whom?'

'It is for Ismat Chughtai. Call her.'

---

* Extract from Ismat Chughtai's autobiography, *Kagzi Hain Pairahan*. New Delhi: Raj Kamal Prakashan (1998), 2000.

The servant was relieved.

'But tell me…'

'Please call her. It is a summons from Lahore.'

I was cooling the milk bottle for Seema, my two-month-old daughter.

'A summons from Lahore?' I asked, shaking the bottle in cold water.

'Yes, from Lahore,' Shahid was irritated.

I came out from the kitchen barefoot, the bottle in my hand.

'Arre, what summons is it?'

'Read it, please,' the police inspector said in a gruff tone. And I burst out laughing when I saw the very first line. It read: 'Ismat Chughtai v. The Crown.'

'Arre, what complaint does the King Emperor have against me that he has filed a case against me?'

'Don't laugh!' The inspector said harshly. 'Sign it after you have read it.'

I read the summons, and took a little time to understand its import. The government had filed a case of obscenity against my story, "*Lihaaf*" ("The Quilt"), and summoned me to appear in the court in January next. If I failed to do so, severe action would be taken against me.

'No, I am not going to accept it,' I said, returning the papers to him and shaking the milk bottle. 'Please take it back.'

'You will have to accept it.'

'Why?' I was arguing out of sheer force of habit.

'Arre, what is the matter?' Mohsin Abdullah asked, rushing up the stairs. He had just come back God knows from where and was covered with dust.

'Look, these people are trying to serve a summons on me. Why should I accept it?' Mohsin had studied law and had topped his class.

'Hoon,' he remarked as he perused the document. 'What story is this?'

'A stupid story, which has been like a millstone round my neck.'

'You will have to accept it.'

'Why?'

'Again the same stupidity,' Shahid flared up.

'I am not going to accept it.'

'If you don't, you will be arrested,' Mohsin growled.

'Let them arrest me, but I will not accept it.'

'You will be jailed.'

'Jailed? Arre, I am keen to see a jail. I have asked Yusuf to show me one from inside time and again, but he just laughs. Take me to the jail, Inspector Sahib. Have you brought the handcuffs?' I asked him rather tenderly.

The inspector lost his temper, but restraining himself, said, 'Don't make a joke of it—please sign this.'

Then Shahid and Mohsin both came at me. I was still treating the whole thing as a big joke. When Abba Miyan* was a judge at Sambhar, the court was held in the outer apartments of our haveli. We had often watched common thieves and robbers, handcuffed and fettered, from the windows. Once, some very dangerous dacoits had been arrested and there was a beautiful and coquettish young woman with them. She was dressed in a pair of breeches and a coat; she had light eyes, a slim waist and long black hair. I had been deeply impressed by her.

Shahid and Mohsin had upset me. I tried to give the milk bottle to the inspector so that I could sign the documents, but he retreated as if I had turned a pistol on him. Mohsin snatched the bottle from me and I signed the papers.

'You have to come to the police station for the bail… a bail of five hundred rupees.'

'I don't have five hundred right now.'

'Not you, someone else will have to stand bail for you.'

'I don't want to involve anyone else. If I don't appear in the court, the bail will be cancelled and the money will be confiscated,' I tried to impress him with my knowledge of the law. 'You arrest me.'

This time, the inspector was not annoyed. He smiled and threw a glance in Shahid's direction, who was sitting on the sofa

---

* The author's father.

with his head in his hands. Then he told me, 'Let's go. It won't take very long.'

'But the bail?' I asked. I was a little ashamed of my foolish behaviour.

'I will stand bail,' Mohsin said.

'But my daughter is hungry. Her ayah is new and just a young girl at that!'

'You feed your baby,' the inspector said.

'Please come in,' Mohsin ushered them in.

The inspector was a fan of Shahid's, and with sweet talk, his mood was also restored in no time.

I went to the Mahim police station with Shahid and Mohsin. After completing the various formalities, I asked, 'Where are the prisoners?'

'You want to see them?'

'Sure.'

Some ten-fifteen men were lying about anyhow in a cramped space behind a grating.

'They are accused, not prisoners, and will be presented before the court tomorrow,' the inspector informed me.

'Their crime?'

'Rioting, pickpocketing, public nuisance while drunk.'

'What punishment will they get?'

'A fine or a few days' imprisonment.'

I was rather sorry for myself that I got such weak criminals to see. It would have been different had I got a couple of murderers or dacoits to look at.

'Where would you have put me?'

'We don't have any arrangements for women here. They are taken to Grant Road or Matunga.'

Shahid and Mohsin fought with me on coming home, and Shahid kept on the fight right through the night. It almost came to the verge of divorce! I had got Mohsin to shut up by threatening him to go underground if he fought with me any more. Then he would have to face the music and would lose his five hundred in the bargain! But Shahid was not ready to countenance any slander and dishonour. What would his parents and elder brother think?

When the news was flashed in the papers, we received a very sad letter from my father-in-law. 'Advise her. Tell her to write about God and the Prophet so that life hereafter can be happy. A lawsuit and that also for obscenity! We all are very upset. May God be merciful.'

I learnt from Manto's call that he had also received a similar notice from the same court and had to appear the same day. Then Sophia and Manto came over. He was very excited, as if he had been awarded a Victoria Cross. Though in my heart, I was ashamed, I put up a brave face. Shahid, having met Manto, was somewhat comforted and I was also consoled.

Earlier, I had been frightened, but Manto encouraged me and I lost all my fears.

'Arre, you have written only one outstanding piece. Shahid, what sort of a man are you! You also must come along. You have not seen Lahore in winter. By God, we will show you our Lahore. What sharp winters we have! Fried fish... aah... whiskey... fire in the grate as if lovers' hearts are on fire! And blood red *maltas*! Aah! Like lovers' kisses.'

'Arre, calm down, Manto Sahib,' Sophia was nervous.

Then there was a flood of abusive letters. Such strange, complicated, heavy abuses that if one were to utter them even in the presence of the dead, they would also be startled out of their eternal sleep. Not only I, but my family, Shahid, and even my two-month-old daughter were the targets of these abuses.

I am very scared of sludge, chameleons and lizards. Many brag a great deal about their brave deeds, but are frightened even of a dead mouse. The letters that came for me scared me as if they contained snakes or scorpions. I would open them with fear in my heart, and throw them away after reading a couple of lines. But if a letter were to fall into Shahid's hands, then divorce would loom large on the horizon.

Besides these letters, there were articles in the papers and meetings held to discuss this issue. Only a strong person could face this storm. I gave no explanation and also did not refuse to accept my mistake. Sure, I was at fault, I admitted my crime. Manto was the only one who would flare up at my 'cowardly' behaviour. I condemned myself, but he defended me. None of our friends gave all this any importance. I do not exactly remember it, but perhaps Abbas had got the English translation of my story, "*Lihaaf*", published in some paper. The Progressives had neither been annoyed nor praised me. And this attitude had given me great satisfaction.

I was living with my brother when I had written the story. I wrote it at night and read it out to my sister-in-law in the morning. She had not said that it was obscene, but had at once known whose story I had written. Then I had read the story to my fourteen-year-old cousin. She said, 'What have you written? I can't understand anything!'

I had then sent the story to *Adab-e-Latif*. They had made no comment, but had immediately published it. Shahid Ahmed Dehlavi was at that time bringing out a collection of my short stories and had included the story in the book. The story had been published in 1942, and by this time, my friendship with Shahid had reached the stage of marriage. Shahid had expressed his dislike for the story after reading it and there was a tiff, but the attacks that were made on the story at that time had not reached Bombay as yet. I subscribed only to *Saqi* and *Adab-e-Latif*. Shahid was not put off and we had got married.

It was in December 1944 that we had received the summons for appearing in the court in January. Everyone was saying that there would be no sentence, only a fine would be imposed. We had started getting woollens made for our trip to Lahore.

Seema was very small and weak and cried in a very loud voice. The child specialist we took her to said she was fine and healthy, but it was not right to take her to Lahore for she might not be able to bear the harsh winter. We, therefore, left her at Aligarh with Sultana Jafri's mother and went on to Lahore. Shahid Ahmed Dehlavi and the printer who had printed the book had both joined us, for they had also been indicted by the King Emperor. The case was not against *Adab-e-Latif*, but against the book which had been published by Shahid Ahmed Dehlavi.

Sultana came to the railway station to receive us. She was working at the Lahore radio station those days and was living at Luqman Sahib's. He owned a palatial bungalow. His wife and children were away on a visit to her parents and we had the whole house to ourselves.

Manto had also reached Lahore and there was a round of parties after our arrival. Most of them were Manto's friends, but they came to have a look at me as if I was a strange creature. We went to the court, but nothing happened. The judge asked me my name and whether I had written the story. I admitted that I had. That was all.

It was a big letdown. My lawyer kept talking all the time. We could not understand what he was saying because, most of the time, we kept whispering to each other. Then another date was given and we were free and had lots of fun. I, Shahid and Manto went shopping in a tonga. We bought Kashmiri shawls and also shoes. At the shoe shop, I felt envious of Manto's fair and delicate feet. Glancing at my own ugly feet, I wanted to mourn like a peacock.

'I hate my feet!' Manto remarked.

'Why? They are so pretty,' I argued.

'They are very effeminate.'

'But you are so very keen on women!'

'You are arguing for argument's sake. I love women as a man. This doesn't mean that I should myself become a woman!'

'Forget about men and women and talk about human beings! You know, men with delicate feet are very compassionate and refined. My brother, Azim Beg Chughtai, also had pretty feet. But... .'

And the image of my brother's feet as he lay on his deathbed flashed in my mind. Swollen, misshapen and ugly. At that moment, the beautiful city of Lahore, with all its grace and beauty, seemed to turn into the bleak sandy dunes of Jodhpur where my brother is buried under tonnes of sand. His freshly made grave had been strewn with thorn bushes so that no wild animal could dig it up. The thorns seemed to prick my nerves and I put the soft delicate *toosh* shawl back on the counter.

How beautiful was Lahore! Brimming with life and laughter, welcoming one and all with open arms. The city of bighearted people! The heart of Punjab!

We had a lovely time, going round the city. Our pockets always full of dry fruits, we wandered around on the roads, deep in conversation, eating fried fish at the street corner. We seemed to be hungry all the time. We walked and we ate, and that was all that we seemed to do. We went into a restaurant and when we saw hamburgers and hotdogs, our mouths watered.

'There is ham in hamburgers meaning pork, but we can eat hotdogs,' Shahid handed down the judgement, and we ate hotdogs to our fill, like it behoved God-fearing Muslims, and drank it down with fresh pomegranate juice.

It was later that we learnt that this white race is extremely devious. There is meat in hamburger and sausages in hotdogs. Though two days had passed since we had eaten the hotdogs, Shahid started feeling sick the moment he heard this. Then, a maulwi advised him that if one eats something in ignorance, one can seek forgiveness, and that stopped his nausea.

In the evening, after Shahid and Manto had got drunk, they felt that it was hamburgers that were not 'kosher' and it was better to eat hotdogs. When the argument seemed to be taking a dangerous turn, it was decided to shun both, for it was difficult to know what was kosher and what was not. Therefore, it was decided to eat chicken tikkas. We went around Anarkali, strolled through the Shalimar Garden, visited the mausoleum of Noor Jahan, and thoroughly enjoyed ourselves at dinners and mushairas.

At that time, I blessed the British emperor for suing me and giving me the golden opportunity of visiting Lahore and enjoying myself. I was impatient for the second appearance and was not upset, and were I to be sentenced to death and hanged in Lahore, it would be a martyr's death and I would be given a grand funeral by the people of Lahore!

The second hearing was in the pleasant month of November, that is, in 1946. Shahid was busy with his film and Seema's ayah was very capable, and now even Seema was a healthy and bouncing child. I therefore left her in Bombay and flew to Delhi, taking a train for Lahore from there, accompanied by Shahid Ahmed Dehlavi and his printer. I was very sorry for the printer. The poor man had been dragged into this for no fault of his. He was a silent, simple man, eyes always downcast, signs of boredom on his face. I always felt guilty in his presence. Poor man had got embroiled in all this for merely printing my book.

I asked him, 'What do you think? Will we win?'

'I can't say. I haven't read the story.'

'But you have printed it!'

'I look at the words separately. I don't think about their meaning.'

'Strange! And you don't read it after it is printed?'

'I do read it to see that there are no printing errors.'

'Separate words?'

'Yes,' he answered, bowing his head. Then, after a moment, he added, 'May I say something? I hope you won't mind.'

'Not at all.'

'You make many spelling mistakes.'

'Yes, that is so. Actually. I get confused about 's' and 'sh'. I also make mistakes over 'z' and 'j'. The same thing happens about a few other letters.'

'Were you not made to write as a child on the wooden board *(takhti)*?'

'Of course! And was regularly beaten for these very mistakes, but… .'

'Actually, the manner in which I only look at the words and pay no attention to their meaning, in the same manner, you are so impatient to have your say that you disregard the distinction between different alphabets.'

May God bless printers with long lives, I thought, for they help me hold my head high.

I stayed at M. Aslam's home with Shahid Sahib. We had barely exchanged greetings properly when he started scolding me. He shouted at me for the obscenity and frankness in my story. I also lost my temper. Shahid Sahib tried to stop me, but I went ahead full steam.

'And you have used such dirty words in *Gunah Ki Raaten*! You have described the sex act in detail and so openly. Just for the fun of it!'

'It is different for me! I am a man.'

'But how is that my fault?'

'Meaning?' He had turned red in anger.

'Meaning that God has made you a man and I have nothing to say about it, and made me a woman and you have no say in that. You have not asked for the right to write what you want to, and I don't need your permission to write what I want.'

'You are the educated daughter of a respected Muslim family!'

'And you are also educated and belong to a respectable Muslim family.'

'You want to be the equal of men?'

'Never! I tried to be at the top of my class and often scored higher marks than the boys.'

I now realised that I had succumbed to my family weakness—argument. Aslam Sahib's face clearly showed his rising anger and I was scared that he would either slap me or himself suffer a stroke. Shahid Sahib was frightened and near tears. Softening my tone, I said with all humility, 'Actually, Aslam Sahib, no one had ever told me that writing a story on the subject that I have used in *"Lihaaf"* is a sin. And I have not read in any book that... one should not write on... this addiction... or illness. Perhaps, my mind is not like the brush of Abdur Rehman Chughtai,* but a cheap camera, which clicks whatever it sees, and my pen goes out of control. My mind leads it astray. And I do not interfere in whatever happens between the mind and the pen.'

'You have not received any religious instruction.'

'Arre, Aslam Sahib, I have read *Behshti Zevar (Heavenly Jewels)*.**

---

* The reference is to the well-known painter, Chughtai.

** A well-known conduct book for women by Maulana Ali Thanawi, laying down their roles, a book often given to Muslim women as part of their dowry. Barbara Daly Metcalf has translated extracts from it under the title, *Perfecting Women* (OUP, 1992).

It is written in a very explicit style,' I said with an innocent look on my face. Aslam Sahib was a little upset. I continued, 'As a child, I was disconcerted when I read many books, for their contents were obviously dirty. Then, after my graduation, I read that these things are not dirty, but are normal and no one in his senses should be ignorant about them. That way, people can also call books on psychology or medicine obscene.'

Tempers had cooled down and we were now talking in normal tones. Aslam Sahib was more relaxed. Breakfast had been served by this time. There was too much food for just the four of us—fifteen people could have eaten what was laid before us. Three or four dishes of eggs, *shami* kababs, mince *paranthas* as also puris and toast. White as well as yellow butter, curd, milk, honey and dry fruits, egg halwa, carrot halwa and halwa sohan.

'Ya Allah! Do you want to kill us?'

Because I had earlier been very critical of him, now I started praising his writing. I had read his 'Nargis' and *Gunah Ki Raaten* and now lauded them sky high. This had the desired effect and he had to accept that frankness was necessary at times. Then, he himself began explaining the high points of his books and, soon enough, was in a happy mood.

'You tender an apology to the judge,' he said in a soft tone.

'Why? Our advocate says that we will win the case.'

'No, the fool is lying. If you and Manto apologise, then the case will be dropped. It is a matter of five minutes.'

'The case has been filed against us by the government because the respectable people of Lahore have put pressure on it to do so.'

'Nonsense,' he said, but could not look me in the eye.

'Then has the government or the emperor read these stories that it was decided to prosecute us?'

'Aslam Sahib, it is correct that some writers, critics and reputed citizens had drawn the attention of the government to these books, saying that they were immoral and should be banned,' Shahid Sahib added.

'If immoral things are not banned, then should they be honoured?' Aslam Sahib burst out. Shahid Sahib looked a little crestfallen.

'Then we deserve to be punished,' I said.

'Again that obstinacy!'

'No, Aslam Sahib, it is not right that one should commit a crime, mislead respectable people, then apologise and go scot-free. It I have done some wrong and it is proved, then punishment alone can give me peace,' I said with all sincerity and no trace of sarcasm.

'Don't be stubborn. Apologise'.

'If I am sentenced, then what would it be? Fine?'

'And plenty of slander and infamy.'

'That has already been done. What else is left? This case is nothing,' I answered. And then asked, 'How much will the fine be?'

'About two-three hundred,' Shahid Sahib replied.

'Only?'

'It can also be five hundred,' Aslam Sahib tried to scare me.

'Th.....at's all?'

'You have become very rich?' Aslam Sahib was annoyed.

'Due to your blessings,' I said. 'Even if I did not have the money, would you not pay the fine to save me from prison? You are one of the wealthy men of Lahore.'

'You talk too much.'

'My mother also had the same complaint. She always said that I would earn by tongue-wagging.'

Everyone laughed and the tension passed. Then, after some time, he again insisted that I should apologise. I wanted to break his head and then my own, but kept quiet.

Then, changing the topic, he asked, 'Why did you write "*Dozakhi*" ('One Who Lives in Hell')?'

'Whether he was hellish or heavenly, I wrote whatever I wanted to, who are you to comment on that? He was my brother.'

I had never told anyone what had I undergone when I had written that piece, through what flames of hell I had passed and what I had lost. I had finished writing the piece at two at night. What a frightening night it had been! The sea had come up to the steps of the house as the boundary wall had not yet been built. I seemed to be caught in a strange spell of madness.

Whatever I had written seemed to be unrolling before my eyes like the reel of a film. I had put the lights off, but felt suffocated and hastily switched them on again. I was frightened of the dark. Images of that grave haunted me, and for months, I could not sleep alone after visiting it. I felt scared and I persuaded my young cousin to sleep with me. I hated being at Jodhpur and I came away to Bombay. One of the ten pillars had collapsed. Who could fill the vacuum?

I made no answer. Going to my room, I packed my suitcase and phoned Sultana, asking her to come immediately and to pretend to force me to go with her. I told her that if Aslam Sahib should try to stop me, she should insist on my going with her. She asked, 'What is the matter? I will come after five, straight from my office.'

'By that time, someone is bound to be killed. You must come immediately.'

Sultana had come at once, but Aslam Sahib refused to let me go with her. Sultana insisted and I laughed at the farce! Then I went away with Sultana.

We were present in the court on the day of the hearing and the witnesses who had to prove that Manto's "*Bu*" ("Smell"') and my "*Lihaaf*" were both obscene, gave evidence in support of the contention. My lawyer had given me strict instructions that I should not open my mouth till I was asked a question. Whatever had to be done or said, he would do or say. First, the case against "Bu" was taken up.

'This story is obscene?' Manto's lawyer asked.

'Yes, sir' the witness answered.

'Which word made you decide that it was obscene?'

Witness: 'The word, "breast".'

Lawyer: 'Milord, the word, breast, is not obscene.'

Judge: 'Right.'

Lawyer: 'The word, breast, is not obscene.'

Witness: 'No, but here, the writer has used the word, breast, for a woman's chest.'

Manto stood up at once and said, 'If I should not call a woman's chest 'breast', then should I call it peanuts?'

There was laughter in the court. Manto also laughed.

'It the accused cracks another joke, then he will be held up for contempt of court and charged, or turned out of the court.'

Manto's lawyer advised him to behave himself in a low tone, and he understood. The argument went on around the word, 'breast', which could not be proved to be obscene.

'If the word, breast, is obscene, then why not knee or elbow?' I asked Manto.

'Nonsense!' Manto was furious. The argument went on. We got up and came out and sat down on the benches in the verandah. Ahmed Nadim Qasimi* had brought a basket of *maltas*. He also demonstrated how to eat *maltas* with great delicacy.

'Soften the *malta* with your hands, then make a small hole at the top and suck the juice.'

We finished the basket in no time, but were still hungry, and rushed to a restaurant at lunch time. I had been very ill at Seema's birth and had lost a lot of weight. We had chicken and naan for lunch and washed it down with pomegranate juice. I blessed the people who had sued us!

Luqman had arranged a small dinner for writers and poets. It was here that I met Mrs Hijab Imtiaz Ali for the first time—too much make-up on the face, eyes loaded with kohl, a sad air, a little indifferent to all who were around. It you asked her something, she had a habit of staring blankly into space.

'She is a fraud,' Manto whispered.

'No, she is lost in a dreamy haze, which she has created around her by her own pen.'

Hijab Imtiaz Ali went on staring into space and I looked around for Imtiaz Ali and fell into conversation with him. How different were these two! Imtiaz Sahib was very talkative, happy-go-lucky and an open-hearted man. We were having a lovely time. I felt I had known him for years. His conversation was more scintillating than even his writings.

I met Hijab Imtiaz Ali again recently on my visit to Pakistan. She looked much younger and prettier, with little make-up, talkative and outgoing, as if she had taken a new birth.

---

* A well-known writer of Urdu.

I was very keen to see an organon that Hijab had often mentioned in her stories. I had never seen one before. On my visit to her, I had asked her, 'Do you really have an organon?'

'Sure. Would you like to see it?'

'Definitely. The very word is intoxicating and makes one want to cry.'

I also told her that I had tried my hand at free verse at one time; later, I had burnt all that I had written.

After one look at the organon, all my curiosity abated. It was the same small piano-like organ that De Mello often plays during the recording of a film song and the recordist often scolds him and keeps pushing from one side to another, and is the same instrument that is used to create the necessary musical effect for the background music when the heroine is really yearning for her love. How crude is the word, 'organ', and by merely adding an extra 'on', it becomes delicate and cute.

The court was crowded. We had been advised by many of our friends to tender our apologies to the court, and that they would willingly pay the fine on our behalf. The witnesses trying to prove that *'Lihaaf'* was obscene were getting upset by the cross-examination of our lawyer. None could cite a single word that could prove obscenity. After a great deal of deliberation, one of them said that the sentence, 'collecting her lovers', was obscene.

'Which word is vulgar—"collect" or "lover"?' the lawyer asked.

'The word, lover,' the witness answered with some pomposity.

'My lord, the word, 'lover', has been used by various poets and has even been used in religious songs. This word is considered sacred by those who are devoted to God.'

'But it is shameful that girls should collect lovers around them,' the witness asserted. 'Because... for... it is not respectable.'

'Is it not bad for those girls who are not respectable?'

'Aan ... no ...'

'My client has referred to those girls who may not be respectable. Then, sir, as you say, girls who are not respectable collect lovers?'

'Yes.'

'Then it is not vulgar to talk about them. But for an educated woman of a well-known family to write about these things—she must be condemned,' the witness said rather loudly.

'Then condemn it as much as you want. But it is not a ground for a lawsuit.'

'If you people tender apologies, then we will also pay the cost of the case and...,' someone who was not known to me had come up to make the offer.

'What do you say, Manto Sahib, shall we apologise? Whatever money we get, we can buy things with that!' I turned to Manto.

'No, you don't realise how quarrelsome this person is. He will make things very difficult for me. The punishment that the court may give me will be better than his anger.'

The gentlemen were put out for we were not given any punishment. The judge summoned me to his chamber and, with great cordiality, told me, 'I have read your stories and they are not obscene. And "*Lihaaf*" is also not vulgar. But there is plenty of dirt in Manto's writings.'

'The world is full of obscenity,' I said very sweetly.

'Then is it necessary to describe it so explicitly?'

'That is the way it can be seen by everyone and then alone can we think of cleaning it up.'

He laughed.

I had not been upset when the case had been filed, nor was I elated after winning it. On the other hand, I was sad that I might not get another chance to visit Lahore again.

What a beautiful city is Lahore! Lahori rock salt! Sparkling like gems! Pink and white! One is tempted to string them into a necklace and put them around the swan-like neck of a young girl.

'Dim is the light of the stars!' sings Surender Kaur in her voice like molten gold. When her husband, Sodhi, joins her, the sweetness weaves a strange yet peaceful ambience around you. A cry for the unknown beloved echoes in your heart. Lahore has an aura all its own. Silent music is played by unseen hands, evoking memories of days of romance which are no more. Then what happened?

Read Charles Dickens, his *David Copperfield, Oliver Twist,* and H.G. Wells' *Tono Bungay*!

And Gorky's *Mother* brought me down to earth.

Chekhov, Emile Zola, Gogol, Tolstoy, Dostoevsky, Maupassant!

All the castles built in the air came crashing down!

And I crashlanded into this bungalow with a thatched roof on the edge of Lal Diggi in Aligarh. These bungalows were built of mud bricks and it was impossible to put even a nail in a wall. Pigeon droppings fell from the thatched roof and bats hung on the trees. The floors were also made of clay, the house shook with the wind and there was neither electricity nor water. Water was brought in by a water carrier, who always had a red scarf tied round his head. The charpoys were covered with durries and dirty sheets with greasy pillows. Amma had given up wearing the billowing pajamas that swept the ground and taken to wearing five-yard cotton dhotis.

There was a time when there were twenty servants in the house. Amma would give shelter to anyone who was hungry or needed a job. Then Abba had used the scissors of economy on all unnecessary expenditure after his retirement. Only Ali Baksh, his wife, Shiekhen Bua, who was also the cook, the coachman and his wife were left. We still had two horses and a buffalo.

Perhaps, I was jealous of the romantic ambience Mrs Imtiaz Ali had woven around herself. As it is, no romance could flourish in my family, and it was after a great deal of thought that I had written my first story, "*Bachpan*" ('Childhood'). At that time, we subscribed only to *Tehzeebe Niswan*, and I had sent the story to that magazine. It came back, and along came an admonitory letter from the editor, Mumtaz Ali, who also happened to be the father of Imtiaz Ali 'Taj'. I had compared my own childhood with that of Mrs Imtiaz Ali in the story. The editor had objected to my writing that the Maulvi Sahib often thrashed me for reciting the Quran Sharif and I could also not enunciate certain words clearly and properly, and was sick when I tried to do so. He had written that I had made fun of the recitation of the Quran Sharif and proved that I was both irreligious and a sinner.

After I had become a known writer, that very story was published in *Saqi* and was appreciated. I did not like Azim Bhai's frivolous romantic comedies. They seemed unreal, with not an iota of reality. He depicted the openhearted mischievousness and gallantry of my other brother's as his own.

I felt chastened. I had often been scolded for speaking the truth, but whenever the matters reached Abba Mian, he would always decide in my favour. Badi Apa (elder sister) had been widowed at the age of nineteen and was now an embittered woman, deeply influenced by the upper class families of Aligarh, particularly the women of the Khwaja family, and I never got along with the women of that family. I was headstrong and argumentative and frank to the point of rudeness. Though I was not in purdah, my tongue was like a naked sword and uncontrollable. I myself become a follower of the Progressives and was trying to create a revolution with full energy and enthusiasm.

The label of "*Lihaaf*" is still sticking to my persona, and what people call popularity was the ill-fame earned by that story and in such a large measure that it made me feel sick. "*Lihaaf*" had become my aversion. Whatever I wrote was buried under the folds of "*Lihaaf*".

When I wrote *Terhi Laqeer (The Crooked Line)* and sent it to Shahid Ahmed Dehlavi, he passed it on to Mohammed Hasan Asqari to review, and he gave me the suggestion to make my heroine like the one in "*Lihaaf*". I was incensed and asked for the manuscript to be returned to me, even though the printing had begun. I sent it to Nazir Ahmed of Lahore. At that time, Lahore was a city in India.

"*Lihaaf*" created many problems for me along with the ill fame. Shahid and I had so many fights that life became a battleground.

But there were many rewards as well for "*Lihaaf*" and all my aversion disappeared.

I had gone to Aligarh after many years. I was apprehensive of meeting the lady on whom I had based the story, for people had taken care to inform her that "*Lihaaf*" was based on her life.

We came face to face at a party. The ground shifted from under my feet. She looked at me with her big eyes and seemed to blossom. She rushed to me and, embracing me, took me aside and said, 'You know, I got a divorce and remarried. Now I have a lovely son!'

I wanted to hold on to someone and cry. The tears kept rolling down my cheeks and I was laughing. She gave a lavish party in my honour. I was happy to see her child and felt that he was someone close to me, an offspring of my mind, a child of my intellect, of my pen.

And I realised that flowers can bloom even among rocks; one only has to nurture them with one's own blood. And another thing: In the passing, I asked a gentleman:

"*Lihaaf*" is immoral?'

'True,' he answered.

'How?' I asked.

'One is sexually aroused by the story.'

'Really? Do you want a quilt at that time?'

'No, actually, the begum is very sexual. She is a stunning beauty with a lovely body. Drenched in colour. Her entrancing eyes and inviting lips! An intoxicating and heady mixture!'

'And then?'

'Satan tempts one'.

'What does he say?'

'That ... that ... one should ... her.'

'Satan is really very wise. This is exactly what I had wanted, that some brave man should snatch her from the clutches of that witch, Rabbu, and give her so much love that she should be able to forget all her pain. To give water to a thirsty sparrow is a pious act.'

'What is her address?' He enquired with a smile.

'You were born too late! She is now a grandmother by the grace of God. Years ago, a prince rescued her from that prison and gave her all the beauties of life.'

In some flat in the neighbourhood, Nayyara Noor* was singing Faiz's lyric:

* A well-known Pakistani singer.

Un bahatayon ke naam

Jinke badan
Be-mohabbat riyakar sejon per
saj saj ke ukta gayen hain.

To those married women
Whose bodies
Are weary of adorning the
Loveless beds of deceit.

And the thought came to me: Where is that great woman of India? The virtuous lady Sita, whose delicate flower-like feet put out a fire.

And Meerabai who put her arms round the divine neck?

That Sati Savitri who rescued her Satyavan from the land of the dead, and Razia Sultana who rejected the proposals of kings and princes and made an Abyssinian slave her faith.

Is she huddled under a quilt today? Or is she waging a constant battle for survival at Faras Road?

Translated from Hindi by **Tripti Jain**

S.H. Vatsyayan 'Agyeya'

Popularly referred to as Ajneya or Agyeya, Sachchidananda Hirananda Vatsyayan (1911–87) was born in Uttar Pradesh, but the family soon shifted to Punjab and he received his education in Lahore. During the freedom struggle, he was in prison for six years—1930–36—and his most important novel, ***Shekhar Ek Jiwani****, is located in Lahore during the peak of the revolutionary period. Agyeya's work was recognised early for its remarkable lyrical and philosophical content. Besides several volumes of poetry, some fiction and a travelogue, he also established and edited* ***Dinmaan****. His editing of* ***Tar Saptak*** *marked a coming together of a range of talents, who, even though ideologically different, were all engaged with experimentation. In 1978, Agyeya was awarded the Jnanpith Award and, in 1983, the Golden Wreath Award for Poetry. Agyeya has twice done teaching assignments at Berkeley and a spell at Heidelberg during 1970–71.*

The essays included here are the two Samvatsar lectures delivered in the 1980s. The two lectures together offer a remarkable hold on the Indian psyche and sensibility and are directed at setting the time-space concepts in our own culture. These concepts are closely connected to the way we imagine and think.

In "Memory and Time", Agyeya expands on the idea that the Gregorian calendar does not and should not dislocate other calendars or ways of measuring time. The moment we restore other perspectives, locations in both time and history also change. It is through the dominance of the Gregorian calendar that imperialism has defined progress and backwardness, and it is through the denial of unrecorded histories that a western tracing of conquests and defeats is defined. In "Memory and Country", Agyeya takes up the whole question of space. The word, 'desh', literally means the place where one belongs. It can also stand for country, nation and space. The shifts in the locations of time and space alter the whole perspective on how we look at ourself, our histories, our cultures and the processes of creativity. Without memory, there is no imagination, and without imagination, belonging, relationships and even otherness have no meaning.

Indians have a whole group of religious calendars. If we adopt the Samvat calendar, it immediately becomes obvious that we entered the twenty-first century in and around the early 1940s, and in all else, the time-lag theory becomes infructious. Again, Agyeya dwells on the difference between 'itihaas' and 'mithihaas', what is recorded to have happened and what is believed to have happened. Perhaps both kinds of history are incomplete if considered only by themselves. The validity of each needs to be acknowledged for the human frameworks of knowledge. The significance of Agyeya's ideas lies in opening out new directions for conceptualising, removed from the 'surrender' mentality imposed by postcoloniality.

Memory and Time*

The times that we are living in today, we keep hearing—sometimes as a full war cry, and at others, as a suppressed echo—that we are standing at the threshold of the twenty-first century. I do not know how many of us feel the same in our hearts, but one does hear some people say that the whole country is physically preparing itself to take a big leap, and this leap will take us straight from the murky darkness of the last years of the twentieth century into the brilliant light of the open, cloudless skies of the twenty-first century. To explain what this leap will be like, some have even borrowed the phraseology of science. It is not that we will enter the twenty-first century as a result of the progress achieved by us in the twentieth century. The way we see in the nuclear world that the smallest atom of matter is in one condition at one moment, and immediately after that, it is in a different condition, and we do not see the journey in between, nor do we see the path of that change—in the same manner, we also will leap from one condition to another. Neither will the leap be seen by anyone, nor will anyone be able to map the path of that journey. By borrowing this concept of the **quantum leap** from science, the propagators of this view derive a double benefit. In the world, where the idea of a **quantum jump** is relevant, we do not consider time and space as distinct; we cannot do that because it is only in the continuity of time and space that this concept becomes meaningful. There—our

---

* Sahitya Akademi has published the essays in Hindi in the Samvatsar series; here, the essays have been taken from Agyeya's collection of essays, *Khule Mein Ped*, edited by Nandkishore Acharya and published by Vagdevi, Bikaner, 1999.

leap—that is the leap of the smallest atom is continuous—from matter to energy and energy to matter. In other words, we also can say that matter is continuously jumping from the dimension of space into the dimension of time and from the dimension of time to the dimension of space—space and time are continuously interchanging. Thus, it is clear that this aspect of the scientific concept does not apply to this leap which our country is going to take into the twenty-first century, but the people who are using this phraseology are big people, and it is discourteous to criticise what they say; it can only be repeated.

In this country, this question has been raised even earlier—whether the way in which we can jump from one place to another, can time also move forward by leaps and bounds, or does it inevitably move at an even pace that is perpetual and uniform? Does time also have atoms and can a living being pass through such nuclear situations, one after another, which are not in any way interlinked because of continuity and eternity? In the west, this question was raised in the form of a scientific puzzle in the nineteenth century itself—as an aspect of the **quantum theory**—and an integral and inherent consequence of this was the curiosity: What is the 'self' of those experiencing this time speed and what is our memory? But, as I have just said, in our country, this question had once been raised earlier and, here, I was not talking about the development of western scientific thought and the intellectual wave that it created here in the east. In this country, this question was originally raised a little before that—'a little earlier' meaning only about two or two and a half thousand years back by the Buddhist logicians. But, at present, I am not raising that ancient controversy here—some preparation is essential before it can be discussed in a meaningful manner. When we talk about **quantum leap**, then, naturally, the possibility arises that if this leap can be forward, then it could also be backward, or it should be possible—when we find the idea of space being independent of time impossible, then how can the concept of forward or backward be sustained? We will have to return to this problem of forward and backward (coming back meaning moving forward!). But, as an introduction to it, it would be appropriate to raise a few other contexts.

For those who talk of standing at the threshold of the twenty-first century, their century is based on the Christian calendar. But, in this country, the Christian calendar alone is not being followed. In this age of propaganda, this calendar has become very popular and now it is being widely used even in those areas where, a few years earlier, when using this calendar, we had to make things clear that this was the 'English date' *(Angrezi* date). But in a country where two-thirds of the population is even now illiterate, in such a country, even though we may say it sarcastically, or link the use of the indigenous calendar with their illiteracy, it is true that millions of ordinary people, while using the Christian calendar and English dates in daily life, yet live according to another calendar and other dates at another level. If you tell them that in reality, they are living in two different worlds, they would not even think you were being sarcastic—they would very simply accept that reality has two levels. To take the discussion further, I select one out of the various different calendars commonly used by these millions of people, Vikram Samwat, which is widely used in north India. There is a difference of fifty-seven years between the Vikram Samwat and the Christian calendar. According to the Vikram era, talk of 'at the threshold of the twenty-first century' is now old. According to that calendar, India entered the twenty-first century when the slogan of 'Quit India' was being raised in the country. Not selecting the exact point of entering the twenty-first century that we stand at today, and keeping the same difference that there is between the twenty-first century and this day, then, in 1986 (1929 A.D.), the country was in the grip of the second 'Satyagraha movement'. The actions of revolutionaries were giving it greater momentum. Getting a little closer to the threshold, if we look at the year 1996 of the Vikrami era (1939 A.D.), then we find the world on the brink of World War II. In brief, we can say that if the idea of standing at the threshold of the new century implies important and unimaginable changes, then at that stage, such an idea was widespread and relevant to the Vikrami era. Today, two generations have grown up since we entered the twenty-first century'. Forty years have passed since we attained freedom. The quantum jump that is being talked about today would have seemed to be more meaningful then. The path of the jump from slavery to freedom cannot be seen, and to draw a map of that mental journey is also difficult. Such a journey is actually a **quantum jump**. And those who are in the situation of recalling the experience and feelings of those moments of freedom may, perhaps, be able to recall the sharp truth of this statement. Many had even danced on the streets at the proclamation of freedom at midnight, but even if we let this extreme reaction be, even then, millions of people felt they had entered a new era. It is difficult to see this momentous change in the form of a continuous journey; it can only be experienced as a transformation—an epoch-making change—a **quantum jump**, a rebirth… .

Had we linked 'entering the twenty-first century' with the epoch-making beginning of freedom and seen some meaning in that connection—the significance of hope, enthusiasm and faith in the future—then it would have been more relevant to discuss the 'midpoint of the twenty-first century'. Perhaps, the same questions would have been raised that are being asked in connection with 'the threshold of the twenty-first century', but the feeling underlying those questions would have been more restrained and appropriate. Then the context of the questions would have been that half of the new century has also been crossed, isn't it time to evaluate what has been done during the journey so far, to prepare a plan for what has to be done in the future and to resolve to achieve it? Perhaps, such an idea would have been more appropriate despite the tumult to which I have already referred. This outcry has been raised mostly by politicians because they have ulterior motives; their method of work is also different—creating a tumult is a part of their methodology. But I am not a person of politics. Without totally rejecting political motives, I can say that I have other motives, or I should be having other motives—as a litterateur, my goals are different, or should also be different. And, also this, that an outcry would not be a part of it, but a purposeful silence might be more useful for it. But whether it is the Christian era or the Vikrami Samwat, there is another context to the reckoning of time, and it is this context with which I am concerned. At the beginning, I had referred to these calendars because the difference between these two is as much as that our average age span can be proportionately balanced and the two kinds of possible emotions compared. But the intellectual stream to the edge of which I want to take you is a little beyond this. The two different emotions, attitudes and tendencies that I have referred to may be apart by fifty-seven years, but for any meaningful discussion on them, one needs to rely on memory, and it is this **perspective of memory** that is my subject. To revive memories of events that occurred fifty-seven years ago may not seem very difficult (though it may be equally true that it can be difficult to recall the memories of even a day earlier), but at times, it is extremely difficult to revive the emotions or mental condition one had experienced an hour ago, or even a minute ago. The warp and woof of forgotten or unforgotten memories of forty years before, or fifty-seven years before, or four hundred or four thousand years ago, which are inspiring and also uninspiring, constitute the foundation of our cultural identity, which defines our personal, social, civil and national experience and aspirations. Giving priority to the concern that I have for this land, it is as a man of letters that I want to talk about the perspective of memory.

If, without an introduction, I were to simply say that accepting the Christian calendar as the only method of reckoning time historically has limited 'our comprehension of reality', it would appear to be a statement made out of religious prejudice. But actually, the Christian calendar has no relation whatsoever to Christianity. In the same manner, without any explanation, I can say that the Vikrami Samwat also limits our comprehension of history. Putting them together would render any charge of religious prejudice baseless. An explanation would still be necessary, but a clue to it would also emerge.

We believe time to be 'without a beginning and also without an end'. Yet, we always begin counting it from one point and this point of origin is not very distant to us in the past. In the process of creation, the distance is negligible and not very distant in the history of mankind. The point of origin is not far behind even in the process of development of civilisation. It is essential to measure the bigger against the smaller—there can be no measure without that—but what are the consequences of fixing a point to measure something that is without a beginning? I once read a story in a book on child psychology about a child who was very smart and who would invent some story or the other every day to tell his parents about what all he had seen or what all had happened to him. His parents were sick of his habit of lying, but also felt that his lying did not amount to a moral or social crime and that, as such, the child should not be punished for it lest it create feelings of guilt in him. Finally, using their imagination, they used the idea of a river and its two banks. After listening to the child's story, they would ask him whether the event he had described had taken place on this bank of the river or the other? By degrees, the two banks of the imaginary river became the dividing line between reality and imagination for the child. After narrating a made-up story, he would himself say, 'This happened on the other bank of the river.' In this way, his parents succeeded in bringing the child back to the hard ground of reality, without giving him a feeling of guilt. Perhaps, they had also realised a deeper truth about the flow of time because the real picture of the river of time is not complete without the other bank, where all that occurs in our imagination takes place. There is a **function of unreality** also, like there is a function of reality, which is also a *dharma*, meaning a function. That book on child psychology did not say whether that imaginative child grew up to become a famous novelist or not, but we can always hope that he did. But here, in the present context, this question can be asked whether an origin point of reckoning time is not like an imaginary river where history is on this bank, and all mythology on the other.

This question has probably exaggerated the issue because whether it is the Christian era or the Vikrami calendar, we do include things that happened a few centuries before their beginning point in our history; for example, following our tradition of reckoning time, we put Buddha or Ashoka or Alexander in a certain year or a certain century B.C. But while referring to the *Ramayana* or the *Mahabharata*, when we put them in 1500–2500 B.C., then are we putting the writing period of these great books in the category of the historically true in which, for example, we also put the attack by Mahmud Ghaznavi and Babar's invasion? Possibly, this question may not elicit a single answer, but by asking this question, we will realise that the totality of our experience of time is influenced by where we place the beginning point of time—year/samwat 0—year 0 A.D. or Samwat 0 Vikrami.

This, at least, is equally applicable to the Christian or Vikrami or any other calendar. But once curiosity is aroused, then many other questions come to the mind and many finer details of the structure of our experience, the perspectives of our memory jostle each other. Vikramaditya, with whom the Vikrami calendar begins, was a king, whereas Christ is a messiah. There have been many Vikramadityas, but there has been only one Christ, and He is the chosen and the only son of God, who is not only a part of God, but for millions of faithful believers, more important than God—a greater emotional force. The reckoning of time may have nothing to do with religion, but what do we do with this bond of love? The historian may be neutral, but an ordinary man with some knowledge of the past does not know that he is expected to maintain such a neutral stance.

Then, that same insistence on historicity that has established the reputation of the Christian era in Indian thought and research—that historicity did not only tell us that there have been many Vikrams, but also that the period of each Vikram is ambiguous. In this way, the system of reckoning years on the basis of the Vikrami calendar, which was even earlier an ad hoc system, became more uncertain because there was no authentic knowledge about its propagator or even of a definitive period of origin. I have heard that some Russian folktales begin this way, 'No one knows whether he was or not, but there was a king.' Does it not seem that the effect of the linking of Samwat and reckoning of time with a Vikram whose own period is indefinite is somewhat like: 'We do not know who he was or when he was, but there was a king called Vikram, and if we begin the counting of time with him, we can say', et cetera.

Then the question has also arisen—and it has not been solved, only suppressed—whether there was one and only one Christ, who was a historical individual, or whether he was a persona created by religious leaders by amalgamating the personalities of three-four persons. And this is a living question—a question that has been buried alive!—whether the one and only Jesus, with whom the Christian calendar begins, was born in 0 A.D. or some twelve, fifteen or eighteen years earlier. If these questions could remain in the forefront or could be kept there, in the manner in which questions related to Vikramaditya are, then the situation would have been somewhat different, But, as I have said earlier, these questions have been buried alive because Vikram is only a king, while Jesus is the propagator of a religion, the Son of a historical God (!), and an historical Christ. Nothing much is gained or lost by questioning the existence of Vikram, but, by raising any such question concerning Christ, a whole religious establishment seems to dodder.

It is not our aim to create any problems for a religious establishment. But it becomes clear how the structures of entire civilisations and cultures shake and totter when you raise such detailed questions connected with pre-eminent men (because most civilisations and cultures are based on religion and faith). In this way, questions related to eras and calendars become questions about our cultural identity because the perspectives of our racial memories are linked to that.

Indian culture is also a religious culture. Actually, the use of the word, 'culture', in the Indian context can only be accepted as the result of the effect of English education, and it would be more correct to say that not only has religion been the basis of culture in India, but what is called culture in the modern context is an extension of the 'ritualistic' aspect of religion. However, religion in India does not have a form in the way in which Christianity is connected with a propagator and a point of origin. Sects are one thing, but the consequence of following these new tendencies of accepting sects as religions (going into the reasons behind this is not relevant here) and the havoc they have played, and are still playing, with history validates our argument. Claims such as the historicity to which Christianity lays claim has no meaning in the Indian context. Here, numerous sects and their founders have existed within the boundaries of religion and, therefore, it can be said that various historical traditions have evolved here, each with its own point of origin. But these points of origin have not been turned into origin points of reckoning time, eras have not been named after these founders, though some sects have followed the tradition of working that period along with the accepted calendar. It can be asserted that it is because of this that Indian culture is multicentric and this can be accepted as its strong point. Because of this multicentrism, this culture has been able to save its identity from breaking up, despite being beseiged by historicism.

This condition of plural centrism may also be compared with the Chinese situation and some interesting results derived, China has neither had the same sort of religious foundation for its culture as India's, nor has its time reckoning process given any importance to a religious propagator or any point of origin linked with him, as has been done in Christianity. China has based its calendar on its royal dynasties and the periods of their reigns. In this way, one finds a clear perception of historicity in Chinese culture, and also the preservation of a secular multicentrism. It can be said that because of this, the structure of Chinese racial memory is different from India's on the one hand, and from that of the Christian world on the other.

The issue of Jewish culture and racial memory can also be raised in this context, and the indelible mark of that memory and its inspiring power with reference to the present century may also be discussed. However, we do not have the time to discuss it in detail. It is enough to refer to the impact of that memory. It is also necessary to point out that our historical epochs are far more ancient and longer than Creation as accepted by the Jewish religious tradition, meaning that the Jewish Creation is proportionately younger than our Samwats. There is, thus, no possibility of any traditional system of counting time in that culture. There, some other factors are selected to establish a fundamental relationship with racial identity, such events which are not the origin point of any epoch, but help in fostering that self-impression through which the Jewish race becomes at once God's own chosen people and also a race which has been oppressed by others through the centuries. On one hand, nomination by God, and on the other, such a feeling of self-protection—memories of both help a great deal in maintaining racial identity.

Memories can be suppressed. Memories can also be buried alive, and are buried alive. Such memories cannot be destroyed—what form they may take in the future and explode like volcanoes is very difficult to assess. But even examples of the power of such subjugated memories, their force and motivation to action, can be found in modern history. Such suppressed memories lie at the root of most of the turmoil prevailing in many areas of the world in which we live. Had they not been subjugated, they would have died a natural death—would have withered away—for it is necessary for the mind to forget or to shed what is unnecessary. Any living unit forgets many things; racial groups also forget many things, they also constitute a living unit in their collective form, which has a racial mind. But as they have been suppressed, they cannot dissolve in the natural process and they generate considerable energy within them, the consequences of which are unimaginable.

It is not my purpose to delve into the history of races or social psychology. Also, it is not my subject and I do not possess the ability to do so. But awareness of historical epochs, knowledge of periods and experience of the flow of time—they all have a literary aspect as well. Our memory is itself the basis of that consciousness and the source of its creation. If there is no memory, then there is no individuality; also, there is no time and also no creativity. 'I know who I am because I am what I can remember!' That and only that much. Though science talks of such a time that is neutral to any experience of life, there is an idea of time in geophysics and also in astrophysics. We cannot say that that time is not real. But if we want to reverse it and say that 'our reality is not based on that time', we cannot say that. Then a definition of reality would become essential. In different contexts, scientists say that what has happened in the last fifty years has not occurred in the earlier five thousand years (and fifty years is not long with reference to our average life span and does not go beyond the limits of our personal memories); otherwise, statements such as 'what happened in the first three minutes of creation did not happen in the next three crore years' are also there; not that they do not seek definition of the word, 'happen', but the second statement takes us where new definitions of even time and space are expected. And the scientist himself accepts that there even definitions become uncertain because we go much beyond the normal use of language and we do not absolutely know the real meaning of what we are doing. To associate reality—in the context of literature or creativity—with our consciousness is as necessary as is associating it with memory.

In the context of creativity, the reality of literature is experiential reality, which is beyond experience, or can be, but it also does not permit that experience-neutral reality to deny our experience. One quality which makes literature valuable lies in this that it continuously goes on extending the dimension of experiential reality and provides to us the standards to test all other dimensions, and in this way also makes it possible for us to accept those other dimensions—and extend our experience and also the sphere of our consciousness. This expansion is reflected in the extension of our memory. **In the context of creativity, all the perspectives of reality are the perspectives of memory alone.**

And here we can also say that **our language** is our memory. A deep emotional bond with language is a common fact of our age. The tensions, agitations and eruptions because of this emotional bond have been a common occurrence of our contemporary life. Many people who consider themselves enlightened thinkers are astonished at the intense and inflammatory form of this love for language and many would also make sarcastic comments on it. But the pressure of language is—wittingly or unwittingly—the pressure of the protection of social memory and the persistence of the protection of identity. We have said earlier that if there is no memory, there is no self, if our language is our memory, then the relationship between language and identity becomes clearer. The so-called intellectual will say that this argument gives rise to terrible fanaticism and prejudice, that it is chauvinism in the present condition our country is in, and a threat to emotional integration. These dangers are there, but any power does not become a lie because it is dangerous and also cannot be cancelled by saying this. The only solution to this danger is that we preach about a larger identity and rekindle those memories, use their power, which are linked to this larger power. That enlightened thinker has not performed this task.

But are we not creating confusion when we say both 'our language is also our memory' and 'our history is also our memory' at the same time? No. Because it can further be said that 'language is also history'. Second, I am not restricting myself only to these two things. Whatever I have said, that also means that even 'time is our memory'. It is our memory which is continuously and creatively weaving the past, present and the future in an organised sequence. It is memory alone which goes on continuously modifying that structure and presenting new modified perspectives. We can condense T.S. Eliot's famous lines and say that *'only in time is time remembered'*. And we also can say it in a different way: *Only in memory is time time*. A scientist, insistent on neutral materialism, may only smile at both these statements. But both are poetic statements and both would be considered meaningful in the poetic world and importance given to the meanings inherent in them.

I had initiated this discussion by talking about the calendar; making it the focus, I had referred to perception of reality, and along with that, I have also then tried to link it with history, literature and also language. **Memory alone is that dynamic creative element which goes on inventing new perspectives of time, history, literature and, yes, also language.**

The trends of modern life are constantly trivialising the significance of memory. The preoccupations of the present that we are living in—we are allowed to live in, are compelled to live in—are continuously increasing so that we should neither have the time to recollect nor should our minds be so inclined. New inventions are meant to create new demands and new informations tend to make memory rigid. The fast developing means of communications are fully helping in this process: They turn consumption into a quality and make sensationalism the equivalent of pleasure. That 'public memory is very short' is accepted, but all modern institutions are involved in the process of making public memory shorter. No one wants that we should be able to recollect anything because when we cannot remember anything, only then does it become possible for us to accept whatever we are told every day. That would be the 'scientific truth', it would also be 'the historical truth'—it would be the modern view! Even if we were unable to accept all this, at least we should not get any free time to remember and compare it with the past. The communication media is all out to create a situation where we should forget the past—or not be able to recall it—and this is a part of our daily living experience. It is this media which is impoverishing language every day, which is a part of this process that increases our knowledge, and where the possibility of the development of reason shrinks/lessens. Vocabulary goes on increasing, but the words are constantly losing their real meaning. This process will gain speed with the invention and use of sign languages for machines and mechanical translations. And, now, can one say that we do not need development?

In the context of continuous impoverishment of language, of experience and of our memory, what should be the duty of the litterateur? Even if he finds free time to comprehend and understand what his duty is, would he be able to decide how many possibilities are open to him, or how many possibilities he can open up? Standing at the threshold of the twenty-first century, the question still remains of what he will do with the historical experience of the twentieth century, which has just ended; also, what will he do with the forty centuries, which at least the history of this country cannot put outside its boundaries? We may have accepted the Christian era for reckoning time for our convenience—and we have officially adopted the Shaka Samwat and, yet, still widely use the Vikrami calendar—but the real question is not which one of these we should accord importance to. The question is that under the name of 'standing at the threshold of the twenty-first century', we are being compelled to bind ourselves to the history of twenty centuries, but what should we do with the history of those forty centuries which preceded them and which are, for us, as bright as ever, for our sun does not rise at the origin point of the Christian era, but wakes up much earlier—and illuminates many earlier eras.

It would be natural for the western system—and why forget that it is being given through an English medium of education—to consider a certain era 'historical' and, on the same basis, to consider certain other periods as 'prehistoric' or 'before history', and to put all that is the most ancient behind the smokescreen of legendary or mythological narration. Should we be compelled to accept this construct of historical periods?

Then, we also have to remember that because of the origin point, the resulting construct of time casts a long shadow on the future, it does not affect only the past. Moving the dividing line between historical and mythological from one place to another can have concomitant consequences. One result of looking at Indian history from the western point of view is that we seek the causes of movements that have begun here, not here, but there. Put aside the matter of train and telegraph, the national movement here also began because we were taught the value of freedom through western education and this created democratic sentiments in us! Let us go still further: Our poets, who wrote about the love of their country, took part in the nationalist movement, went to jail and bore all the tortures of imprisonment, did so because they were inspired by Sir Walter Scott, not by the struggle which they were perpetually living in! I am giving this example because I have read that this is being said in the history of Indian literatures; otherwise, such a foolish statement is not even worth mentioning. Take another example—not in books that I have read, but from my personal experience in this great city of New Delhi. You must have heard Gandhi's name. Now, what will you do if this name reminds you of Richard Attenborough's English film of this name, not of the Mahatma who lived amongst us, who taught us, made men out of us and who was sacrified in our midst?

Surely, in this our own country (and through that direct personal experience, not in this great city, but elsewhere), there are such people who do not want to marry their daughters in Awadh, because the Lord of Ayodhya, Ram, was cruel to Sita *maiyya*. Here also, it is one aspect of memory which is at work, although a very distant perspective. And these perspectives are linked with our experiences.

Let me think of that enlightened thinker once again, to whom I have referred earlier. He may object. This memory that I am alluding to—is it about the historical personas of Gandhi and Ram, or only a book called *Ramayana* on the one hand and a film on the other? I am not disheartened by this objection. On the other hand, I may say that as long as people can raise objections, there is hope because such an objection is based on faith in the book, in literature and art, and in the creative word. This faith is our support.

Perspectives of our memory begin from this point at which we stand. The literature of any country presents perspectives that are established and accepted by the viewers, which communicate their memories in a creative manner. I am myself a writer, and as a writer, I do not ask this of other writers that they come forward and declare where they stand, as I do not accept anyone's right to ask such a thing of me. **But, whatever we write, whosoever we want it to reach, it would inevitably influence him as to where we are standing, and which light we are writing under, and what sort of construct of memory is projected from there.** He also must have memories, for he also has language. He also must have a perspective, which we will influence by the perspectives that we present. The touchstone of our reliability is here—where these perspective clash—reliability for him and also for us.

Translated from Hindi by **Tripti Jain**

Memory and Country

'We live in time'—this is such a self-evident fact that it is not necessary to say it. That is why when it is said, the listener is suspicious that the speaker may have some other motive behind this statement. Is he actually saying what he wants to tell us, or does he want to convey some other meaning to us? If we were to reverse this statement and say, 'Time lives in us'—and this has also been said many times in this way—then the listener is alerted: Is this an assertion of a relationship of time with man or is it an attempt to create a different sort of relationship? Time in which we live and time which lives in us—what is it? We cannot tell. Rather, when the question is asked, then we realise that we do not know the answer. St Augustine said something of great significance: 'As long as this question is not asked, I know the answer, but when someone asks me, then I do not know.' Time, in the form of the present, a continuity and a progression, is a thing for us to experience, but experience cannot be communicated. We can only describe it. We define time and each one of our definitions uses the dimensions of place and space to explain the concept of time. Every definition of time includes a dimension of space, just as our definitions of space also include dimensions of time. But this is the difficulty of the limit of our apparent experiences, which is reflected even in our description or narration of those experiences. In the world of our apparent experiences, the aspects of time and space cannot be separated, our awareness of power and **reality** is inbuilt in a **space-time continuum**; its structure has been woven by the warp and woof of time-space.

But as far as the question of awareness goes—the question only of our perceptions, shorn of all anxiety about communicating our experiences—we have a very natural awareness of time. The time we live in, the time which lives in us, both are parts of that natural perception; we feel this natural flow of both in each part of our body. We perceive the continuity of our existence (even though it is a continuity that changes every moment): 'We were, we are.' We have a natural awareness of a strong and complex feeling of the oneness of the two. It is evident that here, our memory is working. If someone wants to say it in this manner that it is this awareness of continuity which is memory, then raising any question of antecedent and consequent at present is not necessary.

But is there a natural perception of space like the natural awareness of time? Is the continuity and vastness of space a part of our general awareness like the continuity and constancy of time?

When we say that time and space are so deeply integrated that they cannot even be defined separately, or when it is insisted that it is relevant only to talk about the four dimensions of the time-space continuum, then we have implicitly accepted that we have a natural perception and intuitive knowledge of space. By saying 'we are', we do not only assert our temporal existence, but are also making a claim about our physical being and also establishing ourselves in the dimension of space.

But various difficulties arise about this 'I', which underlies our perception of continuity and expansion. 'This body that I am', 'this body which is mine'—is the 'I' which is found in both these statements one and the same? 'I', 'I am', 'mine'—what does this mean? I am not going to answer this question. I am aware that it would be like putting my hand into a hornets' nest. But even then, I think raising this question would be beneficial because it would help us get answers in other areas, and at least it would light up areas of curiosity. Looking at our physical being in the light of these two relations at least gives us the basis of our awareness of the vastness, of the distance between the two. We become aware of the reach of this body, that 'I' am and which is 'mine'; we have a natural experience of this and this is our perception of the space. For instance, 'I am what I can remember, I am to the extent I can remember', this we say in the dimension of time; in the same way, 'I am this area or this country where I am, I am only this area that I occupy'—this is what we can say in the context of space. We dwell in the continuity of time, and continuity of space is our reach. If this reach of ours has some apparent physical features and some which by degrees become subtle, then it also becomes possible for us to arrange the different categories of our powers in a sequence, even though we may not fully comprehend the relationship between the different categories of this sequence. I can extend my hand and lift a pen, or press a switch to put on a light—this is a perception of this capacity. Boys can throw stones at a tree to bring down a fruit, or break the glass panes of someone's house—this is awareness of another type of power. A spacecraft can leave the earth and, after a certain period, reach some other planet, which is not in our direct neighbourhood, and which is itself in orbit—this is the third category of this expansion. It is not enough to say that this difference between these categories is only quantitative; big or small, the difference is there. **There is also a qualitative change**. But what role does our memory play in our perception of each category and in what way? This question can cause some difficulty. We must give some indication of this difficulty and let it be and talk about a different kind of awareness of space. A child feels safe in his mother's lap. If he climbs down from her lap and plays at some distance, even then, that feeling of security is with him. A little further, even where he cannot see his mother, he still has the same sense of security. The mother also does not worry when the child goes out of her sight. But then, a certain distance comes and the child suddenly feels insecure. It may be that he is able to see his mother, even that he feels as if he has gone beyond the boundaries of the circle of security his mother gives him—as though the bond of safety has snapped. The same feelings can assail the mother—after a certain distance, she suddenly becomes tense with worry about the child. What is this awareness of our power? What is this dimension of awareness of space with which the feeling of security-insecurity is linked? I do not know the answer to this question. I know of various scientific and unscientific theories and some that appear to be scientific conjecture. And I believe that the experience that I am talking about has been felt by all of us. Because, as we all know of this experience, therefore, I believe that we will all accept that this instinctive consciousness is somehow linked with the memory of the example of the child and the mother. There is an innate memory of vastness. There is a natural awareness of the expanse, of the dimensions, of space with which we are very closely connected. This awareness is destroyed only when memory is destroyed—that is, when the personality itself has been destroyed.

This dimension of space is connected with our very being

The manner in which we categorise the understanding of time—or we can say it the other way, that the way in which we categorise our personal experience of time and our present—influences our whole history and understanding of our historical situation, in the same way where we put ourselves in the structure of space that determines our geography and, consequently, our situation in the time-space continuum is also determined and defined. For the sake of saying so, we can say that the expansion of space is a scientific reality, even though there may be a mythological version of it and the mythological version is only imaginary and mythical. Apparently, calling this dimension of space mythological or mythical does not destroy its reality or its effectiveness—we are only conceptualising another dimension of reality, which impresses us with its vastness.

The way in which time structures begin at that point at which we are standing—our perception of time begins at that point—in the same manner, the structure of space for us also begins at that very point at which we stand and look around us. That we are standing in the vast expanse of space is a scientific fact and also a mythological fact, but these two are different kinds of expansions, at the centre of which we place ourselves. It can be said this 'we' is also linked with two different kinds of self-awareness.

We can see the expansion of science in many different ways, and scientists do so whenever it is necessary. The cosmic spatial expanse can also be seen in the sun-focused scenario, and on the other hand (keeping in mind the fact that there are other solar systems like ours scattered in the skies), we can conceive of some other centre of the vast cosmic expanse. It can also be that we should talk about some other multicentred space. In the same way, we can talk about the mythical or mythological dimension of space. Here also, there is an all-seeing consciousness at the centre. 'But centre of what?' This question elicits more than one answer, despite the fact that there can be one simple answer, which is always there: 'I am the centre of this expanse of space', and 'The cosmic expanse is this where I am the centre'.

'I am the body which I am.'
'I am in this body, which is my body.'
'I fill one place in this vastness of space; that is me or it is mine.'

Jambu Dweepe Bharat Khande
(Bear-Faced Island, that is, the Land of Bharat)

Reciting this solemn resolve on numerous ceremonial occasions, we establish ourselves at a certain point of time, *'Massanamah massottame amuk masse amuk wasre'* (name of the month, on this particular day of the month, in this particular place), and, along with it, we are establishing ourselves at a particular point in space. The whole universe becomes a witness to our vows because, ceremonially, we stand at a point in the mythical expanse of space. These are different forms of space structure, which expand in different ways and with different dimensions, but at the centre of each structure, it is the same consciousness, which we call 'I'. Keeping in mind the meaning and the power of these concepts, it would not be appropriate to say that these dimensions of space are mythical and, thus, imaginary and, therefore, false. They all are as false or as true as our experience, the memory of our experience, and our self-impression, which is based on the collective memory of our experience.

The specific purpose of connecting experience and memory of experience to space awareness is that there is a mental and psychological dimension to space structure. In other words, we can also conceptualise the inner mental or psychological country. 'I am that (or as much) space which I fill'—The way this sentence also has a meaning at the physical and geographical level, in the same way, it has a mental, psychological and cultural dimension as well. Birds, while making their nests, keep flying within solid boundaries to create a small expanse of space and, perhaps, this small structure is the bird's real nest. (It may or may not be the real nest of the bird, but man, when he conceives of a nest, then he gives more importance to this delicate structure, which becomes the basis of a metaphor, gives rise to a proverb and enriches the language!) Various four-legged animals also, before sitting down to rest, perambulate and create a small area that will be the place of their rest, and only then will they rest therein. The manner in which birds and animals create a country of 'their own' in space and live in it, the human being also does the same. One aspect of this tendency to create a subtle world is that it pervades the whole of mankind, and another aspect of this is that it is affected by various cultures in different ways, and we can call whatever is created a cultural country or space. A reference has already been made to the consequence of looking at the human body as a physical unit or as the dwelling place of a microbe. The process of space construction goes on creating circles even outside the body. The poorest Indian makes all efforts to keep his body clean, even though he puts on dirty clothes after his bath. The Indian housewife cleans her house and throws the garbage in the lane outside. If we forget the effects of modernity, then people coming into a house take off their shoes and then enter the house, so that the house is not polluted. On the other hand, a westerner wears clean clothes, but is indifferent to the cleanliness of his body, which is not always because of poverty. He is very much concerned about the cleanliness of the lane, road and street, and the entire scenario outside his home, but inside his house, he leaves dirty utensils unattended for days. Many such examples can be given, which make it clear that the subtle space structure I am talking about is deeply influenced by culture. There is no need to emphasise that our relationship with the structure of the subtle or inner country inevitably influences our physical scenario, because the structure of this country, of which our consciousness is the centre, has a regular and continuous dialogue and flow between its subtle and solid forms. Wars are fought for cultural or mythological countries—rather, wars are mostly fought for this and it is this which inspires pugnacity: Physical extension of territory is only a pretext. On the other hand, races which are forced to flee their country reconstruct their cultural space in a new country—another Ayodhya or Kashi comes up, a new Kailash mountain or Vrindavan is made—and, in this way, it re-establishes itself even in its displacement, and does not let itself be uprooted from its own earth. This re-establishment of its identity is linked with the awareness of its own power and its basis is also memory.

Power and memory. Memory and imagination. Imagination and reflection. **Remembrance, imagination and poetry.** It is not impossible, without making any explicit or implicit claim to knowledge, to discuss these categories, or any such other categories related to them, only on poetic or fictional premises. But in doing this, a practical question also arises. It would be better to take some examples from poetry—creative literature—and then to proceed on the basis of the premises taken from them, but even if we accept this method as practical, we cannot rely on its utility in the present context and in this society. Because even granting the scholarship of this society and its sensitivity, it cannot be definitely decided from which literature or which different literatures examples should be taken. A multilingual society is bound to have different linguistic influences, its memory storehouses are also bound to be different. Surely, there may be shared materials there, but I can only guess at its existence. Therefore, even though I accept the practical possibility, yet I feel it would be more useful to take the other road—of shared ideas and beliefs, where one can sometimes give such examples which one can believe to be familiar to various linguistic groups.

The *Upanishads* mention a strange tree whose roots are spread upwards and branches grow downwards. Is this tree—*urdhavmoolmagh:shakha*—only an allegory, a metaphor, or is it in any way seriously linked with our experience? If it is related with our experience, then it is also linked to our memory. But one level of memory is this that the tree is there and it has roots and branches—roots spreading down in the sweet earth and branches reaching up towards space—full of light. Going beyond this, imagination is reversing this memory symbol and creating a unique tree. But is this strange tree only a concept, a mere allegory? Or is not this image of an inverse tree actually a part of our deeper experience? **Is it that this symbol of an inverse tree may not be a product of our imagination, but a part of our memory?** To find an answer to our question, however long and free a rein we may give to our imagination, is this image not a memory image of the beginning of human existence? Isn't the position of a human embryo like this tree, *urdhavmoolmagh: shakha*, where the earth nurturing it is above and the sky giving it the chance to expand in its own space, below? The ancient memory of this position is accumulated in this image of an inverse tree; we also consolidate many other images of other situations in which trees are upright and their roots are deep in the nurturing earth below them, and the sky which gives them the freedom to expand, above. And the link between these two opposite images—establishing an image reflection effect between the two—we can see the tree actually as well as carved in stone, and this banyan tree also gets anchored in our memory. It opens up new avenues of symbolism and imagination for the poet. But the significance of memory is not in this alone. Its real importance is that it gives us 'above', 'down' and 'centre', it becomes a basis of our knowledge of *'urdhavadhaita'* (verticality) or *'anulambta'* (proneness), our knowledge of the structure of space. The word for 'man' in the Japanese language itself means 'middle human', meaning that this awareness of *'urdhavadhaita'* (verticality) has been made the basis of defining humanity there. This awareness of straight/upright and being suspended in the middle, and also of right side and wrong is, on one hand, the result of our lived experience and, on the other hand, the result of our creative imagination.

With this fundamental awareness of space structure, other aspects of knowledge of that structure are added on. A square cell which gives an appearance of stability is a symbol for earth, but before it becomes a symbol, it becomes a part of our consciousness as an ancient image of home. It is this ancient image which is extended: Our memory, our imagination and our intelligence all erect structures on it, create images, invent signs in their own style and way. The image of a house or a cottage is not the sign of security or stability; it is also a basis of our understanding of 'up' and 'down', 'vertical' and 'horizontal'. If there is a house, there is an 'interior' and an 'outside'. And if there is a house, there is also a roof and a basement. And beyond the roof, there are palaces, and under the ground, there are lower regions. A question that may be asked is, while talking of them, are we drawing upon our memory or using our imagination? But as I have said earlier, there is no imagination without memory. And then there is the fact that the worlds that we create with our imagination—and imagination is constantly creative—**these worlds of our creation go on to become a part of our memory.** In the same way, our dreams, and also daydreams, go on enhancing the treasure of our memory and create possibilities of new imagination. They make the storehouse of our memory richer and go on increasing its capacity of culling any image from it and enhance its vocabulary. Along with this, the capacity of our dreams and daydreams to assess and measure actuality and reality also goes on increasing.

Above, below and centre, stable and secure. These interwoven and mutually exclusive images of a home are the fundamental images of our world. I have already talked about home and basement, but castles, forts, towns, villages, Durg-Dwarka and the city of Ayodhya also begin here. It is the power of the fundamental memory of the cottage which is the basis of our imagining all these and the basis of their construction. And, because our idea of up and below, inside and outside, is integrally linked with this cottage of our memory, that is why we look at our body also in the form of a fort—eight circles, nine doors, divine Ayodhya city or the House of God—and recognise the cosmos as our residence—that is home, *yatra vishwam bhavtayakindam* (Here, the world becomes a house).

And we also recognise this vibrant and lived in space which is our world and also know that great void, which is the sky of modern science—**empty space**—but which we call the **vacuum**, meaning not empty, but that which fills a vacuum, the way honey fills a honeycomb, which is itself without light, yet whatever goes into it, brightens up and shines.

I have called these square cells ancient home or cottage and then talked about the expansion of fort and town. As long as the house is a cottage, till then the roof and the floor of the house have a different place in our structure of space. And sources of memory are linked to the house-cottage in which one was born and also to the conditions of the womb before birth. Daydreams open the door of that memory and the writer's imagination gets new sights. Forts, towns and buildings with many levels give a new extension to our space structure, and distort it also. **In a town house, there is no sky above the roof, there is only the floor of another house. Mostly, there is no land under the floor, but there is the roof of another house.** Man does live in an upward environment, but he is on top of other people's heads, or is being trampled under their feet. There is another important aspect to this distortion, that is, whereas there was a door and a small verandah to the cottage where an earthen lamp (a *diya*) gave light—a complete image exuding security and also hope—in the urban situation, its place is taken by various distorted and broken images. There is scope for a feeling of loneliness even in the ancient cottage—watching the light of the lamp in the distant verandah, the mind can experience the empty expanse in which it is alone:

The small sacred lamp of my cottage
Has been put
In the vast courtyard
of your temple.

Even in that loneliness, the relationship of the mind with that cottage is reassuring. The room in the town does not leave any place for this feeling of assurance. Looking at the room in the town, consciousness finds itself solitary, and this loneliness is not the loneliness of an empty, open expanse, but the loneliness of a tunnel or a cave.

As we are talking about the village house and the town house, it is appropriate to point out that when the town house takes on the form of a cave, then there is no possibility of a qualitative relationship with space. The distance is there, one has to walk it, but there is no feeling of reassurance or sense of achievement attached to the end of the journey. Loneliness is there, so is desolation, there is a feeling of deprivation, a violent reaction—an aimless, blind desire to kill. On the other hand, the verandah of the cottage is like the eye of the cottage—waiting for someone, without blinking. We can say that in this manner, the cave and also the cottage are as much images of space as of time, but in one, time is dull and lacklustre, and in the other, full of spirit and pulsating.

The structure of country and its distortions and disruptions that I am talking about—examples of all these can be found in plenty in contemporary literature, the way in which examples of early images and symbols are found in Sanskrit and folk literature. Awareness of village, knowledge of town and consciousness of the metropolis will also join them in the contemporary discussions.

It can also be indicated that the concepts of vertical and horizontal structure that I have referred to earlier are not limited to space alone, but also present before us a structure of time. 'Above', 'middle' and 'below' (or like the strange tree of the *Upanishads*, the sequence can be below, centre and up—*bhu:bhuv:swah*). Shifting this from the space structure to the time structure, here they become 'future', 'present' and 'past', 'ahead', 'here' and 'behind'. Actually, it is not a parallel structure, but it is about that contiguity of space-time, which can be explained in the two different statements to which I have alluded earlier. Ultimately, space and time are an integral part of an indivisible structure.

I should be apprehensive that in the discussion so far, I have dabbled in different fields of study, subjects in which I have had no formal initiation. I have no knowledge of any. 'Where even the sun cannot reach, the poet reaches there' and 'Fools rush in where angels fear to tread' are not very much dissimilar! But the poet lays claim to being open to formal and informal knowledge, or doesn't make any such claim, but believes that he may sometimes receive the benediction of that divine light because of this open-mindedness as that alone leads to creative action, and he also accepts that he may commit such unauthorised acts from time to time!

I have said that I should be apprehensive, but apprehensive I am not. Because it is not the task of the poet to link the scenario which opens up in the moment of enlightenment to some scientifically approved system. This is the job of learned people, people who are experts. I have called the light being given to the poet divine because it is the light of memory, and that memory is beyond logic. The perspectives of memory are not the scenarios of history, but rather, the perspectives of freedom from history. This divine light surrounds the facts with values; if we deny these values or sweep them aside, then those facts become meaningless. For the poet, this liberating value is the central element and the whole world revolves around it. For the poet, the outer structure of space-time is an attempt to safeguard this awareness of the core of space-time. Surely, there is an integral relation of identity and mutual difference between these two structures; the outer structure is not Kabir's *'jhini chunariya'* (gossamer-fine veil), which can be taken off and put aside, the way it is; and the inner structure also is not a mere product of the outer one. The poet is not defeated by the internal inconsistencies that exist, even though he may not issue a challenge like Walt Whitman: 'There are contradictions within me, so what? I am vast and encompass many groups within me.'

It is the consciousness of vastness which is a significant perspective of the creative memory. The narratives of poets about their awareness of vastness are not preserved the way the narratives of ancient great men or religious leaders are preserved. One reason for this may be that when the poet glimpses any such scene, he does not accept that he has seen the final form of the whole truth, or that he has been able to capture it in words; then, the effect that it has had on him also does not always stay with him. The divine light touches this crazy man now and then, but then it moves away. Mahaprabhu Chaitanya saw a vision in the waves of the sea, which had assumed the form of his beloved, and he wanted to immerse himself in it. Bhagwan Buddha had another vision of this vastness, which gave him enlightenment; this vision was also like the ultimate truth, although the Tathagatta had ordered that whosoever sees that truth must do so in his own light, not on the basis of their faith in him: *App deepo bhav*. This poet also has this light of the soul—*atma deep*—and rather, it is the light of his lamp—*diya*—which lights up numerous other lights. But the poet's vision is not final. Perhaps, it also may not be unjust to say that the poet has no vision, that he does not see any vision, but only feels that presence of the spirit and that also now and then, in rare moments. It is the glow of this awareness which illuminates his words and makes his language unique and symbolic. Language is a social time; only that can be a medium of communication in society which is not only predictable, but each word should have a definite connotation. By implication, language binds one and many with each other, the way it binds the usage of words to time. Creative language rises above time, is inferential and symbolic, and it does not only create new methods of communication, but also a new world that is communicable. In this way, creative language liberates from bonds and shows new dimensions of freedom.

It would be rather useful to allude to one thing here. All those who read creative literature know about the unpredictable power of language that I am talking about, that it lives in the word. I have linked language to a larger social time because the very first basis of conversation is that, but creative language rises above this time and takes us beyond it; it is in this that its creative power and unpredictability lie, it is this which liberates us from time. It is clear that this power will not be in ordinary words—ordinary meaning is tied to the social time. But this power is also not only limited to the roars and echoes of the creative word. The creative word has an echo, then its resonance spreads into various directions. That word of poetry which gives this process depth and vastness, it is on the basis of that word that we attach so much significance to poetry, and its influence is also lasting. It is also necessary to know that this is not the final limit of the liberating process. There are some amongst the critics who accept that this is the resonance that has been talked about by ancient experts in ancient poetics. Actually, resonance is something beyond this—it is another dimension of influence and expansion. We keep on linking echo and re-echo with only one source and point of origin. Resonance is the widest effect which becomes multicentrist; it goes on receiving energy from other sources of power. The best of poetry has another echo, which becomes evident with the passage of time. It impacts other fields of study and becomes active in other areas of knowledge. Such unpredictable influences are also resonance, and not only an echo.

It is this far-reaching effect of poetry which must be accepted as a form of memory, but because it is difficult to understand, it is accepted as a fragment of memory from an earlier birth. But it is a creative dimension of memory.

What is the basis of this creativity, where is the source? The simple and easy answer to this is: 'in the imagination'. But this imagination, this power of creation, what is its basis? Definitely, there can be other answers to this, and some of them would seem easy and also simple. One kind of straight answer would satisfy those who believe in God, and the other kind of simple answer would satisfy those who deny God, and want to insist on fundamental physical power. For the poet, none of these two conditions is essential because it is not necessary for him to deny any of these. If anything is essential here, it is to know whether beginning with any of these, is it possible to create, can one become aware of the enlightened spirit, can the inferable symbolic power of language be attained, and can one seek liberation, then what is it that can bridge these two? What perspective can it be which can, while keeping the paths of both open, keep the possibility of our getting a glimpse of the enlightened spirit open, illuminate our minds with that divine light to which I have alluded earlier? That scenario can only be the perspective of memory. It is not necessary that we accept that memory as the happy memories of earlier births, which make us 'nostalgic', as Kalidasa said, and it is also not necessary that we accept this as racial memory, which is safely inured in our subconscious mind, as conceived by Carl Jung. It is also not necessary that this should be awakened only when we see beautiful and sweet things, or that we must roam villages, forests and dales, moving from rivers to springs to trees, to be able to feel it. The only condition to find it is to keep one's mind open to one's own self: This connection with the self is in itself the forests, the rustic, the urban, the ancient as also the contemporary; it is this which stores memories and also arranges and edits them; it is this which makes them available when called upon to do so, and which makes their energy worthwhile for the creator.

The memory of prehistorical reflections remains unbroken in both concepts. It is these prehistoric symbols that arouse a feeling of curiosity in us and also inspire us towards liberation. These prehistoric symbols are symbols of memory alone. The perspective of memory is the perspective of our restlessness and also of our anxiety, and also of our creative imagination and our possible liberation. Modern technology and communication systems all seek to emphasise that an increasing load of information should constantly surround us and be stored in our storehouses and, consequently, we should be relieved of the habit of remembering and the necessity of remembering anything. And the poet's imagination, his creative memory, vows that it will not let us forget. Sometimes, people ask that—in the twenty-first century—the century of computers—**what would be the need of poetry? The perspective of our memory gives strength to our answer that, if at that time, we need anything for ourselves, then it would be the need of poetry—the act of writing poetry.** Then, and if, we would have rendered ourselves superfluous, it would be a different matter. And this is for others to do, not for the poet, not for the sensitive.

Translated from Hindi by **Tripti Jain**

Gopalkrishna Adiga

Born in an orthodox Brahmin family, Gopalkrishna Adiga (1918–92) inherited the family tradition of scholarship. His full name was Mogeri Gopalkrishna Adiga. For his education, he had to travel daily to a school located at a distance of fourteen miles from home and, had it not been for a generous aunt, his college education might never have taken place. Graduating from Mysore University, he first worked as a lecturer in English in the college he had studied and later became the principal. He also edited the journal, **Sakshi**, *and was deputy director of the National Book Trust.*

But bare facts hardly tell us anything about the writer, who preferred to stay away from the public eye. Adiga belongs to the generation of writers who introduced the Navya movement. He was mainly a Kannada fiction writer and his novels had a wide readership. His writings have a deep existential content and are about the angst and disillusionment of our times.

In the present essay, he debates the meaning of the word, 'renaissance', and points out that the movement of the nineteenth century known as the Renaissance was incomplete and engaged only the upper and middle classes. Beginning with a review of the country's intellectual history, Adiga dwells on its religious and spiritual heritage and the belief of the people in the stability of those systems. In this, India was no different from other cultures. But the difference emerged in its slowness to come to terms with the new scientific discoveries and its inability to either react or absorb them. The encounter with the west led to a forked sensibility—part imitative and part defensive. It punctured the complacency of the intellectuals who, even as they responded to and appreciated the new ideas, felt compelled to reassert their own heritage and were driven towards traditional fixities.

In Adiga's view, the Bengal Renaissance and the accompanying political awakening did not go either deep enough or far enough. Neither of the two was able to address the challenge to creativity, and the much awaited resurgence never really came into being. Instead, art, which was essentially a part of life, distanced itself as each art form distanced itself from others, retreating into its own cocoon. For creativity to be meaningful, a certain connectivity of art forms is essential both with each other and with society. There has to be a total resurgence. The true renaissance, in Adiga's view, still awaits a birth.

The essay reflects Adiga's uncompromising stance and intellectual honesty.

The Renaissance Yet to Come*

In a country like India, where the life of the mind got stratified about a millennium ago and the mode of living changed from the creative to the conservative, renaissance could mean only a rebirth, not a revival. The ideas and attitudes and norms of living which came into being during the earlier creative epochs and which were refined and perfected through centuries seemed immutable and ultimate. For many centuries during the middle ages, before the arrival of the age of science, the old religious and philosophical knowledge accumulated and fused during centuries seemed to say the last word about the world of man, nature and the gods. Our country, of course, was not at all peculiar in its total reliance on the old mythology and its credos. This was a universal phenomenon then, but was specially fortified and hardened in India, where people seem to be, to an extra degree, slow to learn new things and slower still to unlearn. In fact, by the time our country first came in contact with the domination of the West, it had for long ceased to be creative. A wholly conservative life devoid of any decent vent for revolt or dissent gets reduced to a mere animal or vegetable existence. For such a country, bowed down by its ancestral wealth, renaissance could only mean a rebirth, a re-growth and a new fruition. When symbol replaces reality and the other world subjugates this world, there could only be death. In such a situation, what is required is a total intellectual rejection of the past, a new design for the future, a new beginning and a rediscovery through experience of the wealth of human culture lost in the debris of tradition and repetition. A rebirth means a new lease of living, a new face of

* From *Indian Renaissance*. Ed. K. Ayyappa Paniker. New Delhi: Sterling, 1983.

adventure and a new spurt of creativity in all fields of human endeavour. Such a rebirth has not yet taken place here, though there have been persistent attempts on the part of a few great individuals to bring it about. The past is too much with us and the present has not yet mustered strength enough to dominate it.

Our attitude to the impact of the West was naturally ambiguous. It called for a search for identity on the one hand, and an assimilation of modernity as presented by a new and dynamic society on the other. The impact was at first a great shock that reverberated through the length and breadth of our country. It picked the swollen ego of the typical Indian and punctured his complacency and even his self-confidence. The thinking Indian was forced to notice the stagnant life around him and reconsider traditional values and ideas. But it was also dangerous for any nation to lose self-confidence, for, with its loss begins thoughtless imitation and an enslavement of the spirit. Therefore, it was felt to be the first duty of a responsible Indian to reassert the validity of our ancient philosophy and religion in a newer, rationally acceptable manner. At the same time, he had to imbibe the spirit of the scientific West so that a new upsurge of creativity might be occasioned in this country. Thus, our early efforts at a rebirth of the national spirit were at once a promoter and a subverter of a real renaissance.

Hence, the impact of the West was a challenge at once to our identity and also to our creativity. The thinking minds in India began to probe the roots of our culture and prepare themselves to meet the challenge. The great men that Bengal produced in the latter half of the nineteenth century had the depth and sweep of the renaissance heroes and, gradually, such cultural heroes arose all over the country. Their work and worth cannot be underrated. Yet the effect of the work of such great men as Vivekananda, Tilak and Gandhi has been proved ultimately rather superficial, touching only the English-educated classes and leaving the masses where they were. While the modernist aspect of their teachings was not heeded, the revivalist one caught the imagination of the people. This led to a blind self-assurance and an ugly national egotism. Real creativity, social and intellectual, became rather sporadic, not a systematic resurgence. The emphasis on the 'greatness' of India, its 'spiritual leadership' of the whole world, did reinforce the nationalist fervour of our youth, but failed to pinpoint the ingrained defects of our culture and the need for a total reconsideration of our national ideals and restructuring of our society on new egalitarian lines as demanded by the times. This failure has led to the present social chaos, uncertainty of the spirit and the lack of dedicated pursuit of a new national goal. We are still impelled by out-of-date hierarchical principles, even though we have learnt to render constant lip service to the democratic ideals of equality and freedom. Thus, we find that what started as a prelude to rebirth has resulted in a vain effort at rejuvenation of what is on its deathbed.

A renaissance in the particular context of India could not be just a revival of ancient learning or spurt of creativity in a few chosen fields by a few eminent men. It ought to have been and ought to be now a total one. It has to reject the festering overgrowth of custom and dive deep for essences and go in for new bodies for those eternal principles enunciated by our ancestors. The new spirit of reconstruction would then have expressed itself in all fields of activity, not only in literature. It could not have confined itself to the upper layers of society, but would have sunk into the vast masses throwing up newer heroes of culture from all levels. What has actually happened during the last few decades is, on the contrary, an isolation of art from life and of each branch of art from others. On account of this, every branch of art suffers, especially the visual arts and music. While some individuals, conscious of the times and the interdependence of life and art, were able to produce remarkable works, the general trend has been to oversimplify and shirk the responsibility of meeting the challenge. The poets and painters, for example, who feel kinship with each other, are rather few. Each form of creativity has suffered impoverishment because of its ignorance or neglect of others.

A true renaissance is, for one thing, a nationwide quest for the highest truths of life—artistic, religious and spiritual. It would not take anything for granted. Everything has to be tested against the touchstone of life experience and shaped on the anvil of a burning zeal to create afresh on unprecedented lines. Secondly, it would put the utmost stress on the sacredness of an individual human spirit, encouraging it in its untiring effort at new creation. What we find now is that even the highly educated are content with the second best, willing to live at the lowest ebb and make do with secondhand themes and ideas borrowed either from our own past or from the West. We have also failed to note the gravest defects of our tradition as it has come down the ages. The first of these is a strange dissociation of sensibility, wherein the educated man converts himself into a cramming machine and is lost in abstractions, having no contact with concrete things. The vast multitudes of the uneducated are lost in the mine of the concrete, unrelieved by sunshine or a downpour. Our educated men still continue to be the abhorred wordmongers, finding fulfilment in verbalisation, while the uneducated remain inarticulate, content to live on a subhuman level. The second grave defect is an inordinate respect for authority, divine or mundane. We find today a citizen in this democracy cringe and crawl even before a minor functionary of the government.

I should like to make it clear here that I am no denier of the past. Nor am I prepared to jettison the great universal truths enshrined in our tradition up to the age of Kalidasa. What I want to affirm is that in the present state of our country, what is needed is a rediscovery of the past truth through personal experience. This is possible only through an absolute commitment to one's own experience in the context of our tradition and the modern conditions of living. Only those aspects of our tradition could be accepted when tested through experience and the rest thrown overboard. At the same time, the gamut of personal experience has to be widened. Every phenomenon has to be looked upon as something new and wonderful. It ought, in fact, to have been a renaissance of wonder first, a return to nature, and an all-consuming curiosity to know.

Among our writers in Karnataka, there is a lonely figure of this eminence, who can stand comparison with the great renaissance men of Europe such as Leonardo Da Vinci and Michelangelo. It is our great fiction writer, Shivarama Karanth, who has been recently and so rightly honoured with the conferment of the Jnanpith Award. His interest in life and living is an example to follow for those who desire and work for a rebirth for our ancient nation. He is an embodiment of the sense of curiosity that lies behind both artistic and scientific endeavour. His interest in science is something not to be found in any other of our celebrated writers. His pursuit of knowledge has been total and persistent. Even now, in his seventies, this great man has the mind of a youthful adventurer combined with the poise and the gravity that go with age. His achievements are bewilderingly manifold and various, stretching from writing a great novel to preparing a dictionary in Kannada when there was none. He is as much interested in art as in science. He himself has painted, sung and danced. He has written and talked continuously on burning social and political problems. Starting as a heretic, he has, through his own experience, arrived at some of the eternal truths enshrined in our religion. A selfless seeker after knowledge, he has upheld the highest standards of life and stood by them through thick and thin. He has always thought in terms of the whole nation and upheld truth and justice. Living all the time an honest life of hard work, he has proved that he is the most religious man we have had in recent times. There should be and should have been such men of genius all over the country. Your revered poet, Vallathol, himself was perhaps such a man. Unfortunately, however, their number is still very small. They have shown the path that will lead to the renaissance here. But our verbalising experts, who are unfortunately our intellectuals, are still abroad. They are all very happy with words. In actual living, they are one with the poor masses who live on a subhuman level.

Unless the bold experimentation and the lively curiosity of Karanth become the very life breath of our society, no new birth is possible here. It requires a radically new system of education, wherein the accent will be not on learning things by rote, but on actual personal experience through doing and reflecting. Unless the whole nation becomes again a child with wonder and curiosity, always eager to know and grow and unless the old men give up their vain effort at *kayakalpa* or rejuvenation, we shall continue to be as we are today, a set of lost souls moving inexorably towards a limbo.

Mohan Rakesh

Mohan Rakesh (1925–72) gained all-India fame when the new dramatic mode he used caught public attention. Badal Sircar, Vijay Tendulkar, Girish Karnad and Mohan Rakesh were clubbed together as representatives of the new dramatic wave. But there is much more to Rakesh than only drama. He wrote novels, short stories, criticism, travelogues and memoirs.

Born in Amritsar, Rakesh's education took place mainly at Punjab University, Lahore. Of his novels, ***Andhere Bund Kamre*** *and* ***Na Aane Wala Kal*** *heralded a new movement. He was considered a pioneer of the Nai Kahani wave and Mani Kaul made a film based on one of his short stories in 1971. His plays, mainly* ***Aashad Ka Ek Din, Lehron Ke Rajhans*** *and* ***Aadhe Adhure****, brought him the Sangeet Natak Akademi Award.* ***Aadhe Adhure*** *is about incomplete human beings who fail in their relationships. It is a modernist play with a bold theme and has often been staged experimentally and continues to have a tremendous appeal due to its connectivity with modern life.*

In the essay which has been translated for this volume, one of the issues discussed is the connection between reality and fiction. What indeed is reality? Though a much used word, it is still very difficult to pin it down to any one meaning such as what we see or what we experience, and whether it is always visible or not. If we contrast it with the ideal or the imaginative, where does it lead us?

Rakesh, after entering into an initial discussion of these issues, takes up two other concepts—consistency and authenticity. They assume significance when it comes to representing reality. Fiction is an imagined narrative, hence consistency and authenticity are both essential. If the character and the situation are portrayed with conviction and reflect a possible consistency, it is reality. The writer needs both sensitivity and perception to portray believable situations and to be able to establish a connection with the reader. But if the narration is interspersed with long speeches or religious discourses, which fail to connect and stand outside the construct, the presentation of reality does not hold.

Rakesh asks whether an element of psychological truth is also required for the depiction of the real and for consistency in the character and situation. Further, a consciousness of the 'real' or the 'possible' does not in any way restrict presentation of the ideal, the imagined or the sentimental. The function of the narrative structure is to place them in balance.

The Novel and Depiction of Reality*

The first question we are confronted with is what is reality? Is it what surrounds us and which has a solid physical existence and is visible to us? Can that experience alone be considered an experience of reality in which the awareness of this material existence is constantly present in our minds in some form or the other? We use two words—ideal and imagination—as opposed to reality. The ideal means a situation, state or condition which is beyond our reach, but which we are impelled to achieve. Desire is an intrinsic element of the ideal, and as we always have a mental picture of what this unattainable is like, ideal is, therefore, a half-way house between reality and imagination. The hypothesis may be inspired by the ideal, or it may be devoid of any idealism. The consciousness of having to go beyond reality to achieve the unattainable is always present in the ideal. It is not essential that the consciousness to progress should be inherent in a precept. Imagination is that state of consciousness which has the ability to transform an inconsistency into a consistency. A consistent precept which begins with the possible may be the ideal or even its opposite. But any consistency which is based on the impossible, ends up as a figment of the imagination. It is true that man has imagination. It is also true that he has a fine sensibility. When a writer creates a character that is both perceptive and sentimental and draws the character with conviction, he is portraying reality. The problem begins when the writer abandons the authenticity of life and seeks to depict a situation that is either unrealistic or unattainable. To the extent he deviates from the genuine conditions of life, to that extent his writing is

---

* From *Parwesh*, Bhartiya Jnanpith Publication, Calcutta, 1967.

removed from reality. We can find numerous examples of sentimentalism nurtured by the circumstances of life. And we may safely conclude that human emotions and sensitivity form a part of the range of realistic writings—as long as the characters are drawn with perception and understanding. The appeal of a half-whispered word, uttered in a befitting harmonious atmosphere, may be greater than the effect of saying sweet nothings fifty times over in an incongruous atmosphere. The impact of pain is heightened if it is depicted in a realistic manner. A rational acceptance of the fact that anguish is real does not make anyone sensitive. Pain touches our heart, but the philosophy of pain doesn't move us. The tragic conditions of Jean Valjean in *Les Miserables* move us profoundly, but the philosophic acceptance of pain by Bhuvan and Rekha in *Nadi Ke Dweep* does not touch our hearts.

In this context, we must also look at the tendency to fill novels with long ideological interpretations and explanations. In some novels, the whole narrative structure seems to have been devised as an appropriate frame for readymade speeches and explanations. Supporting realism or idealism through such speeches does not make writing realistic or idealistic. If a new concept is presented systematically, then, at the most, it can be called a book on a doctrine written in the form of a novel. It becomes a novel only when its characters behave like real people and their conduct and behaviour are shaped by the circumstances of their lives. Only then does it become a powerful book. Then, even if there are long speeches in the book, they will not appear contrived and imposed on the narrative. We can quote the example of the assertions of Kironmayi in Sarat Chandra's *Charitraheen*. Kironmayi's angst is the consequence of the circumstances of her life, and that is why each one of her utterances has the power to hurt. This impact, however, is missing in the expressions of the cynical characters of contemporary literature, who assume a pose of anger as they find themselves in the position of heroes. In the same manner, the long-winded speeches of Dostoevsky's characters on religion and morality and other related issues do not detract from the quality of his novels, for these long speeches constitute integral links in the narrative flow. They are rooted in life. But the speeches that we have in *Muktidoot* do not spring from life. The flavour of such a novel is surely not realistic.

There is another question in connection with the portrayal of reality, and that is: How far is it desirable to bring in the local colour for creating an authentic environment? The argument advanced by some that any introduction of local colour reduces the appeal of the novel and limits it to only a specific section of society does not seem to be relevant. It is true that human nature is the same everywhere, and that there are certain elements in our natural surroundings that are similar, and their depiction should be in general terms. Yet, it is also true that because of geographical, historical and various other reasons, a country, or a part thereof, acquires certain peculiar features that set it apart from other areas or countries. For Josh Malihabadi, the earth is '*zarrate*-khaki' or khaki coloured motes of dust, but for the writer from Travancore, the earth is not khaki, but reddish brown. We see many different shades of colours on the beaches of Kanyakumari, which the combined waters of the Arabian Sea, the Indian Ocean and the Bay of Bengal have spilled on to those sands. Cultural history is strewn with innumerable examples of such intermingling of races. Truth demands that our writings should reflect these colours and that these diversities be portrayed accurately, whether they are the colour of the soil or the social behaviour of human society.

Indians are generally believed to be sentimental. Emotionalism is a volatile state of mind and it is natural for the people of a tropical country to be sentimental. But it has also given us our tolerant, sympathetic and affectionate attitude. Also, it is the reason for our nervous debility. Our sentimentalism has assumed different forms in different parts of the country. At one place, it appears as strong conservatism, and at another, it has taken the form of blind faith in modernity! It is our mawkishness that turns politics into religion, and religion into politics. The economic conditions of our country are also responsible for many distinctive attributes of our behaviour. We come across characters endowed with these qualities in the writings of Sarat Chandra and Premchand, but rarely do we meet them in the period that followed. Sarat's Vipradas and Premchand's Surdas can be products only of this soil, and are. But Agyeya's Shekhar can belong to any society. It is difficult to establish any relation of sensitivity with such an independent character—at the most, such characters may be the subject of adoration as icons. Romain Rolland's *Jean Christophe,* on which the author has based the character of Shekhar, is rooted in his own milieu. German blood runs in his veins, and though he lives in France, yet he cannot hide his diversity. Christophe's character has that balance which keeps his feet firmly on the ground. The measure of success of any writer does not lie in creating characters which represent either their own egotism or some ideological opinions, but in portraying characters which are close to real life—their physical features, gestures and even the smell of their sweat should be familiar—and about whom we should be able to say that their behaviour was very natural under the given circumstances, or that in those conditions, such a person cannot behave in this manner. Such characters are very close to us and it is natural for us to establish a rapport with them.

Some of the novels written in Hindi during the last thirty-five years are historical, and they are a class apart. Premchand, Jainendra, Yashpal, Bhagwati Charan Verma, Ila Chandra Joshi and Upendra Nath 'Ashk', et cetera, are novelists who have portrayed life and the conditions around them, and though they were guided by the prevailing circumstances, yet they strove to give a new direction to them. Premchand's novels are a vivid portrayal of his times; we are able to instantly establish a rapport with his characters. His characters, however, are weak where they have acted as propagators of his idealistic realism. They are weak to the extent that they are not the products of realism, but of idealism. It is realistic to be inspired by idealism. A balanced depiction of an idealistic character keeps it from becoming unrealistic. It becomes unrealistic when the portrayal, not the character, becomes idealistic. A sentimental portrayal of a character is not the same as a sentimental character.

By the time we come to *Godaan,* Premchand's views were no longer sentimental. By that time, he could see reality in a more authentic and genuine manner. That is why the appeal of that novel is greater than that of his other writings.

Jainendra has written about politics only at the intellectual level. His characters are not profoundly affected by political events, but they think a great deal about them. The ideals inspiring his characters are also not the ideals generated by the conditions and times in which they live. The life and events that are depicted in *Sunita, Sukhda* and *Vyatit* appear to have been created and lived on the table of an intellectual and seem to have no connection with life surrounding and influencing us. The conditions that induce the acute emotionalism of a woman like Sunita seem to be more appropriate to a fantasy. Despite his political awareness, Jainendra's writings lack the essence of his times, which began with the massacre of Jallianwala Bagh and come right up to the present age of 'me, myself'.

Our life today is overshadowed by national and international events. We are living in troubled times. There are some selfish interests, envy and animosity, petty ambitions, over-bloated venomous egos, and an underlying feeling of resentment, a wish to rebel and a strong desire to demolish all this. Also, political anarchy has come to dominate life in such a manner that it seems to be losing all sense and meaning. Barring a few big centres, everywhere else, our cultural life seems to be on the decline. Old traditions are being abandoned and new customs are yet to be evolved. This is the confused world that we have inherited, and this heritage constitutes the backdrop to a fast-changing history to which we are witness. Whatever we are watching and experiencing, the manner in which we are living, and the way we want to live, why are all these not being portrayed in the contemporary novel?

Translated from Hindi by **Tripti Jain**

Rahi Masoom Raza

Rahi Masoom Raza (1927–92), poet, lyricist, scriptwriter and novelist, was born in Ghazipur. Closely associated with films and TV serials, he is well known as the script-writer for the TV serial, ***Mahabharata****. Earlier, he won the Filmfare Award for the dialogue of the box-office hit,* ***Main Tulsi Tere Aangan Ki****. But his work as a sensitive novelist, responsive alike to political events and social concerns, is lesser known but equally significant. The novels work with ideas different from the frames of readymade plot lines or characters as dialogue or scriptwriting requires. His work is in Hindi.*

Amongst his notable contributions are ***Aadha Gaon*** *(Half a Village),* ***Topi Shukla, Neem Ka Ped*** *and* ***Katra Bi Arzoo****. While* ***Aadha Gaon*** *is about the 1940s and the partition of India,* ***Katra Bi Arzoo*** *is an anti-Emergency novel. Raza has also written an autobiography,* ***Chhote Aadmi Ki Badi Kahani****.*

The two extracts that are included in this collection are from ***Aadha Gaon****. They are presented here in the order in which they appear in the novel. The first is the opening chapter, the setting. The second is the "Preface" ("Bhumika"), which appears after two-thirds of the novel is over. Both connect with each other and the discourses they present are extremely significant for the contemporary world, which is an age of dislocations, migrations, violence and uprooting and preoccupied with the extreme sense of non-belonging of an individual. These sections discuss the idea of space, significance of location and their role in the individual's psychological make-up.*

"The Slumbering Town" demands a very close reading in order to respond to the images it evokes as land and river play with each other, as forests are visible in the distance from the manmade fort and as stories of

the past are replayed. Amidst this, the call from urban centres is viewed as a separation, imposing an exile. Time and history are contrasted, are seen as different. The "Preface" turns to dislocation with greater emphasis. Belonging is not a sense of prosperity, or of religion, or acceptance by the community, but one rooted in memories. The first extract is a first-person narration, with the narrator adopting the role of sutradhar, but the second is autobiographical and inward looking.

The Slumbering Town

In the old fort of Ghazipur is a school where the sound of the waves of the Ganga can be heard, but the sounds of the hum of history and its cold sighs are not heard. No sentry guards the walls of the fort and no student walks up to them to look at the waves of the river Ganga rippling under the brilliant rays of the setting sun, or to talk to these waves, or even to listen to what they are saying.

This grandly flowing current of muddy water knows innumerable stories. But mothers are engrossed in relating the tales of ogres, fairies and spirits, and this restless town on the banks of the Ganga does not ever think of going up to it and listening to the recital of the stories of its ancestors.

If someone were to sit on the old walls of the fort and close his eyes, it is not improbable that the villages, plains and fields across the river might vanish to turn into thick and deep forests; one may also see the *tapovans*—the settlements of the rishis. One may also espy the two princes of Ayodhya, with bows and arrows slung across their shoulders, protecting the sacred precincts.

But no one ever sits on these walls now. For when the age to sit on these walls arrives, young shoulders are saddled with the burden of earning their bread and have to watch their life seeping away under this burden, and their dreams crumbling.

Laga jhullani ka dhakka
Balam Kolkata chale gaye.

(With one shove of fate/My beloved has gone to Kolkata)

The dreams of this town are woven into the warp and woof of the hemp flax churned out by the machines of Kolkata and shipped abroad. Only vacant eyes remain, as remain lonely hearts, yearning for the mud paths, ponds, fields of rice, barley and peas, as they lie in broken-down rooms.

Kolkata!

It is not the name of a city. For the sons and daughters of Ghazipur, it is also the name of separation. This word symbolises the entire story of pain and anguish which, God alone knows, has made so many lives forlorn and miserable. Each year, thousands of messages are confided to the fleeting clouds by those who are far away from home. Perhaps, for this reason, the monsoon pours in Ghazipur. The agony of separation makes everything cry—the old and new walls, the roofs of the mosques and temples, and even the apertures of the doors of the school weep for the loved ones—and the pangs of love are expressed thus:

Barsaat main koyo ghar se na nikse
Tumhi anuk bides javaio.

(No one leaves home during the monsoon/You alone are unique that you have to leave home.)

Kolkata, Bambai, Kanpur and Dhaka are the boundaries of this town. Far flung limits... those who leave the town still live here. A balloon may fly a long distance in the sky, yet its links with its centre do not break, as the hands of a child still hold the other end of the slender thread to which it is tied.

This story, if you ask me, is about such balloons or, perhaps, about those children who are still clinging to one end of a thread even after the thread has snapped, and looking for their balloons, not knowing what has happened to them.

The Ganga caresses the head and cheeks of this town, the way a mother loves her sick child, but when it gets no response to this love, then it weeps, bitterly, and the town drowns in its tears. People say there is a flood. The Muslims offer prayers and the Hindus make offerings, so that the angry Ganga may be appeased. This insult to her love annoys the Ganga all the more, and it bangs its head against the walls of the fort, and its shining white hair gets tangled and is spread far and wide. We call this foam. When the Ganga realises that no one feels its anguish, then it wipes its eyes, and we say that the water has receded. The Mussalmans assert that their prayers are answered and the Hindus declare that their offerings have been accepted by the Ganga. But no one says that the tears of the mother have made the land more fertile... the soft soil is spread far and wide, like a cover. But what else can the Ganga do? She knows that the bullocks and other animals do not have the strength to bear the burden of the plough.

This town is unaware of history, it does not even have the time to sit under the shade of a banyan tree and ponder over its history, which goes beyond the *Ramayana*. And the future... it does not have the courage to think of that. There is a fine crack in the pitcher of time and time is seeping away, moment by moment. This town lives by the moment, dies by the moment, and comes alive again by the moment.

Who knows when its austere penance will come to an end? Ghazipur is not on the road traversed by the caravans of life. Sometimes, when the wind blows this way, some dust raised by the caravans is blown along with it, and this settlement accepts this dust as perfume and spills it all over its body and clothes.

This is my town. Whenever I pass through the lanes of this town, it puts its hand on my shoulder. It meets me at different points on the road to my short and long stories. But I have never been able to grasp its reality fully, and that is why I want to meet it again.

This novel is, in reality, a journey for me. I am looking for Ghazipur, but before that, I will halt at my Gangauli. If I am able to understand the reality of Gangauli, then I will have the courage to write the epic of Ghazipur. This novel is actually a preface to that epic.

But listen to this. The story is neither about some people, nor about some families. It is also not the story of the village, where the good and bad characters of this story are trying to make themselves better. This is neither a religious story, nor a political one, for time is neither religious nor political... and this is a story of time. This is the tale of that time of Gangauli that has been. Many old people have died and young ones grown old, many children are now grown up, and infants have been born. This is the story of dreams, of passions caught up in the vicissitude of time. This story is of those ruins where houses stood at one time, and of those houses that have been built on ruins.

And this story is as true as it is false.

I know the art of mixing falsehood with truth and truth with falsehood. I am using the term, 'I', time and again in this story so that it may not go away from me, and so that I should be able to touch it whenever I want to. I am trying to console myself that the story I am relating is to give you and my own self the confidence that I am like this story. That is why it is as much my story as that of others.

Time is an open book without a cover, lying in a field. Its leaves flutter even in the weakest gust of wind, and the pile of pages keeps shifting, so the reader is at one time ten pages ahead, and at another he goes back ten pages. That is why I am using the first person without hesitation, so the pages may not change their position by themselves, and the sequence remain undisturbed, and I may be able to see what was, and what is, and what is yet to pass.

It is said that on a dark rainy night, Syed Masood Ghazi, one of the chiefs of Tughlaq, crossed the flooded Ganga and annexed Ghadipuri. Thereafter, the town became Ghazipur, instead of Ghadipuri. The roads were the same, and so were the lanes, the houses the same, but the names had changed—a name is perhaps an outer covering that can be easily changed. A name has no integral link with personality, for had this been so, then Ghadipuri should have changed after it became Ghazipur, or at least the ones who had been defeated—the Thakurs, Brahmins, Kayasths, Ahirs, Bhars and Chamars—should have continued calling themselves Ghadipuris, and the victorious Syeds, Sheikhs and Pathans would have called themselves Ghazipuris. But this did not happen. All are Ghazipuris, and had the name of the town not changed, then all would have been Ghadipuris. These new names are very interesting. The Arabic *fateh* mixes with the Hindi *garh* and becomes one unit, Fatehgarh. That is why even after Pakistan has been created, I fail to understand the reality of

Pakistan. If 'Ali' is separated from *garh*, 'Ghazi' from *pur*, and 'Dildar' from *nagar*, then these areas will become nameless and deserted, and if 'Imam' is separated from *baras*, then where will we have the congregations for Moharrum?

The Ganga has taken this Ghazipur to its heart in the same way it had embraced Ghadipuri. Thus, the name may be Ghadipuri or Ghazipur, it makes no difference, for Masood Ghazi's descendents must have taken over the villages near and far. And in this way, this family from Delhi would surely have been split into many zamindari families, and even then I would have written this story.

One of Masood Ghazi's sons, Nuruddin Shahid (how did he become a martyr and why, I do not know, and perhaps no one does), crossed two rivers and annexed Gangauli, which was some twelve-fourteen miles away from Ghazipur. It is said that the king of this village was called Gang and the village was named Gangauli after him. But even after the consolidation of the control of the Syed family, the village did not become Nupur or Nuruddin Nagar—the name of my Gangauli is not worse than my Ghazipur. But the interesting thing is that Nuruddin Shahid's *samadhi,** which is later than Gangauli in time, seems older than Gangauli... . This small brick structure must have had a roof at one time. But for the last thirty-six or thirty-seven years, I have been seeing it in ruins. Only on the tenth of Moharram, when processions from both sides of Gangauli arrive here, is there a semblance of an assembly, and at some distance from the samadhi, the crowds from Lakri Ka Akhara congregate. They stand there armed with sticks, clubs and swords. Suddenly, one man raises his hand holding a sword and shouts, 'Bol Mohammadi', and the whole village answers, 'Ya Hussain!'

These days the number of Gangauli-*wallahs* is decreasing and the number of Sunnis, Shias and Hindus is increasing. Perhaps that is why the gathering at Nuruddin Shahid's *samadhi* is no longer as large as it used to be earlier, and Gangauli's skies do not hear the cries of 'Bol Mohammadi–Ya Hussain' with the same enthusiasm they did before. Perhaps this is why the *samadhi*

* A replica of the samadhi of Imam Hussain, where *tazias* are buried.

wears a sad look these days and peers about with its blind eyes, pondering where has my Gangauli gone! The *samadhi* is, however, rooted in the land of Gangauli. That is why it stands where it has always stood—all by itself. This is to the south of the *samadhi*, and the *samadhi* itself is in the north of Gangauli. They also got a pond dug, which lies in the western corner of the village. This pond must have been constructed by the heirs of Nuruddin Shahid, because there are no remains of any temple nearby. There are mango and *jamun* trees on the mounds of earth that must have been excavated from the pond, and the Mirs of the village come to offer their prayers on the tenth of Moharram on these mounds. To the west of this pond is a three-door structure of lime where *neel* was being produced and which we, no one knows why, call the *godam* or storehouse. This is a memorial for John Gilchrist, which means it belongs to another era. Now it is either being used by the shepherds who sit there and chew sugarcane or else by lovers. Heer may not be able to find her Ranjha here, but a body does find another.

This village lives between a *samadhi* half in ruins and a deserted factory. The Syeds live in two corners of Gangauli. All told there are ten houses. Those in the south are called Dakhan Patti and the houses in the north are called Uttar Patti. In between are the houses of the weavers. From the house of Sibtu Da starts the area of the Rakis, and the dirty mud lane enters the bazaar of Gangauli and, passing the low-lying shops and itchy scratching dogs, it heaves a sigh of relief as it ends in the open area around the *samadhi* of Nuruddin Shahid.

There are many settlements of huts around the village, each called a *pura*, some belong to the Chamars, others are occupied by Ahirs. There are three large gates in Gangauli. One is in the Uttar Patti and is known as Pakkad Talé (under the Pakkad tree). It is a big wooden gate. There is a Pakkad tree nearby. As you enter the gate, there are many Imami courtyards on the south, on which beautiful wooden *tazias* are placed on the ninth day of Moharram, and then you enter a very large courtyard. These courtyards were of great social significance during the days of the *zamindari*. This is the place where all the weddings of the clan were held. This is where the community was fed on occasions of death and birth. Recalcitrant tenants were punished here. It was here that the affairs of the *zamindari* were tangled and untangled, and again, it was here that parties for visiting police inspectors, deputies and collectors were held. Were it not for these courtyards, it would be difficult to run the *zamindaris*.

There is one large gate in Uttar Patti and two in Dakhan Patti. One belongs to Zahir Cha's ancestors, meaning it belongs to Dadda's family. This gate is called Barka Gate. There is another large gate belonging to the family of Abbu Da, which is known as Abbu Da Miyan Ka Phatak.

We have to go to these three gates to the Syed families living all around these gates.

Yes, another thing! This Gangauli is no imaginary village and the houses that we will see here are also not imaginary. All that I have done is to get the people living in these houses to vacate them and put the characters of this novel in their places. These characters will not seem out of place in this milieu and you may also feel that Phunnan Miyan, Abbu Miyan, Jhangtiya Bo, Maulvi Bedar, Komila, Babar Mua, Balram Chamar, Hakim Ali, Kabir, Gaya Ahir, Anwarul Hassan Raqi and all the others are inhabitants of Gangauli, but along with these imaginary characters, I have also put some real people. These real people are from my own family, who have helped me in laying the foundation of reality, and because of them, even the imaginary characters have become frank and open with me.

Come, let's go!

(After the narrative is two-thirds over,
there follows a "Preface", a "*Bhumika*".)

Preface

I, Syed Masoom Raza Abdi, son of Syed Bashir Hasan Abdi, am extremely perplexed. I often wonder where I belong! Azamgarh or Ghazipur? Is my home in a village called Gangauli in Ghazipur or in a village called Thekma Bijauli in Azamgarh? I havn't seen it! Even after accepting that my grandfather, Mir Ali Mohammad Sahib, was from Bijauli District, I am not enthused at hearing its name. Azamgarh, for me, is one town in thousands of towns in India and Bijauli only a village! My grandfather may have belonged there! I belong to Gangauli. I know only Gangauli. I do not know anything about Bijauli. I do not even know what the house—which can be called my ancestral home—looks like! What is the colour of the doors of the *Imambara* of that house? What *marsia* is recited in which *majlis* and who recites it?—meaning that I have no emotional attachment to that house in Bijauli. I am from Ghazipur and I accept that my grandfather had come from Azamgarh. Ghazipur, for me, is not one town, nor is Gangauli just a village for me. It is my town and my village. You must have understood my meaning—and my grandfather had not come with a girted sword to Ghazipur!

You must be wondering what this preface is doing in the middle of a story! I was also thinking the same. But this is not some other story. The task of saying what I want to say is becoming increasingly difficult with every sentence. Because the village and the people I am talking about are my village and my people, and I love them. It is this love that is acting as an obstruction to my desire to say what I want to. At this juncture, the story of this half village is at a very delicate point. I knew that this twist would come in this story and that is why I did not choose the entire village, but only that part of the village that I know extremely well. It is essential for a storyteller to know all that there is to know about the people whose story he is telling. I know all these people, but even then, I am breaking all the rules to write this preface. The matter is that our story has now reached a point where one era is drawing to a close and another is about to begin. Does not every new era demand a preface?

And, therefore, I thought it necessary that I should declare that my grandfather was from Azamgarh, but I am from Ghazipur. I am from Gangauli. Gangauli is the village of my father's maternal family. It may be possible that my Abba's loyalty may have been divided between Bijauli and Gangauli, but my loyalty is not. I belong only to Ghazipur. I am of that indigo storehouse that Gilchrist Sahib had got built. I am of that pond which has taken Gangauli in its lap like the Ganga. I am of the rounds on the fifth and the eighth day of *Muharram*. I am of those voices of the looms that work day and night and never stop. I am of Ganga Ahir, Hariya Badhai and Komila Chamar. My grandfather may have come from Azamgarh because everyone's grandfather or great-grandfather comes from some place or the other.

It does not hurt me to know that Sifarva has proclaimed himself a Syed in Pakistan. He may have done so. And who can say that the blood of some very high and pure Zaidi Syed does not flow in his veins? But I am worried about Sallo and her daughter, Shahida, who have been abandoned here by Tannu, and whom Rabban Bi curses day and night. Hearing those curses, Sallo beats Shahida. The question is, what sort of mother will Shahida become when she grows up? The question is that this Quddan has married again in Pakistan, and what will become of the whole lot of grandsons and grand-daughters of Hakim Ali Kabir in India? ...

There are many more such questions.

The Jan Sangh says that Mussalmans do not belong here. How dare I say that this is a lie! But this has to be said that I am from Ghazipur. My relationship with Gangauli is unbreakable. It is not only a village, it is also my home! Home! This word is found in every dialect and every language of the world, and in each dialect and language, it is its most beautiful word. Though I am saying this again, I am of Gangauli, not because it is only a village, but because it is also my home. 'Because'—how strong is this word! And there are thousands of 'because-s' like this—and no sword can be so sharp that it can cut this 'because'! And as long as this 'because' is alive, I, Syed Masoom Raza Abdi, will remain of Ghazipur, even though my grandfather may have been of somewhere else. And I do not give anyone the right to tell me, "'Rahi', you are not of Gangauli. Therefore, leave Gangauli and go, for instance, to Rae Bareli.' Why should I go, Sahib? I will not go.

This preface was essential to take the story forward.

Wali Manzil
Badr Bagh
Aligarh

Rahi Masoom Raza

Translated from Hindi by **Tripti Jain**

Jayanta Mahapatra

Jayanta Mahapatra (b. 1928) looks back upon his life as one marked by several happenings, both personal and political. Mahapatra grew up in Cuttack, where his schooling took place in the Stewart European School run by a missionary organisation. Though he was fascinated by the English language, he chose to do his Master's in Physics at Patna University. One of three siblings, he was the eldest and has memories of World War II when he was in senior school. Family tales, as he has heard them, place the conversion of his grandfather to Christianity as the result of a terrible famine. This is how histories pass on, parts of it recorded and communicated to the future—in Mahapatra's case, it was the 'torn and moth-eaten' diary of his grandfather.

As a young lecturer, he fell in love and succeeded in winning the young woman's hand. Somewhere along the way, the poet in him was born—out of his sensitivity to landscapes, nature, the emaciated people around him and his baggage of mixed cultures. At one point, he tried his hand at fiction, but it was the poet in him that gained supremacy. His first collection, ***Close the Sky, Ten by Ten****, came out in 1971 and happens to be a Writers' Workshop publication. And since then, there has been no stopping him. His poems are close to the soil. One can see that he is a poet of nature, but not one of isolation—his poems are inhabited by human beings. Despite his emotional conflicts and political experiences, Mahapatra has not allowed himself to be distracted extensively by the life of the external, he has continued to communicate the connection which he has always felt between man and his world.*

Mahapatra, who has been a visiting writer at Iowa, has written several collections of poetry. Some of his work has been translated into other Indian languages. He has also written for children and translated the works of some of his contemporary writers. There is an aura of sensitivity about him and his poems stand apart from many another on account of their rootedness and closeness to the soil, to the landscape around him, and his empathy with the anguish of his people.

Face to Face
with the Contemporary Poem

Once again, I feel it would be audacious to speak about the poetry I write, plainly because I realise that my years have *not* been spent learning the makings of verse, its art and craft, studying the procedures which distinguish the good poem from the bad, in academic centres. In other words, I admit that I am not an academic and that I did not read any poetry until I started writing it myself (which was rather late in life), except for a dozen poems in my last year at school, the usual which ranged from Keats to Wordsworth. Therefore, whatever I might have to say will only be a limited voice because of my lack of proper critical approach, but certainly will move toward an honest realisation of my innermost convictions. Secondly, and this is what seems of primary importance to me, is that, as a practising poet, my job is to write poems and not to go about exploiting the suggestions of my verse.

I would say *conscience* matters because what else is the poet responsible to? Nothing else is as consequential as this 'inner thing' to him, this secret root of his being, and which acts as the hidden code behind his writing. A poet is, perhaps, only right when he says in his poem what he has actually known. This appears as the only relevant truth—that one's experience in the world is the raw material from which the poem is made. Usually, writers do rely on their individual, personal experiences—on those things which can be seen and heard, touched and trapped by their senses, which threaten their ephemeral existence—to produce their own poems. For it is then that the poem becomes the only reliable authority to which one can turn if one is to recognise the shapes and movements of life.

I do not, however, wish to discuss whether such an experience is appropriate to the making of a memorable poem, and that, besides the central experience, nothing else matters. For I am not going into the process or build-up of a *significant* poem; it is simply that a poem becomes a testament on the page, a testament of the poet's ability towards life, and his own way of breaking forth an experience into a responsibility that cannot be dismissed. William Carlos Williams said it without jargon, 'Because it's there to be written', in the manner of the Everest mountaineer who lost his life years ago, 'Because it's there'. And it is hard, most of the time, to ascribe any rationale for the writing of a particular poem; it's just that a part of the mystery of one's self comes out, perhaps in the manner of a truth, or a decorative gesture, or in virtuous attire—a reality that endures that specific instant of thought. A good number of my own poems have their roots in day-to-day common experiences. (I should like to cite "The Report Card", "The Abandoned British Graveyard at Balasore, India" and "Grandfather" as examples, and these have probably turned out to be 'ordinary' poems.) I shall label them 'insignificant' in the broader context of poetry because the experiences from which they originate are trivial ones and, therefore, to the general reader, insignificant. I do not (here) put forward any pretensions that any one of those three mentioned above be called memorable or significant. Perhaps thought, language, imagery and metaphor are all present in the poems, but then, do only these factors qualify for a poem's greatness? Not the honesty and meaning of a poem? And should a great poem be the only grand occasion for taking stock of a society's artistic capabilities?

It is my intention here not to refer to this unity of fullness in a poem (and how a great poem lets us embark on a sort of journey or voyage through symbols and allusions to encompass the human condition), but to deal with any poem or verse that qualifies enough to be called poetry, arising out of the commonplace experiences of our time. In such a poem, the experience emerges as the core around which the whole writing structure is built. And yet, how strange it is that the act of making or writing the poem itself becomes a *full* experience! I am afraid it is not in my thinking to explain this apparent discrepancy; I see it as a question one has to live with. But no one can deny that the act of writing any poem, significant or small, is only the poet's concern, the poet's secret deal. And this writing of it is a lonely and difficult affair. The poet himself cannot pretend to know how the poem will progress, and *how the poem wants him to be*. For it is only the poet who finds himself at last, after the word has been written down. His private life does not remain private for too long, and as the poem imposes itself upon him in the process of his writing, the poet is unable to tell whether he has suffered his realisation of what he is.

It appears correct for me to insist that the manner of writing a poem is a painful one. This is true also of today's poem, the contemporary poem, in which according to popular comment, meaning is neither clear nor explicit—to extract a statement or understanding from the poem becomes 'difficult'. When the 'confessional' poetry of the 1960s in America (markedly) gave way to a new 'surrealism', it evidenced a new ambiguity—not what the lay or common reader could follow, not something they had come to regard as poetry through the years. Generally speaking, today's poem utilises a number of images and symbols to form a whole, leaving the reader to extricate for himself the valid meaning or argument from them. Thus, the reader is left to find out his own meaning from the poem; this, I admit painfully, is true of much of the poetry I have written. If contemporary life is no longer what it was, say, twenty-five years back, can one expect the same content, the same form, the same substance from contemporary poems? And yet, poets are expected to create a unifying sense from contemporary existence, not to portray or reflect the fragments and pieces they encounter in their day-to-day living.

How far a poet is able to relate to the reader thus becomes the crucial thing; a seemingly obscure poem does, in its content, contain the hidden voice for its ultimate understanding. For even though the poetry of the past two decades or so has become a very personal matter (as evidenced by the poems in anthologies and periodicals, and which don't concern many people), a true poem should make the reader feel how the poem *wants* him to feel, should build that relationship by making him feel and not merely telling him a certain thing. Certainly, therefore, the poet faces a difficult task. But besides this, the reader—whether he be layman or critic—is responsible, and he should be aware of the poet's predicament in order that communication between them be possible.

This feeling or *wanting* of the reader for the poem can be poor or good; often, the reader reads the opening (first/second) lines of the poem and then ditches it for another thing—another literary form, like a story or essay. Why does this happen? Is it because the first two lines of the poem are trite and uninviting, or is it that they remind the reader of the refuse of a greater poet he has read and admired? Is it because our existence today has corrupted our normally open instincts by the excessive interruption of politics so that the ordinary reader is turned off simply by the sight of a poem? Or has our culture become so 'popular' that serious poetry has lost its readers for good? Or, coming to the poem itself—and this from a writer's viewpoint—*is* the contemporary poem too poor to evoke a response in the reader?

All poems cannot be good and powerful and, often, the ordinary reader is confronted by a poorly written poem. He is justified thus to deride the state of contemporary poetry in our day. This is a general statement and covers both Indian writing and poetry being written in other countries as well. And this is not the reader's fault. The relation between a poem and reader is a reversible process, a two-way affair. And how an individual poem is able to put forth its experience so as to touch the reader is important and decisive: This experience might (i) reach the reader almost immediately, spontaneously—in the manner of an electric charge passing through a good conductor such as copper or iron, (ii) reach the reader with difficulty, slowly under great stress, like that of a charge passing through a bad conductor like glass, or (iii) not be able to pass or communicate at all, as though there was a break or gap between them.

It becomes safe to conclude that the capacity or power for conducting the essential experience of the poem will primarily depend upon the poem itself—on the poem's design. Together with this lies the responsibility of the experience in the poem, perhaps to its awe, to its delight, and to its hopes and fears. And no one can refute the fact that experience is an ambiguous thing, difficult to explain—an unknown quantity 'x' that the poet wishes to give concrete form to in a poem, in order that it may reach out for another unknown.

I feel, therefore, that the reader's experience is a necessary one, for the reader to be *wanted* by the poem, to share the poem's mystery and its content in full. Otherwise, the reader's response becomes a partial, superficial one. Also, confront here an encounter between two separate cultures, belonging to the poet and to the reader, because the poem is never addressed to a single, homogeneous audience. For instance, a reader from a westernised or technologically advanced culture (usually considered a superior culture) will come upon a number of obstacles in reading the poems of one who is reconciled and (apparently) content with backward conditions at home. I am aware of this grouping when a city reader reads my work. Taking my poems in the last two books, *A Rain of Rites* and *Waiting,* where the poems deal with Orissa—an area where I have lived almost all my life—I meet the befuddled reader/critic. The poems are woven from the unchanging ways of life in the temple cities of Puri and Bhubaneswar, with the unquestionable rituals of a predominantly agricultural society. How then could a reader living outside Orissa react to such a poetry abounding in local detail? How could he react fully to the poems, feel himself wanted by them? What reactions could one then expect from a non-Indian reader? And how can one blame the reader (or reviewer) for being blind to some of the important aspects of this verse? And this does explain somewhat the state of criticism of western readers toward Indian poetry.

As I remarked earlier, the contemporary poem stems from a confused and loose earth, quite unlike the one our forefathers lived in. Values have changed considerably through the years;

indeed, so much so that they have come to resemble abnormalities. The sensibility of an earlier century is not here any longer, not here any more to push man into the continuum of nature, to establish him close to the banyan bark and to the leaf, to the owl's hoot and the mantiss, to those symbols which enabled him to reach beyond himself. Will it be a cruel thing to say that the reader of today's poem needs an external set of antennae to feel his own knowing? To feel pain and sadness and infinitude? Or has the taste for the poem been robbed by a new, technologically oriented culture? A culture which is excited, nourished by flamboyant media—by a system of super advertisement that strips symbols and words of their time-proved meanings?

Perhaps the pedantic, intellectual poetry which many significant twentieth century poets wrote was responsible for this loss of popular appeal (the poetry suffered from a loss of coherence); it would be easy to name these modernist poets, poets who had among their audience other poets and academics, and this probably led to their poetry being confined to the English departments of universities. Outside the campuses, their poetry failed basically because of a difference in outlook between poet and reader. And this still ails the state of poetry today.

The medium being language in poetry, language makes greater demands on the artist. An almost pure art like music is capable of creating an immediate response. Musical sounds are not ordinarily used for other purposes, visual arts like painting and sculpture are also in an advantageous position because the pictorial element can at once relate to the viewer—maybe not on the truly aesthetic plane, but on some other. Poetry becomes the most difficult of the arts because it operates on language, and language is used to relate to, to communicate with the world every moment of our lives. Thus, for language to be successful in poetry, it must be made to work for the poet, with an additional boost. In other words, poetry has to make use of *language plus*—that is, a human language (not utilitarian like science or day-to-day speech), a language of over-and-above noumenal concerns.

Strange that everyone feels a poem is easy to make. For on the page, it appears exceptionally neat and ordered, perhaps resembling a convenient piece of architecture. Therefore, all kinds of people find it simple to talk about it, to dismiss it lightly, but not any other art form such as painting or sculpture. I am at a loss to know what sort of pleasure poetry gives. Is it of a different kind, bringing a refined delight? Or is it capable of producing a reverse, numbing effect on the mind?

When I reread the poetry I have written, I find many of the poems confused, made up of abstractions that fail to connect with the reader. (This is especially true of my earlier work.) For every poem one makes is a step forward, a process—just as thought itself is a process—and gradually, the language changes, expanding and contracting as time passes by, the words curve and straighten and vibrate with the silence around and inside the imagination. How unfortunate that, unlike a scientist, one is unable to wash out all the errors, the absurd and poor arguments, when he arrives at a fruitful conclusion? But with verse, each poem one leaves behind becomes witness to a crude experience of the poet, becomes an anguish that he cannot overcome, on the way to a continued growth as a writer. One discovers that the old ideas still continue to condition his emotions. So, I am very tentative in admitting to myself that I am a poet. Governed as one is, as I am, by the unconscious—which, in more ways than one, acts like a power generator, behaving like a god—I would be satisfied if I can reveal a consciousness in my writing in agreement with today's realities.

To conclude, the pertinent question: How many would read the poems I've written? Perhaps twenty or thirty people at the most. It won't be an understatement when I say that in Cuttack, my home town, a small number (say, about ten) read my poems, discuss them and walk home perhaps with unfinished feelings. They are all youngsters in their late teens or early twenties. I keep on asking myself: Do they like what they read? Are they really interested? Have the poems been able to expand their moments of sensibility in some way? I don't have any answers. And here I have to admit truthfully that the college where I've been teaching all these years does not have a single collection of my poetry on its library shelves. Doesn't this confirm my fears that my readership is severely limited? Isn't it right that I assume that nobody cares a damn about the stuff I write?

It is not always possible to make meaning and sense of life, and poets are expected to do just that. Auden wasn't uncomfortable when he said 'poetry makes nothing happen'. And yet, when one looks at a poem on a page, he faces a response to a part of himself: The poem looks back at him; it is there, taking care of itself and, perhaps, that's enough.

Nirmal Verma

Nirmal Verma (1929–2005), during his literary career, worked freely across genres and across different ideological positions. A novelist, short story writer, travel writer, activist and translator, Verma's intellectual journey is amazing.

Born in Shimla, he graduated from St Stephen's College, Delhi University. Like many of his contemporaries, he came from a large family and some of his siblings were equally talented. He lived in Prague for ten years, during which period he translated nine world classics into Hindi and also wrote seven travelogues. As a young man, he used to attend Gandhi's prayer meetings in Birla House though he was also a card-holding member of the Communist Party. It was only on his return to India that he opted out of communism and his mind turned towards more philosophical and reflective concerns.

Nirmal Verma is amongst the pioneers of the Nai Kahani movement. His story, "Maya Darpan", was made into a successful film. He chaired the creative writing programme in Bhopal from 1980 to 1983 and the Yashpal Centre at Shimla during the years, 1988–90. His last novel, ***Antim Arney****, is about love, old age and relationships and makes a sensitive and powerful contribution to the Hindi novel.*

The essay included here reflects Verma's concern with language and the identity that is vested in it for the people of the nation. Beginning with the necessity of language for constructing and asserting identity at all levels, he begins with the smallest unit: the individual. Language is the basics of self-expression and self-realisation, for self-discovery and analysis. In brief, we need words to objectify ourselves and to share our feelings with others as much as we need it in order to think. We need it for our dreams and for the shaping of our culture. As such, it looms large over us, enveloping us in multiple ways.

The important question is not how essential is language, but what colonialism has done to it, diverting it from its natural path. Western thinkers and philologists pushed the language of culture into the past, but strangely enough, also projected a picture of its continuity in other languages.

Contextualising it in the international theoretical frameworks, Verma also takes note of positions closer home such as Ananda Coomaraswamy's, tracing a historical continuum and locating the problem in a larger discourse of self, identity and nation in an international context. The history/histories of language are significant for understanding our own cultures. Time is intimately connected with the shape our ideas take as they relate to the flow of history.

Language and National Identity*

To say anything about language is like chasing your own shadow. It may be more appropriate to assert that we are its shadow, we create our reality with it, and define ourselves through it, and with it. Man can never be defined fully, not only because there is something in him that is still unknown, but also because he has not yet completed the process of recreating and reinventing himself. We are unable to accept man as a finished product. There has been much speculation about the manner in which he may fulfil himself, the direction this fulfilment may take, and the form it will acquire and how he will project his innate potentialities in the future. Various scholars—from Nietzsche to Sri Aurobindo—have made predictions about his innate capacity. The question is not how correct or relevant these prophecies are; the point to consider is that man being what he is, all these predictions are born of a painful disillusionment with what he is. Man is the only creature—between a god and an animal—who finds himself in a strange situation of being incomplete; he lacks the self, the involvement, of the animal and does not possess the fullness of god. Even in the historical framework, man appears as a figure—half-drawn and incomplete, as if thwarted in the process of acquiring a proper shape, its colours lacklustre and faded. The 'full figure' of man—if there is such a thing—is not without, but buried deep within him. In order to realise himself, man digs 'within' and raises himself from his own grave.

Language is the most efficient weapon of self-discovery or self-analysis. It is that invisible part of the human body, which

---

* From Nirmal Verma, *Doosre Shabdon Mein*, New Delhi: Bhartiya Jnanpith (1997), 1999.

gives man an inner sight. The link between language and self-awareness puts man in a separate and unique category from all other living beings. This consciousness of his own incompleteness makes him yearn for fulfilment... thus, the determination to attain it is also intrinsic to its realisation. No culture is limited only to its reality, but also reveals itself through its dreams, and that is why language plays a very significant role in the shaping of culture.

The vision of a culture is largely formed by the memories that it carries. If the word is symbolic of a dream, it also has the hint of the memory. No language, as long as it is, can, therefore, be a dead language. If all else of our past were to perish, even then the languages would remain through which the members of a society communicate with each other, and though living in the present, are unconsciously linked with their past, and the past flows imperceptibly through the present. Language, in this manner, plays a double role; besides being the vehicle of communication, it is also the carrier of a culture. Historical upheavals may impair the culture of a country, but its truth and cohesion persist in its language.

Indian culture is an excellent example of this. In the nineteenth century, the European thinkers and philologists—among whom Hegel and Max Mueller were prominent—while declaring that the golden age of Indian culture lay buried deep in its hoary past, dismissed its present on the one hand, yet, on the other, they, specially Indologists such as Max Mueller, were conscious of the fact that as long as Sanskrit and the various languages based on it, continued to be used for communication and self-realisation, its cultural identity would survive. This being so, Indian culture could never be turned into glorious-but-dead exhibits for museums, the way the Greek or Egyptian cultures have been. The national awakening in the first half of the nineteenth century could grow and blossom through this cultural identity alone. A rich and vast wealth of racial memories lay hidden in Sanskrit and other Indian languages, which served as the life-giving current flowing through the past into the present. The seeds of nationalism were nascent in this consciousness, and Macaulay had warned of this: 'We will never be able to establish the domination of western culture in India until we are able to oust Sanskrit completely from the Indian educational system.' The issue of intellectual freedom, which had been raised by the Indian philosopher, K.C. Bhattacharya, had a deep connection with the linguistic and racial identity of a people.

What we call the truth of a culture is nothing but the prearranged order of the hidden meanings of words, and what we refer to as 'reality' is the external world glimpsed through the windows of these connotations. The proportion in which we are alienated from our language because of some historical pressure or oppression, the scene glimpsed through the window becomes dull and hazy in precisely the same proportion. Language links the truth within with the reality without. The interesting thing is that truth and reality are not two different and separate entities; we only treat them as distinct concepts and distinguish between them for intellectual convenience. We live in a single 'word universe'. The manner in which the world outside is a prisoner of language, in the same way, we are also imprisoned by language—the window and the scene outside are not unconnected. If we borrow an illustration from Wittgenstein—then we should say— that when we bang our heads against the walls of language and hurt ourselves, only then do we realise that we are prisoners.

A culture establishes its own uniqueness within these walls alone. There is a stability and permanence in human languages which enables man to shape an identity of his own. Not only on the basis of language, but from this point of view as well, man is different from other living beings. Other creatures also communicate with members of their species, even though the manner of this communication may not be as sophisticated and organised. If human language is qualitatively different from theirs, it is because beyond a certain point, it is not a vehicle of communication alone, but takes on an independent and autonomous entity. The language of animals is born out of certain inner cravings, of sex or of hunger, and disappears as soon as the craving is satisfied. Their memory does not go beyond the immediate. This, however, is not true of human society. Even after the fulfilment of immediate goals, the power of the word persists. From its original resonance, the word is transformed into abstract ideas and takes on a definite meaning. As the early man carved an image of some divine being from his memory of some event, and in the course of time, the image became a venerated icon, its role in the miracle long forgotten, in the same manner, words are like these momentary icons, born in a moment of emotional outburst, and after it has passed away, acquiring an independent existence of their own. Independent only in a limited sense, for they are not mere sounds, but are also carriers of connotations in which the earliest memories are always alive. The myths of a race are nurtured by its very early memories, inherent in its 'word universe'. Language has the same relation to these myths that early man had with his gods—both give a permanent form and image to his earliest memories and perceptions. Myths are the ancient icons of language.

This interrelationship between language, myth and memory is what binds the members of a group to a collective identity. Just as European culture cannot be separated from Greek and Latin languages and their myths, the image of Indian culture has been shaped by the Puranic tales and epics written in Sanskrit, whose archetypal memory still permeates the Indian psyche. A culture has its historical roots, which we take for granted, but it also has an 'internal past', which resonates in the concepts, myths and beliefs of its language. As Heidegger says, 'Each language draws a magical circle around the people who speak it, from which escape is possible only by going into another.'

Two different forms of language appear before us here, and it would be appropriate to call them two different aspects of its character. One is the language that we speak in, converse in—the colloquial form, the core language; the second is its essential form, which lives below the surface, but is constantly echoing in the words spoken above. The words we utter, in some way or the other, express this invisible, internalised and covert form of language. Heidegger has described this in a beautiful and poetical manner. He says, 'Speaking is an internal way of listening, listening to the language we speak. We only speak what we hear, and what our language itself says... and we are capable of hearing it only to that extent to which our essence is related to the internal language.' Perhaps, a poet feels this basic truth about the language the most. He harmonises what he hears in the language—the obscure, mysterious and sombre voices emerging from the dark and gloomy underground of the language—into his own words. In the words of a poem, we hear what language seeks to reveal to us. Thus, the essential language of poetry is very different from colloquial language, both in its nature as also in its purpose. Language, in its ultimate form, is like a 'placid river', which links its two banks and also creates them. One side is what it says, and the other side is what we speak, and which it echoes.

There is a dynamic relationship between this internal form of language and its practical character. Each language, as it develops, establishes a special constitution and structure, which, once having come into existence, influences the inner responses of man. Both processes go on simultaneously; language determines the identity and the special characteristics of a race, and the collective experiences, memories and traditions of a group mould the unique character of its language. This is, in a way, a circular process, in which the question of what comes first remains unanswered, like in the case of the chicken and the egg. What is clear is that there is nothing like one language; there are numerous languages. And the various races, groups and nationalities are nurtured by their languages; languages are their residing places. In this sense, each language, in its ultimate form, is a mother tongue. Man is drawn to the world for the first time through language, opens up, and is linked to it. It is not only a part of the external day-to-day activity of a group, a part of its superstructure (although it has a specific role in the achievements of its worldly goals), it also decides its inner nature, impulses and sensibility, and demonstrates its unique spiritual character. One language differs from another, not only in its sounds, intonations and the meaning its words convey, but also in its 'world view'. Each language looks at the universe in a particular manner, tests it and translates it into its own meanings in a special way. The connotations that the *Rig Veda* conveys through the symbols of Surya, Agni, Dhenu and Space to the Indian mind, and the images of certain divine forces that it conjures up, are distinct in their import from the Greek and Latin symbols, different because their mythical sources and references are distinct and separate. Human languages are born in the same world, but each has its own incomparable quality, manifest and well-defined. When we translate from one language into another, it is not just a translation of the words alone, but the transformation of a whole universe, with all its baggage, into another language.

The warning given by Michael Witzel of Harvard, a Sanskrit scholar, is significant in this context; explaining the difficulty of translating the Sanskrit word, *Rt,* he says, 'Many words in Sanskrit, as well as in other languages, cannot be rendered by a single good translation of the "term", the concept encompassed by the *Rt* is in fact quite similar to the equally untranslatable letter. Hindu "Dharma" on modern usage of the truth does not cover all aspects of the term *Rt*...... *Rt* is an active realisation of truth, a vital force which can underlie human in divine action... . English, German, et cetera, have no word expressing the combination of concepts carried by the term, *Rt*.'

What Dr Witzel has said about the term, *Rt,* is applicable to other concepts that are central to Indian culture—Self, Brahma, *Satya, Asatya*. What has been said about languages having a 'world view' is reflected through the tradition-laden concepts of a language, which are richly endowed with memories. Therefore, any worthwhile translation of these ideas into another language is possible only when they are reproduced not in their literal sense alone, but carry with them all the cultural and philosophical undertones. It is not a question of a good or bad translation, but of the extraordinary profundity of these concepts, which can be highlighted only in their traditional context. Some time back, Ananda Coomaraswamy had drawn our attention to this quality of language. What he says about

Hinduism is, by and large, true of all ancient religious systems that have experienced colonial pollution. In the introduction to his book, *Hinduism and Buddhism*, he writes:

> Brahmanism or Hinduism is considered to be one of the oldest mystery religions, or metaphysical systems, of the world. It is the only religion which has an almost unbroken tradition for the last two thousand years—a tradition which is still observed by millions even today. But it would be no exaggeration to say that it would be possible to properly define Hinduism only after rejecting most of the views and opinions expressed by those European philologists and Indian scholars well versed in the modern European progressive movement.

Coomaraswamy explains the reason for this by the fact that Indian historians, following the European scholars, have misinterpreted concepts like Karma, *Sidhant, Bhasha,* rebirth, self and Brahma in their own languages, and these words have ceased to have any relationship with their true meanings, which is the very essence of Indian culture.

It is obvious that Coomaraswamy does not in any way doubt the competence of European languages, but is only indicating their limitations. Each language has this constraint because each language has a cultural context. The word, secularism, is a very good example of the misunderstanding that can be caused by a mix-up of two concepts rooted in two distinct milieus. 'Secularism' is a product of European culture and history and is not even remotely related to the concept of religious neutrality, which we have adopted in our political system and education since Independence.

A secular political system can also be highly righteous in its ultimate character... provided the word 'righteousness', is not overlaid with the connotation of the word 'religion'. This is a unique example of how many Asians, under the influence of European language, tend to forget the real nature of their own society. It is also suggestive of the fact that whenever there is interference between a society and its language by an outside power, the members of that society tend to forget their own identity.

The threat of the dominance of European languages, which Coomaraswamy has hinted at, has been called 'Europeanisation of the earth' by a European philosopher, Heidegger. He was acutely aware of how this had led to misunderstanding and misinterpretations of the concepts of eastern cultures. He had voiced his misgivings about this in a conversation with a Japanese scholar, and Jadav Lal Mehta, an Indian philosopher, has referred to this. Heidegger's views are so closely related to the present issue that I would like to refer to them at length:

> On his return from Europe, a Japanese philosopher had lectured at the Kyoto University on aesthetics in Japanese art with the help of European aesthetics. Heidegger had objected to this—is it proper for him to rely on aesthetics? The nomenclature and the object, both had originated in European thought and philosophy. The concept of aesthetics would be essentially unknown and alien to East Asian thought, then why is it necessary for him to take the help of this method? The Japanese scholar had answered: 'Because this system gives us the concepts through which we can analyse the elements of our art and poetry.' Heidegger asked: 'Do you need concepts for that?' The Japanese scholar had answered:
>
> 'It appears so, for after interacting with European thought, our language seems to have become inadequate, it appears to lack the capacity of defining objects and cannot arrange them into lower and higher categories, and imagine any coordination between them'. Heidegger's answer was: 'Do you really think this deficiency is a weakness of your language? Is it necessary and proper that you should follow European methods of conceptualisation? If you do this, then, will it not result in your failing to understand your own truth as also the reality of the European point of view, and you will not be able to see them in their distinct and separate forms, and then, the real dialogue between these two will never begin?' Finally, the Japanese scholar accepted that after being overwhelmed by the European concepts, they tend to devalue the uniqueness of the ideas of their own language, which they have received from their own tradition...

We can quote another example of how the philosophy and metaphysics of a culture are moulded and shaped by its own language from another conversation between a German friend of Heidegger, who was translating Lao-Tse into German, and a Chinese friend of his. The German asked the Chinese friend, 'I do not understand why the Chinese speak in this way.' The Chinese scholar remarked, 'Because at that time, we Chinese did not know Aristotle's "Logic".' 'Thank God,' was Heidegger's comment, 'that the Chinese did not know it!'

All of us must have had this experience—at least I have—that when we express ourselves in another language, our thoughts, to a certain extent, tend to be influenced by the concepts of that language. Language is not only a medium, but also becomes an instrument of an autonomous force. We can express ourselves through it, but only in the manner it wants us to. In the words of Dr Mehta, 'The question here is of the dominance of language and to the extent we are under the influence of the language, what do we want to say, and what the language compels us to say.' Indian thinkers, scholars, writers and intellectuals who have been influenced by the English language for the last two hundred years, do they ever ask themselves the questions that Heidegger posed to the Japanese scholar? Do they never feel that when they use a western language to understand and explain the truth of the art and poetry of their country, the foreign language then tends to dominate their inner experiences? We seek to express ourselves through a language whose logical system pulls us in one direction, while our sensory perceptions pull us in the opposite direction. Don't most of us educated people find ourselves in a situation of linguistic displacement, which affects us continuously and makes our national awareness rather lopsided and dubious? A wide gulf opens up between the two, which has been difficult to bridge even after fifty years of Independence.

Critics like Edward Said lay the blame for this on the European Indologists and thus feel absolved of all responsibility. They forget that the colonial intellectuals of most Asian countries and western educated Indians had identified their cultural heritage through the researches and translations of these very western scholars. It is a bitter truth that cannot be ignored. It is true that these European scholars moulded the essential elements of the non-western cultures in the ideas and theories of their own languages and falsified them to an extent, but we are also to be blamed for accepting unquestioningly the conclusions that they propounded about our history and culture. The issue was not whether these conclusions were right or wrong, but did we critically investigate the intellectual framework within which these theories and conclusions had been worked out of our own free will? Sri Aurobindo was the first scholar to analyse this in his *Foundations of Indian Culture*, but his place in our universities and philosophy is still negligible. In Said's book, *Orientalism*, Aurobindo has not been mentioned even once. It is one thing to subject oneself to self-analysis after coming in contact with others, but to define one's own self through their eyes is a different matter altogether.

We had mentioned Aristotle's 'Logic' in reference to the Chinese language. It is worth pointing out that languages that are dominated by 'reason' or rationality are structurally somewhat different from those that are rooted in racial symbols and myths. Here the linguistic roots of the poet and the philosopher are not very different—imagination plays a greater role than reason in both. In a way, the universe of words runs parallel to an experienced life view. The religious sensibilities of a society and its mythical awareness reverberate in its memories. That is the reason it is not easy to draw a dividing line between the philosophical concepts and poetic symbols of languages in Indian philosophy, be it the *Upanishads* or the *Bhagwat Gita*. The entire philosophy of Ramakrishna Paramhansa is based on symbols and metaphors, legends and mythical allusions. He imparts such a uniquely lyrical dimension to concepts like self, god, Brahman, man and nature that the boundary between poetry and analysis of elements is blurred.

There may be various reasons for this. I will not go into them, but would like to draw your attention to two main facts, first that the character of language is indirectly, but internally, influenced by the period of the culture. The time awareness of

Indian culture is vastly different from the western concept of historicity, and this has had a deep impact on Indian languages. Agyeya once made a very penetrating remark about this. Some excerpts from his last diary have recently been published. At one place, he writes:

> A total acceptance of the historic perspective of time led to a weakening of the assertion in the language; it lost its vitality, rather it had to abandon it with a recurring perception of time, our language was flexible, we had no other option but to forsake it... even an indeterminate deviation tended to irritate us... one can see this in the new poetry that is being written ... it has become less flexible than earlier, has become more rigid now—is it not because its sense of historic perspective of time is more firmly tied to chronology?

It is difficult to say how far Agyeya's view on awareness of period in modern poetry is right, but there is no doubt that the knowledge of the chronological sequence of epoch has inhibited the parameters of the modern Indian novel and prose. It is true that the events around which a novel is constructed are more deeply affected by sequence of time than poetry. I have analysed the relationship between the knowledge of historical epoch and the Indian novel elsewhere.* Here, it should suffice to mention that time has been variously conceptualised by Indian intellectuals, and we have given these concepts a unidimensional and afflicted form by moulding them into a sequential concept, and this has had a deep and inevitable impact even on the language of the different creative genres.

There is another element besides a sense of historicity to which we do not pay much attention, but which has a significant role in shaping the distinctive character of the language of a race, and that is man's relation with nature. It is an anthropological truth that in societies where man and nature are not treated as opposite entities, and their mutual relations are more intimate, close and natural, the distinction between the language of

---

* "Sanskriti, Samaj Aur Bharatiya Upanayas" (*Shatabdi Ke Dhalte Varshon Mein*)

perception and the language of thought is not very marked, and its mythical sensibilities are richer. In such a society, language is essentially metaphorical. The famous critic, Northrop Frye, says:

> Nature and man share the same energy and are an indivisible unit. But in societies where man and nature are divided into opposite categories, this metaphorical unity of language is dissipated. Intellect rather than metaphor dominates the language. Then, man evolves concepts rather than symbols. The convention of reflection and imagination lose their metaphorical status and are alienated from one another, as has happened with western language, where man's relation with nature has almost broken down because of the aggressive domination of reason and science.

If Indian language developed within the halo of symbols and images, the major fact responsible for this was that before the assault of modernity, the sacred relation between man and nature was unbroken for centuries. In the manner a person travelling through darkness seeks to find his way by the light of the stars, in the same manner, an Indian asserted his identity through these metaphors and symbols. As planets seem to be in motion despite being stationary in space, in the same way, language remains rooted in its traditional literature, yet keeps extending the frontiers of its connotation. This balance between motion and stability lends Indian languages a sort of unwavering dynamism.

Each language has its own history, and also a geography of its own. We cannot separate its symbolic character from its natural environment. If symbols like Ganga, Saraswati, Himalaya, ocean and space are deeply entrenched in the Indian languages and profoundly influence our sensibilities, it is not because they are the physical attributes of our natural habitat, but because they are the carriers of our legendary memories, which at one time linked Indians to their deities and lent a divine grace to their material existence. The meaning of the word, 'Bharat', was its essence—a region surrounded by divinity. The reason why 'Bharat' was called 'Dev Bhumi'—the land of gods—and Sanskrit was 'Dev Bhasha'—the language of gods—was to underline the eternal and sacred relation between the land and the language.

Language, with all its metaphors and imagery, played a significant role in kindling the national awakening in the nineteenth century in India. The novels of Bankim Babu, Sri Aurobindo's philosophy, Gandhi's *Hind Swaraj* and Coomaraswamy's thoughts on art are ample evidence of this. When a handful of historians call the concept of Indian nationalism a mere 'construct', using the vocabulary of French philosophers, where the very concept of 'Bharat' is labelled an imaginary product or 'invented construct' of some nationalist historians, then the linguistic and cultural foundations of Indian nationalism are totally overlooked, which is a living example of colonial forgetfulness. In India, the desire to seek freedom was inspired not only by political factors, but there was also the desire to retrieve our cultural identity from the darkness of oblivion. From this point of view, it was different from the aggressive, egoistic sentiments that lay behind the modern nation states, which came into existence only after the various races, nationalities and folk languages were annihilated. That the Indian national awareness was free of a self-involved rigidity right from its inception was because it had not been forcibly imposed from above, but its roots lay deep in the Indian cultural traditions. The various dialects and languages of India, despite their distinctiveness, shared an inherent unity, and this could never obstruct the growth of national unification.* Their diversity gave them an openness—they lived in the same house; though the windows were different, their casements opened on a full panorama of the interrelationship of Indian cultures. It is often said that we seek ourselves in our languages; perhaps, it happens in some cultures that they tell their stories in the language of dreams.

---

* This inherent unity of India was distinctive and different from the artificial unity of the former Soviet Union, which had been established through aggression and force and, therefore, broke up with the weakening of the central power. [Author's Note]

The reality of the national identity of Bharat is perhaps reflected in such dream languages.

References

Cassirer, Ernst. *Language and Myth.* (Tr. Susanne K. Langer), New York: Dover Publications, 1953.

Coomaraswamy, Ananda. *Hinduism and Buddhism.* (F.P. 1943), New Delhi: IGNCA, 1999.

Mehta, J.L. *Kavi Karma aur Chintan.* New Delhi: National Publishing House, 1986.

Mehta, J.L. *The Philosophy of Martin Heidegger.* Varanasi: Benaras Hindu University, 1967.

Witzel, Michael. *Inside the Texts, Beyond the Texts: New Approaches to the Study of Vedas.* Harvard Oriental Series, Vol. 2, Cambridge, Massachusetts: Harvard University Press.

Translated from Hindi by **Tripti Jain**

U.R. Ananthamurthy

One of the literary stalwarts of our times, Udupi Rajagopalacharya Ananthamurthy (b. 1932) is a novelist, poet, short story writer, political commentator and educationist. Ananthamurthy has had varied experience—a village school, university education in Mysore, doctoral work in Birmingham, followed by a return home and a lecturership in Mysore. Later, he shifted to Mahatma Gandhi University, Kottayam, as Vice-Chancellor. As an educationist, one of his major concerns has been the need to improve primary education.

In his literary career, Ananthamurthy has also been part of the Navya movement—a fact inevitable for that generation, except for some lonely figures who may have deliberately chosen to hold back. He has held the positions of President of the Sahitya Akademi, Chairman of the National Book Trust and a double term as Chairman of the Film and Television Institute of India. The crowning success has been the Jnanpith Award in 1994 and Padma Bhushan in 1998. Some of his short stories and novels have been made into films. Of these, **Samskara** *is perhaps the best known for the debates it raised on caste, the nature of power, masculinity, and the interpretation of religious scriptural discourses. Ananthamurthy has always been an unconventional writer, a non-conformist.*

In "What Does Translation Mean in India?", he raises several significant questions related not only to our multilinguality, but more relevantly, to the bilingual or trilingual strengths of writers and, in some measure, readers. He further makes a distinction between home language, social language and literary language. There is also the accompanying phenomenon of languages travelling from one area to another, and migrations of communities, which adds to their language acquisition.

One of the questions he asks is: How does the fictional presentation transform or affect language? Given the presence of different kinds of characters, their everyday speech has to be transformed for fictional writing. Amidst all these almost infinite levels, how do we define translation and explore its significance? Obviously, not as a one-to-one transference, but, perhaps, more adequately by realising its embeddedness in cultural frameworks.

This essay was first published in a newspaper. I procured it through the courtesy of the author. It has been included in the ***U.R. Ananthamurthy Omnibus****. Ed. N. Manu Chakravorthy. Gurgaon: Arvind Kumar Publishers, 2008.*

What Does Translation Mean in India?

I must try to change our academic notion of the word, 'translation', and make it more homely if I want to make some sense of what I want to say today. Let us look at ourselves in our everyday speech activity. We are most of the time translating from one language to the other. Many of us use at least three languages, one at home, another on the streets, still another at our office. When you narrate to your old mother what happened in your office, you are translating. And vice versa.

This isn't just an aberration of contemporary urban life. I can imagine the Adi Shankara using two languages, Malayalam in Kaladi and Sanskrit everywhere he went. And he travelled quite a lot, from Kanyakumari to Kashmir through a complex web of languages. Anandateertha in Udupi must have used three languages, Tulu at home, Kannada on the streets and Sanskrit everywhere else. Ramanuja was inspired by the low-caste saints, the Alwars of Tamil, but used Sanskrit for his metaphysical speculations.

We live everywhere in India in an ambience of languages. The word, 'mother-tongue', doesn't mean what it means in Europe. Conrad is an exception, writing in an alien tongue. We can count such geniuses in Europe on our fingers. But many of our writers in Kannada, some of them the best in our times, spoke a different language at home. Masti and Putina spoke Tamil at home and the great poet known for his magical use of language, Bendre, spoke Marathi at home. As he once related to me, in his formative boyhood years, he was not even conscious that he spoke two different languages.

This is true of a large number of writers in Hindi who speak Rajasthani, Bhojpuri and many other languages related to Hindi.

The characters in their fiction may be actually speaking these languages, and they are rendered for us in Hindi.

More significant than this in our understanding of what constitutes a text is a unique Indian phenomenon often bypassed—Kalidasa's *Shakuntala* isn't a text in a single language. An early poet of our times in Kannada, Shishunal Sharief has poems where the first line is in Kannada, the second in Telugu and the third in what may be called Urdu. He came from an area where these languages were spoken. As he was a mystical poet of the people, I am sure his immediate audience would understand all these languages and their copresence in the same poem must have made a unique sense to them. They were listening to the silence beyond the spoken word—especially to the silence celebrated in a variety of words.

Along with this free play of languages, which existed in an ambience allowing for shifts and mixtures, and also because of such a free play aside from the hegemonic indications that languages carry with them, the poets of the past in Indian languages could acquire the territory of Sanskrit for their vernaculars. The use of vernaculars never seemed to threaten free communication with others, isolating each language group in its own territory. Such a process of cultural inclusion and quiet synthesis has gone on in India for more than a thousand years. First, if it was the language of the Gods making way for the languages of common people, now it is the official domain of English making way, however reluctantly, to the vernaculars in the process of the empowerment of the people. Translation, oral as well as textual, was the principal mode in the past as well as the present for such negotiations.

When languages which do not travel (as they lack imperial power) still undertake spiritual and intellectual journeys into the experiential richness of other languages (which travel and, therefore, assume universality), then we don't seem to bother much to be literally true to the languages from which we translate. We have to digest anyhow these languages of power, lest they dominate us. We rarely translated the Sanskrit *word-as-mantra*, in which the *shabda* is supposed to be both sound and sense to the believer. But we unhesitatingly adapt and change the narrative texts, even when they are composed in the language of the Gods or of the white men who ruled us. In Kamba's Tamil *Ramayana,* the cursed Ahalya becomes a stone, and not a disembodied voice as in Valmiki's *Ramayana*. And it wasn't Dryden alone who tried to make Shakespearean tragedies into comedies; our early writers in Kannada did it, too. That is why I would like to propose that if India has been able to digest several influences through her long history, it was mainly because of these vernaculars, the unquenchable imaginative hunger of the people who speak these languages.

I must also add here that these are languages with a difference: They have a frontyard of a self-aware literary tradition as well as a backyard of unselfconscious oral folk traditions that have never been discontinued during our millennium. The oral traditions that flourish in the backyard have vigour as well as an unfailing sense of what is alive on the tongues of men and women, without which a literary language can become heavily artificial.

2

I want now to take up some concrete examples in support of my ideas. The coastal Karnataka has a small town called Udupi, a name made familiar by its inhabitants who have opened restaurants all over India. There are at least three languages spoken in and around Udupi. Tulu is the language of a large number of its inhabitants, the peasants and workers, and it is also a language rich in folklore. Not only the lower castes speak it, but a Sanskritised version of it, considered impure by the native Shudra speakers, is spoken as mother tongue by the Brahmins as well. Next to Tulu is Konkani, mainly the language of the trading castes.

Kannada exists in Udupi along with these languages. One could say it is perceived as the language of high culture, whatever that means. Kannada is also the mother-tongue of a large section of people. However, the point I want to make is this. A large body of Kannada literature in the past as well as the present has come from this coastal region. If one encounters a stranger on the streets, the language used for communication is Kannada. But a Tulu or Konkani speaker encountering other speakers of those languages would invariably use the language native to the speaker. Otherwise, it would be considered arrogant behaviour. And almost every one of the native Tulu and Konkani speakers would understand Kannada *and* if he/she happens to be a writer, most probably, the language of choice for writing would be Kannada.

Thus, *Chomana Dudi*, a celebrated novel in Kannada by Shivaram Karanth, is written in Kannada. Choma, the hero of the novel, is an untouchable, and in real life, he would be mostly speaking in Tulu. In fact, one could say much of the novel takes place in the language of Tulu, and the author, Karanth, while writing the novel, is truly translating from Tulu into Kannada.

I wonder if this is not true also of much of the good fiction in English written by us in India. Isn't Salman Rushdie translating from Bombay Hindi in many of his creatively rich passages? The best effects of Arundhati Roy, I feel, lie in her great ability to mimic the Syrian Christian Malayalam. Raja Rao's path-breaking *Kanthapura*, although it is written in English, is truly a Kannada novel in its texture as well as narrative mode—deriving both from the oral traditions of Karnataka. With most of the truly creative Indian novelists in English, who seem to have made a contribution to the way the English language is handled, I would venture to make this remark: For them to create a unique work in English is to transcreate from an Indian language milieu.

3

I want to conclude by speaking a few words about what we often write about these days. I mean 'the politics of translation'. What do we choose to translate from among the Indian texts into English? We often think that we choose the best. This may be so. Yet, there are notions of the 'best' which need to be interrogated.

We not only write in a language, but write into an ethos. Kumara Vyasa, a great poet of the past in Kannada, would have made sense to a contemporary of Chaucer, but today, he would be read if translated into English by a few interested European scholars only. Kannada has a thriving modern literature which would interest a common reader in the west, but Kumara Vyasa is also a part of the literary ethos in Kannada. But Chaucer in England isn't a part of their living literary ethos. As a matter of fact, a non-literate in Karnataka would respond to Kumara Vyasa more genuinely than to a modern writer like me. This makes me feel humble as a writer because Kumara Vyasa has Shakespearean strength in his use of language and is a greater writer than many of us writing into a modern ethos.

Ramanujan is the best of our translators, and when he chose to translate from the past either from Tamil or from Kannada, we should ask the uncomfortable question: Was he influenced by the ethos into which he was translating? Wouldn't a lot of great literature in our languages remain untranslatable if what is good were determined by the literary ethos of the language into which we are translating? I do not know what we can do about it, or, honestly speaking, whether we should do anything about it. For us writing in India, it should never matter what is translatable into English and what would be acceptable in the literary ethos of the west. If we begin to think that what is good is what is eminently translatable into the modern western ethos, we can't be forgiven. Indian literary ethos has space for the ancient as well as the modern, the written as well as the oral. In the silent process of translation as I have defined it earlier, much more of Europe is coming into the Indian languages as living literature than in the other way. I read Saul Bellow as literature, but Premchand is read in the universities of the United States of America for sociological purposes. That is their problem, not ours. But that may well become our problem, too, if we should also globalise and become prisoners of the homogenised modern world system.

Rā Gă Jādhăv

Rā Gă Jādhăv (1932) is a well-known writer and critic and has had a varied professional experience. Beginning as a lecturer in Marathi, he went on to be the Section Editor for Humanities for the Marathi Vishwakosha (Encyclopaedia) Unit of the Government of Maharashtra, a post he occupied for more than two decades.

Jādhăv is a prolific writer and has more than fifty books to his credit, including two volumes of poetry and three of belles-lettres. Amongst his literary criticism, there are three volumes on Dalit writing. Though himself a Maratha, the understanding he extends to Dalit writing is remarkable. The essay included in this collection is one of the most balanced on Dalit aesthetics. Most Dalits, when writing on aesthetics, have a tendency to stay close to Black aesthetics, which, in the long run, is a limiting factor. Dalit aesthetics, as Jādhăv points out, still needs to work more with experiential aesthetics and sift it in order to approach the position of aesthetic detachment.

Rā Gă Jādhăv's three volumes on Dalit writing are titled **Nili Pohat** *(Blue Horizon), 1993. As a critic, he is both a culturist and an aesthete. His work reveals his strong appreciation of the creative expressions resulting out of tensions between culture and art, life and letters. Jādhăv points out the necessity of social freedom for the cultivation of true aesthetic detachment.*

Jādhăv's work has dealt at length with most of the important issues floating in the literary scenario in the last half century. He has been honoured by his peers and was unanimously elected president of the 77th All India Marathi Literature Sammelan in 2004. This essay has been taken from **The Poisoned Bread**. *(Ed. Arjun Dangle. Hyderabad: Orient Longman. 1993)*

Dalit Feelings and Aesthetic Detachment

The organisers of the conference on Dalit literature in 1976 at Nagpur have evinced a proper understanding of the development of literature by formulating a theme that combines social awareness with an aesthetic outlook. During the last decade, a many-sided, serious analysis of Dalit literature was made, but it was not adequately supported by the actual creation of Dalit literature. The situation has improved since then. Dalit creative writing is slowly growing in substance and showing signs of yet more rapid development. The time, therefore, is ripe to raise issues in a concrete way about this literature. So, this seminar is being organised at the right time.

The seminar has made a categorical proposition, but I don't think this should put any constraint on discussion. A proper analysis of Dalit literature may not be possible if we start with the prior assumption that social awareness and an aesthetic outlook are present in it in a natural way. Such assumptions are not helpful to the appreciation, understanding and evaluation of literature. They cannot enlighten and enrich literary taste. Raw and immature literary taste prevents the proper development of literary creation. This is true not only of Dalit literature, but of literature as such. The assumptions have to be analysed. So, it is necessary to consider the quality and extent of social awareness reflected in Dalit literature and also to consider its aesthetic and formal aspects. Fortunately, this can be done on the basis of actual works. Till now, all consideration of Dalit literature was confined to theoretical discussion, arguments and claims. Now, proper examination can be made and the credit goes to the organisers of the seminar.

The proposition implies a proper awareness of the fact that social content and aesthetic form are indivisible in any work of literature. In a literary discussion, first and foremost, the autonomy of a work of literature as a work of literature has to be granted. Even social awareness assumes significance when it is expressed in the proper literary form. In literary criticism, though the content-oriented and form-oriented positions seem to be separate, in actual criticism, they go hand in hand, or at least they should. The social and formal aspects are blended in a work of literature. The blending is organic; where it is not so, both the purposes are defeated.

It is true that Dalit literature is prominently a literature of social awareness. The novels written by Haribhau Apte are novels of social awareness and content. The novels of Dr Ketkar are largely novels of sociological analysis. But such general statements do not advance criticism significantly. For that, it becomes necessary to enter into the formal aspects of literature, and into the mental attitude of the writer. It becomes necessary to study works of art and know about the aesthetic from which social awareness is achieved. Just as it is important to remember that Dalit literature has achieved its distinction as a separate entity mainly on the basis of its social content, it is equally important to bear in mind that this content takes a distinct form with each individual writer and with each of his separate works. Dalit literature has this double dimension and this aspect forms its special feature. The tradition of social awareness lends a quality of realism to Dalit literature.

Fortunately, the whole of Marathi literature has this quality. As such, Dalit literature has inherited the context of an established tradition. It is possible, therefore, to assess the worth of social awareness in the different streams of Dalit literature and the special distinction of each piece of Dalit writing in the light of the achievements of the whole of the Marathi literary tradition. It may be necessary for both these assessments to take into account the norms and criteria of the Marathi critical tradition. In both these respects, established norms will have to be considered. It shall be the mission of Dalit writing to transcend established norms and standards and to create new ideals and norms emerging out of the characteristic social awareness present in Dalit literature. The success of the seminar will depend on the extent to which the consciousness of this task is impressed upon the minds of Dalit writers.

I shall prescribe for my consideration certain limitations so far as the seminar is concerned. I shall keep out the theme of social awareness in Dalit literature and concentrate on the aesthetic aspect alone—in the sense of aesthetic detachment. I shall further restrict my attention to those Dalit writers who have been brought up in Dalit communities. Anna Bhau Sathe, Shankarrao Kharat, Baburao Bagul and Keshav Meshram as narrative writers and Namdeo Dhasal, Arjun Dangle, Daya Pawar, Waman Nimbalkar and Chokha Kamble as poets, come to mind. Forms of literature, which require greater detachment, such as drama and humour, are yet to be taken up by Dalit writers. It is with reference to such forms that aesthetic detachment can be properly considered. It may be that a detached Dalit sensibility is yet to form itself and that is why these forms have not appeared in Dalit literature. This fact can be interpreted in another way. Perhaps, Dalit writers, for certain reasons, fail to acquire the aesthetic detachment necessary to portray social feelings and relationships objectively. It is also possible that the form of drama can appear only in an atmosphere of social freedom and this kind of freedom is also congenial to humour. Perhaps these forms of literature are not as spontaneous as the narrative forms are. An advanced literary culture appears to be necessary for their successful expression. Dalit writers have not secured the benefit of these favourable circumstances.

I think that from the point of view of Dalit aesthetics, the important thing is to achieve aesthetic distance by liberating oneself from extreme involvement in social awareness. It means that the Dalit writers have to realise their total sensibility towards life from the level of art. I know that this is easier said than done. In this connection, I remember the two short novels, *Hakikat* and *Jatayu,* written by Prof. Keshav Meshram. Out of these, *Jatayu,* in my opinion, is more successful. I have been trying to seek the reason for this. At the outset, it appears as if the author is directly involved in the narrative of *Hakikat*. The story is told in the first person. The story of Abhuman Mangewar in *Jatayu,* on the other hand, is presented in a comparatively detached and objective manner. But this is merely a difference of degree; both these short novels are fine specimens of artistic detachment in Dalit literature.

This can be accounted for in many ways. What strikes me most is the literary personality of Prof. Meshram, which is introspective and self-critical. This personality has been exposed to the influences of modernism. It shares the pains and privations of the Dalit community, but is not involved in it. It continuously examines the right or the wrong of things and events. It is its own speaker and listener. It does not address itself to any outside individual or group. It debates and argues only with itself. Such an introspective personality in a writer can naturally maintain artistic detachment. This means that one aim of the aesthetic outlook in literature is to confine the experience of life to one's own sensibility and to realise its worth and meaning for oneself. The remarkable detachment that the writer maintains enables him to present in *Hakikat* and *Jatayu* the picture of Dalit life in a balanced, realistic and critical manner.

Can it be said that this deeply enriched personality was built up naturally? This is simply not possible. Such a personality is to be achieved through deliberate effort. This personality is not rich from birth as it has not received any specific social influence from birth. To achieve a personality like this, it is necessary to undertake a critical examination of social consciousness and feelings. One has to absorb its meaningfulness through reflection and concentration. One does not interpret the form and literary worth of social consciousness by simply laying claim to it. All this leads to the fact that the vague 'feel' of social consciousness has to be coupled with critical understanding. This alone enables one to liberate oneself from the involvement of this 'feel'.

A different kind of aesthetic attitude is seen in Baburao Bagul's stories. Like the stories of C.T. Khanolkar, his stories form themselves through poetic insight. But they tend to become wild and uncontrollable when confronted with the ruthless, awesome reality. The reality which takes shape in his stories fills their external surface with such a thrilling and exciting plenitude of events that it doesn't allow his poetic insight to turn inward. In Khanolkar's stories, his poetic insight seeks every opportunity to turn inward because of his deep concern for the psychological and pathological elements in human existence. Bagul's stories become dramatic as they are embellished with poetic style and poetic comments. It is however felt that Bagul gets too involved with the dramatic content of his stories. Poetic insight has to be natural and spontaneous, but it has also to be disciplined and developed. Mrs Shirish Pai has written a discerning preface to Bagul's collection of stories, *Jeuha Mi Jaat Chorli Hoti (When I had Concealed My Caste).* She states that his stories evoke joy and fear—the joy given by a good story and the fear generated by its content enveloping the mind. But no story can make you introspect. Gruesome reality seen through a poetic vision creates something which should not limit itself only to the catharsis of fear and pity. It is desirable to transform poetic insight and gruesome reality into a wider creative form.

If Bagul agreed to restrain the poet in him, he would be able to penetrate deeper into this fearsome reality. The introductory portions of stories like "*Mala Lokani Nauhe Tar Manune Marle*" ("I was Killed Not by the People but by Manu") and "*Jeuha Mi Jaat Chorli Hoti*" reveal a restrained, but deeper, poetic insight. Manu also acquires a universality here and becomes the symbol of a mysterious but inevitable social destiny. This is also the case with his incomparable story, "*Sood*" ("Revenge"). In this story, the awful nature of reality is illuminated by revolutionary and poetic insight. However, it seems that, generally, the poet in Bagul gets involved in an unprecedented and fearsome reality. The way to resolve this problem is to make one's sensibility of life adequately objective and then to take it to the narrative form. In her preface, Mrs Pai has made a significant suggestion. She wants Bagul to turn from the short story to the novel with its more extensive form.

Poetic insight has the ability to express deeper truths of life. Great literature is not made out of merely the sensational and thrilling aspects of reality. It tries to bring out the abiding significance of things and events. This is the task of Dalit narrative writers endowed with poetic insight.

In narrative writing, the absence of poetic insight can be a virtue as well as a blemish. *Asmitadarsha* publishes stories by young writers, many of which are highly sentimental. Revolt, protest, humiliation and defeat are the broad feelings and experiences presented in these stories. These stories are nearer the lyric form. This kind of social lyricism is, in a way, natural to young writers. The story of a fallen woman in Chokha Kamble's *"Pimpalpan"* ("The Peepul Leaf") is a poetic story or a story-poem. It is necessary to see that all stories of fallen women do not take this form. Narrative literature should possess the eye of poetry, but it should not lose its inner—penetrating and reflective—eye.

The problem of artistic detachment does not figure in Dalit poetry. The world of poetry is a world swayed and swept by emotional surges. The blind alley in which objective Marathi poetry finds itself today can be broken through by Dalit poets. The poems of J.V. Pawar, Namdeo Dhasal, Daya Pawar and Waman Nimbalkar tend to take a narrative turn. In Dalit poetry, the lives of Dalit individuals appear either in the direct narrative, in descriptive form or in an indirect way. Dalit poets face squarely the stories of social injustice and outrage that appear in newspapers and give them passionate poetic expression.

Dalit life is full of such incidents. It is involved in and afflicted by these incidents day and night. Can the poets not realise them into well-knit story-poems? Chokha Kamble's *"Pimpalpan"* deserves special mention in this connection. In the preface to this poem, Durga Bhagwat has observed that the story-poem is an essential part of the Dalit tradition. The young poets can bear this out in the new context. Even in *"Pimpalpan"*, the Dalit in the poet frequently comes out with poetic and emotional comments. Narrative reality cannot speak out freely. Its objective does not get proper expression.

One important reason for this phenomenon is that the social consciousness in Dalit poetry is getting standardised. This poetry is becoming confined to provocative emotional outbursts. It is getting set into the usual moulds of revolt, helplessness and protest. In a way, this is natural. But it has lent the music of repetitive social notes to Dalit poetry. The situation is not different in poetry written by non-Dalit poets. There is a disturbing conformity in the field of Marathi poetry. Poetic sensibility is taking the form of conditioned reflexes. Dalit poets can find their way out of this stalemate with story-poems. Though Dalit feelings are broadly the same, they require distinction in their individual existence. Though emotional truths natural to and implied in poetry are much the same, the experiences on which these are based are different kinds of Dalit misery. So, if poetry turns from the abstract to concrete forms of experience, it can develop through narrative description and the creation of atmosphere. The new emotional equivalences needed for this can develop, perhaps, through objective story-poems.

I may modestly state that this brief account of the aesthetic dimension of Dalit literature, seen from the point of view of artistic detachment, is presented with a sympathetic and impartial mind. I am aware that Dalit literature is deeply immersed in life's struggles. The actual Dalit world is filled with dreadful, terrible, humiliating events and as such the writers cannot escape being tied physically and mentally to this world. Dalit writers are doing the difficult work of portraying this life through personal experience and empathy, absorbing it from all sides in their sensibility. To live this life is painful enough; it can be equally painful to recreate it on the mental level. Dalit writers are deeply involved in this process. It is not easy for them to extricate themselves from it and write. The creation of literature has its own laws and higher literary creation is possible only on the basis of these laws. Those who have the right to say that 'our humanity is our burden' can easily master these rules of literary art. The gift of art can never be as heavy as the burden of humanity.

Translated by **M.D. Hatkanagalekar**

Sitakant Mahapatra

Sitakant Mahapatra (b. 1937), a well-known Oriya poet and writer, is one of the leading intellectuals of our times, presenting an unusual combination of scholarship and public service. In 1961, he joined the Indian Administrative Service and went on to hold several other posts, including the chairmanship of the National Book Trust. Poet, travelogue-writer and essayist, he is the recipient of many an award, including the Bhartiya Jnanpith and the Padma Bhushan. His work and his sensitivity to the Santali tribal culture reflect his deep understanding of social structures.

In the essay selected here, "Indian Culture, Quest for Perspective: Dualities, Resolution and Transcendence", Mahapatra's concern is with the plural tradition(s) we have in India and to locate our attitudes to the past both in terms of history and the problems of the present. Written almost at the end of the twentieth century, in this essay, he reviews the ideologies that have made the present and the events that have acted as a conduit between our earlier problems and the ones we are now faced with in this global world.

Suffused with the spirit of modernity, it seeks to establish an interface between tradition(s) and modern technologies, political shifts and the collapsing of the nation state. How important a direct confrontation is for the writer becomes evident when we mark the shift from conventional spiritual attitudes, which held tradition to be sacrosanct, to more interrogative stances. Mahapatra questions both its singularity and its existence as a static category, especially now that old power centres are yielding place to new ones.

As the essay progresses, issues of time, mortality and history are discussed both in the Indian context and with reference to European thinkers, placing them in comparative frameworks. Layers and layers of the unseen patterns of our tradition are unveiled—oral, folk, religious—along with its perpetual headache persistent in the caste system as Mahapatra argues in favour of a fresh approach to tradition, one which refutes the unnatural separation between tradition and action, and goes on to put into practice the organic nature of its thought. In all our shortcomings, it is we who are collectively guilty.

Indian Culture

*Quest for Perspective – Dualities, Resolutions and Transcendence**

Indian culture presents unprecedented and complex challenges to anyone seeking to understand its dynamics. This is true not only for non-Indian scholars, but also for Indian intellectuals who live their lives immersed in their own tradition. Possibly, it is truer to speak of Indian traditions rather than a tradition as it is not a single monolithic one. These traditions, which form the bedrock of its culture, often bristle with contradictions, some of them seemingly irreconcilable. Indian culture, for this very reason, is both highly eclectic and integrative. It has always sought to resolve dualities and dichotomies at a higher level. Its capacity for transcendence has to be fully understood so that one is not lost in the forest of contradictions. It is necessary to briefly discuss some of the contradictions between its metaphysical concerns and the social praxis and the cultural approach to certain eternal truths of life like time and death. A look at its art-history, which combines erotic symbolism with transcendence, its complex social structure, and its occasional flair for equality and for being anti-structure is equally necessary. Its highly structured caste system also deserves analysis. Finally, there is need for a highly flexible methodology for the critical discourse so necessary for the task of rethinking on the various facets of its complexity.

II

Any culture like that of India, which has grown over the centuries on the bedrock of a great tradition and a host of little

* Unpublished essay, courtesy of the author.

traditions surrounding it, generates a large number of contradictions, ambivalences, uncertainties and dialectic oppositions within its fold. In the case of India, the latter are so many and so complex that, sometimes, it may even appear doubtful whether there is a unity which connects these apparently diverse streams—an integrity or a specific identity. Multiculturalism is the word often employed in this context. All of us have heard from Milton Singer of what happens when a 'Great Tradition' modernises. We have also heard from Srinivas of the processes of Sanskritisation and Westernisation. Add to all these, the prevailing churnings of liberalisation and globalisation and that would complete the landscape of myriad nuances of confounding intellectual ambience, patterns of thought and dialectics. No wonder it becomes difficult to separate the conflicting strands, hold them apart, examine and then determine what kind of ongoing challenges are generated in the process of action and interaction and what kind of responses are forthcoming. It would be necessary to remember that not all the responses may be clear cut or well spelt out. Some of them may be as confusing and complex as the challenges they are supposed to respond to. Some responses may still be inarticulate and slowly forming themselves and struggling to achieve a measure of clarity and definiteness. It is, therefore, necessary to try and unravel some of these complexities, seek to understand them and only briefly point to the many and various levels at which contradictions appear.

First, let us look at the conflict between Indian culture's metaphysics and the social reality. You may speak that all human beings are children of god and, hence, by implication, equal and brothers and sisters. But then you may practise the caste system with all its stratifications.

Such equality in social terms, as different from equality before the law, can be before god, maybe also after death, but here and now, in this world, I am a Brahmin and you are a Shudra or an untouchable. The bedrock of Hinduism may be tolerance for each other, to accept the legitimacy of all faiths, all religions, and yet there could be conflict between the practitioners of different religious faiths. If Hinduism is infinitely absorbent like the ocean, it also throws up on the shore of that ocean all the garbage that various sects, litanies, liturgies and rituals throw into it. Indian metaphysics may speak of the ultimate reality being one, but the popular pantheon may incorporate three hundred and thirty million gods and goddesses. Both should be correct because have not we known that *ekah sad bipra bahudha bhavanti*—the one becoming the many. If a grand spectacle of over-reaching tolerance, brotherhood and respect for the 'other' is a reality, so too are the intrusions of conflicts, violence, turbulence and intolerance generated by many new influences.

Indian society sometimes throws up images of intolerance, barbarity and shocking lack of consideration for others, which totally negate the cherished values of tolerance, of universal brotherhood and of the whole world being one family, much as of humaneness, tolerance, concern for others, compassion and brotherhood. One can say they are aberrations, but how and why do such aberrations happen? Are they not the challenges emerging out of the manifold contradictions within the system that need to be faced and not swept under the carpet?

Years ago, in Orissa's Dhenkanal district, at a place called Rentlei, a fake sadhu acquired the reputation of curing people of diseases and thousands converged there from all parts of the state. The farce ended in a tragedy with the death of hundreds of innocents. Nietzsche had pronounced the death of god. But such godmen abound today even if gods do or do not exist. Sometime back, I read in a couple of local newspapers about two separate incidents of the appearance of Siva. In one case, he appeared in an earthen cooking vessel placed on the hearth in village Mirzapatna (of Mahanga P.S. in Cuttack district) in the form of not one but six *Sivalingams* (daily newspaper *Sambad* dated 14–11–1997). The next day, the news spread like wildfire, hundreds gathered, there was worship, offerings made, *bhajan* and *kirtan* followed, and naturally, some profit came to some people. In another instance in Mayurbhanj district, village

Itighar, rumour spread that milk was flowing from the cut piece of a bamboo pole which one Jitendra Mohanty had kept for thatching his house, that the milk had a strange aroma and, on the same night, his wife dreamt of Siva telling her that he had come to the village at that spot. Once again, Siva worship started by treating that bamboo as Lord Siva and thousands converged and some funds were gathered by some people (daily newspaper *Samaya* dated 21–5–1997). It is easy to ignore these superstitions of an illiterate society. True, but the roots go deeper and reach into the depths of 'faith', the social psychology of *punya* or virtue, and the possibility of many manifestations of the Supreme Lord.

So, the Vedic Rudra and the puranic Siva and the folk Mahadev or the *Sivalinga* of Orissa villages were of a piece and the last incarnation was when the Lord was reappearing, once in a cooking vessel and the other time in a bamboo pole. And some people implicitly believed and prayed and made offerings as others gathered some profit. The nature of the many faces of faith in Indian culture deserves to be studied in depth from such instances to locate the present variants of Richard Lannoy's *The Speaking Tree*. Most private transport vehicles in the state bear the name of some local folk goddess or other. Sometimes one may wonder that there are so many goddesses or *thakurani* spread over the state. It may be one way of attracting passengers. Parents can cut the throat of their three-year-old child, which is offered as a sacrifice to a goddess, either because they had been so ordained by the goddess herself in a dream, or some soothsayer had advised them that way. Maybe the parents are deeply religious and otherwise very compassionate. Instances can be multiplied. All of them point only to the various levels of contradictions within Indian culture. They symbolise complexities, contradictions and conflicting ideas and beliefs. Briefly, they represent the contradiction between its metaphysics, its philosophical traditions and its social reality, group praxis. Such conflicts are at almost all levels of individual and social life, economic and social values, religious and ritual traditions. This world and the other world, strong attachments and detachment, eroticism and asceticism—all of them coexist in the ocean that is Indian culture. It is more than ever necessary to understand the challenges of these contradictions and the responses that have traditionally been prevalent and the ones that are now being offered or even being formulated.

III

One may look at the way Indian culture viewed the two central verities in human existence: time and death. India did not allow much of philosophic significance to history or rather *time as history*. It was more preoccupied with being. History, on the other hand, was, by definition, the realm of created becomings and, hence, only a form of non-being. But it is necessary to remember that Indian culture also sought to examine the meaning of history. The outline for such analysis was what Western philosophy calls 'being-in-the-world' or 'being-in-a-situation', both of which are not very different from the approach of Sartre and the existentialists. *Yoga, Vedanta* and *Buddhism*—all of them emphasised the essential and the inevitable *relativity of everything* and hence the non-reality of all situations and all conditions. Hence, if time was eternity, the immeasurable and the Ultimate Reality had no beginning and no end and, hence, was outside Time. Time also was history, of human destiny, of the succession of day and night, the seasons, the phases of life, of death and new beginnings, and the punctuations in the endless cycle of Becoming. Hence, time was both eternity and history. In fact, the concept of the relativity of Time that Einstein taught us was practised in its quaint fashion in the Indian philosophical system. Human time was different from god's or Brahma's time. *Brahma Varsha, Deva Varsha,* the Yugas, each of which was on a varying time scale, were concepts built into the system. In fact, the Indian perception had a lot of scientific basis. For example, the duration of a day on our earth is so little compared to what is a 'day' on Jupiter or Neptune. The span of our day is determined by the revolution of our planet earth round the sun. Going further, one may speak of the sun itself revolving around a huge galactic space and, therefore, a solar day, that is, a day for the sun (if there was such a day) would be immeasurable, almost inconceivably larger than us. Even on our tiny planet, as it hurtles round the sun in the pristine dark, we have nearly equal or varying lengths of day and night defining the seasons, while the Arctic zone has the 'midnight sun', six months' day and six months' night. That only emphasises the relativity of time, which is not merely a Western or modern scientific concept. It was a concept applied in its own way in the Indian measurement of time.

Indian culture as an inclusive system of high complexity has evolved its own mechanism of reconciling binary oppositions. On one hand, it has been instinctive, emotionally feminine in its languor, laziness and elegance, other-worldly, mystical, mythical, superstitious and world-denying, obsessed with personal salvation, time as eternity and with the hereafter and the beyond. From another point, it has also within its fold elements that are cognitive, rational, masculine in its energy and pragmatism, historical, emphasising the here and now, obsessed with this world and what it offers and denying anything beyond it and beyond the body and the sense perceptions. In short, the quality of Indian traditions is a surprising reality. It always had an aura of ambivalence, absence of rigidity and a large measure of eclecticism.

We should also remember that India and the West have viewed death differently. For the West, death was a definitive end, a finality—a state from which there was no return. It looked upon death as a full stop and not a punctuation mark, and tried to overcome the anxiety it created by insulating it from day-to-day living. Slowly, it became a dirty word, something to be forgotten, to be kept away, with great difficulty and sustained efforts in lonely old age homes, hospital corridors or equally lonely homes. It was neither a new beginning as in Hinduism or Buddhism, nor a mere stage in the ever-recurring process of living. As per the sanctified ritual, when a person died, he was to be bathed, anointed and sent away with precisely those things that he loved in life. For was he not beginning a new journey only? And the ancients, the dead ancestors, had a role to play in the world of living. They were propitiated, offerings were made to them. Thus, for India, death was not nothingness, not an abyss, not a blank wall. It was neither definitive nor absurd. Seen in the Eastern perspective, it was homologous with the dialectical moment of the discovery of the final illusory character of everything or *maya*. For non-existence was only a mode of perceiving the void. Buddhism went further to assert it as nirvana, as release from the ever-recurring cycle of life. Death was only an opportunity to take us nearer to this final release by enabling yet another lease to time in which to work towards that end. It may not be out of place to mention here the classical Egyptian pharaohs, their mummies and all the precious wealth that was buried with them in the pyramids at Giza and Luxor, inviting tomb-raiders in search of that wealth. They believed in a life after death. So did the Chinese emperor who, not satisfied with carrying the wealth of the empire into a new birth, buried with him hundreds of terracotta soldiers at Xian, who were to fight his wars.

IV

Perhaps, Indian culture is one which, more than any other, has sought to establish a remarkable continuity between the classical, the folk and even the tribal; between the *desi* and the *margi*, between scriptural religion, folk religion and tribal religion. The tradition also never recognised any binary opposition between religion and superstition. It would appear Indian culture is not the same as Hindu culture and they should be viewed as two different interacting entities even though quite a bit of the former's structure has been determined by the latter. Speaking of the latter, Sontheimer, the German scholar, says: 'Hindu tradition has an organic view of the cosmos and does not make an absolute distinction between the divine and human, the sacred and profane. What is the transcendent source of all existence and value is at the same time the immanent essence of all things in the universe. As a consequence, there is no absolute distinction between good and evil; rather, we must say that there is a sliding scale between those polar opposites.' Sontheimer has studied how the formless Vedic Rudra has been transformed first into the classical Siva and then into Mahadev and his various folk tribal forms, celebrated in various shapes of *lingams* and designated variously as Khandoba, Murukan, Vyagreshwar, et cetera. In fact, the names are many and varied, taking on some particular aspect of Siva. In a state like Orissa, for example, which has seen a rich Saivite tradition, the city, Bhubaneswar, has a very large number of temples bearing different names.

Sontheimer is right in emphasising that scriptural or high religion and folk religion, including tribal religion, should be seen as complementary, an organic whole and not exclusive to each other—that monotheism and polytheism are not incompatible with each other and folk religion should not be written off as magic and superstition and not considered to be true Hinduism. Unfortunately, we view and study tribal folk and scriptural religions as separate entities and Vedic literature and other scriptures are interpreted with the help of all kinds of extraneous, sometimes far-fetched, theories. Sometimes the folk, the tribal and the scriptural are either ignored or considered as extraneous, marginal and irrelevant as far as Indian tradition is concerned.

V

A culture (or cultures) is structured on a set of values, belief systems and social processes, which anchor it and give it meaning and significance. Social anthropologists often use the term, ritual, to describe the social processes and activities through which the structure is formed and rendered visible. A structure has thus the qualities of a frame. Often, it is well-defined, with parameters laid out and concepts and meanings 'given'. Indian tradition has several aspects which are not only unstructured, but are in fact anti-structure.

One can take two instances: the Holi festival associated with Krishna and extremely popular in North India, and the annual Rath Yatra at Puri, when the triad, Jagannath, Balaram and Subhadra, are taken out of the temple in three chariots on *Badadanda,* or the main street of Puri. Holi as a festival is based on the temporary breakdown of class and caste barriers. On this occasion, the humblest and the lowly can splash colours on the mighty and the high-ups. Class and caste distinctions seem to disappear on this occasion and everyone seems to be at one level. This great levelling is in the nature of an anti-structure and the festival has been very well studied by social anthropologists from that point of view. The same is true of the Rath Yatra of Puri. If the Rath Yatra or the Car Festival of Lord Jagannath is a ritual, then it is based on ritual as anti-structure, a syndrome of symbols that embraces almost the whole gamut of human emotions and endeavours. The Car Festival perhaps symbolises this luminal phase of the ritual system in which the all-powerful Gajapati King sweeps the area in front of the chariots before the swirling multitude and the Lord of the Universe leaves the cloistered seclusion of the dimly-lit sanctum sanctorum, the litanies of the nearly secret forms of aristocratic worship, to sit on the wooden chariots in full view of the humble and the lowly and listen to their strange orchestra of private prayers and supplications. This is indeed a form of supreme *communitas*, an egalitarian relationship between persons stripped of status and property. 'Liminality,' as Prof. Victor Turner explains, 'implies that the high could not be high unless the low existed, and he who is high must experience what it is like to be low. For individuals and groups, social life is a type of dialectical process that involves successive experience of high and low, *communitas* and structure, homogeneity and differentiation, equality and inequality.' The achievement of a degree of *statuslessness* by abolishing in one sweep of a symbolism all the multiple personal, group and class identities is, perhaps, the most significant aspect of Jagannath culture. It is based on a concept of submissiveness and silence that lifts grace to the level of a mutual contract between the godhead and the individual. The latter has a prior claim on the godhead. As a matter of fact, the more lowly the individual, the more urgent and pressing his tragic condition, and the greater his demand on the Supreme Lord.

These two extremely popular and participatory festival occasions delineate how Indian culture embraces the ritual system both as structure and anti-structure, adding a strange complexity to it.

VI

Any attempt to redefine Indian culture has also to contend with the past and present of the caste system, which was and has been one of the major aspects of traditional Indian social structure and, perhaps, its most intricate. We have known about what is called India's original four castes. In the *Gita*, the Lord says, 'I have created four *Varnas* by the division of *guna* and *karma* (life quality and ordained duty).' There have been discussions relating to them and the historical formations in subsequent ages of the innumerable subcastes. Discussions have also centred on caste exclusivism and the lowering or breaking up of the barriers with modern education and the modern political and economic system. We are aware of the brilliant work on the subject by Professors Francis Shu, Louis Dumont and M.N. Srinivas. The Chicago School also did a number of theoretical studies on the system. One other kind of attempt to interpret caste is the book, *Untouchable,* by John Freeman, which projects the caste system through biography. All these studies have contributed to our overall understanding of the system. Years ago, Hutton had done primary work on the subject. For him, 'a caste system was one whereby a society is divided up into a number of self-contained and completely segregated units (castes), the mutual relations between which are ritually determined in a graded scale.' Prof. Edmund Leach, in his study, felt that 'there is nothing peculiar to Indian caste. Internally a caste presents itself to its members as a network of kin relationships, but this network is of no specific type', and the kinship systems of caste-oriented societies is not easily understood by societies historically unconnected with the Indian world. It was, however, necessary to fully explicate the concept of 'hierarchy', which originally seems to have the notion of a religious gradation. The most important definition of this concept of hierarchy came from Prof. Dumont, who said that as applied to the caste system, it is 'a principle of gradation of elements in a whole with reference to the whole, it being understood that in most societies, it is religion which provides the view of the whole, and that the gradation will thus be intrinsically religious'. The whole question of purity and pollution has been discussed in relation to the caste system. But in the modern context, caste has lost its earlier relevance and has also intermingled with the new concepts of economic class and general classification of affluence and poverty as well as levels of education. The tradition of looking at caste either as *jati* or *varna* and as linked to a *jajamani* system has, therefore, lost much of its relevance. McKim Marriott studied it when, in the mid-1950s, it had relevance, but today, Indian social ethics has to look into the new idea of community, Panchayati Raj, middle class consumerism and affluence integrate caste into the entire social structure, which is undergoing transformation. Way back in 1932, Dr Ambedkar had made the loaded remark, 'Mahatmas have come and Mahatmas have gone, but untouchables have remained untouchables.' It happened to be a part of the statement he had made thinking of a separate electorate for the depressed classes. If the caste system was given academic sanction in the hoary past by Manu, today in the India of the twenty-first century, namely, when universalisation and parochialisation have almost uninterruptedly gone on, it needs a rethink. The former has an upward movement and the latter, a downward movement. Like little communities and greater communities, or like Little Traditions and the Great Tradition, one has to think how to redefine tradition around the upward and downward movement referred to above in the social fabric and integrate them into the new socialisation process. It would be yet another challenging task in rethinking Indian culture.

VII

Indian culture has a very intense and deep aesthetic orientation. Its long and celebrated art history reflects its tradition and thought in a very vivid way. This history has an organic unity and a remarkable continuity both in time and space and also in genre. The same motifs and symbols could be painted, could be expressed in poetry, carved in stone sculptures, or incorporated into dance patterns. The essence of this history from Gandhar art to Moghul art, Hindu and Buddhist art and art of later times, particularly in Hindu temple sculptures, sought to discern the patterns of human lives and man's cultural self-image. As Lannoy says, 'However abstruse we may find Indian thought and religion, its art makes a direct appeal to the senses. It can be intensely metaphysical without being abstract. It affirms that there is no reality which is not divine, and furthermore, that there is no reality except that which is immediately apprehended. For the West, God and man are, according to the *Bible,* distinct: Man is the image of God; the world, nature, animals, men and women are not within the same sphere of divinity, but outside it. In India, on the contrary, everything is a manifestation of the divine substance. The richness of its mythological imagery is proof of this instinctive, deeply-rooted outlook. Its subject is indeed the divine, but since the divine is in all creation, we know from such works of art how men responded to the life around them, and discerned in the chaos of experience an underlying unity.' The erotic sculptures of Konark and Khajuraho, for example, have been looked upon as possibly a delineation of the other approach of attaining salvation or self-realisation through *bhoga,* where *prakriti* and *purusha* are in interlocked equilibrium. They are supposed to be based on a life affirmation and celebration of the elemental energy of the sun and life as whole. Sometimes, critics have lost track between the *Vedanta* and the *Kama Sutra,* instead of recognising their duality, which Indian culture easily transcended. It was only a higher order of resolution of the spirit and the flesh, of rejection and affirmation, of celebrating life and denying it.

In his Preface to *The Speaking Tree,* Lannoy observes: 'What India requires is not a kind of static hierarchical equilibrium between tradition and modernity; growth arises from conflict, from the open, as distinct from the covert and apologetic acceptance of incessant struggle. So long as social reconstruction is founded on the ideals of an open society, whatever is valuable in tradition will, in fact, survive and grow; what has ceased to be viable in a modern context will then be abandoned. In this way, there is no danger of India losing its identity; on the contrary, it will become more itself. But this is no panacea, for a society remade will ever remain a society to be remade—in tireless experiment (xvii).

What Lannoy says of Indian society applies equally well to Indian culture. A culture or tradition remade will ever remain a culture or cultures to be remade. This remaking will be born out of relooking at it and redefining it, and hence is extremely difficult. For apart from the past and its burden and heritage value, there are also the new challenges of a new era, the new millennium. Such a task would not only involve relooking at social structure, aesthetics and art history, or the approach to eternal verities like time and death and the colonial legacy, but also to its assimilative, integrative mechanisms, its strategies of integrating affirmation and rejection, of the here and hereafter and time and eternity, of eroticism and asceticism, of the natural fear of death and the patient and happy waiting for it on the shores of the Ganges at Varanasi.

References

Dumont, L. *Homo Hierarchicus*, Paris (1967).

Lannoy, Richard. *The Speaking Tree*, Oxford University Press, London (1971).

Leach, E.R. (ed.) *Aspects of Caste in South India, Ceylon and North-West Pakistan*, Cambridge University Press, Cambridge (1960).

Marriott, McKim. *Village India: Studies in the Little Communities*, Chicago University Press (1955).

Sontheimer, G.D. "Scriptural Religion & Flok Religion in India" in *The Realm of the Sacred PY* (ed.), Sitakant Mahapatra, Oxford University Press, Delhi (1992).

Turner, Victor W. *The Ritual Process: Structure and Anti-structure*, Aldine Publishing Company, Chicago (1968).

Mridula Garg

Mridula Garg (b. 1938) is one of Hindi literature's most eminent writers. She broke new ground with form and content in her early stories like "Hari Bind" and "Daffodils Jal Rahe Hain", and novels like ***Uske Hisse Ki Dhoop*** *and* ***Chittacobra*** *in the 1970s.*

She is never averse to experimenting with new forms to suit the diversity of her themes. They vary from suspension of female guilt ***(Uske Hisse Ki Dhoop*** *and* ***Chittacobra)****, the throttling hold of the joint family (****Vanshaj****), the merging of the personal and political against the backdrop of the Independence movement of India (****Anitya****), the conflict between the creative and humane urge (****Main Aur Main****), and the male/female confrontation with its resolution in the concept of Ardhnareeshwara (****Kathgulab****). Her latest novel (****Miljul Man****) is part memoir and part fiction, set in the age of innocence of a newly independent India.*

Freedom is the undercurrent in most of Garg's work, both for the individual and society. She deals with the predicament inherent in the exercise of choice, and the courage of conviction needed to adhere to it. In the process, the individual and society come together as an integrated whole. Memory plays a significant role in Garg's works, be it fiction, travel accounts or discursive essays.

Garg has written in almost every genre—seven novels, three plays, four collections of essays, a travel memoir and short stories now available in two volumes called ***Sangati-Visangati****—in addition to being a distinguished columnist. Recipient of the Vyas Samman (2004), Garg has also moved beyond literary awards to get the Helmann-Hammet Grant from Human Rights Watch.*

"Word as Censor" was first published in ***Economic and Political Weekly*** *(April 29, 2000), and in it, Garg comments on the*

social and moral controls that are imposed on expression of ideas through language. The established norms, usages, codes acceptable to a wider public become hegemonic in themselves. Words too carry their own ambiguity and gender biases, thus creating barriers for the woman writer. The question then is: How does it all measure up in terms of freedom of expression, creativity and gender? These are some of the issues Garg addresses, pointing out that the creative writer has to constantly struggle against such taboos, resist control, face criticism and still continue to invent new languages in order to express new and individual stances.

Word as Censor

Some censorship is inherent in the use of language. Cultural hegemony declares some words to be decent, others, indecent, and goes on to control meaning and thought. In this paper, I propose to examine how the power structure has changed over time to make the graph of control more complex and subliminal. The weapon used is always the word. Starting from direct blotting out of certain words, it has gone on to reduce the shades of meaning a word could have, and finally, a divorce of word from meaning.

Religious leadership has been the first source of censorship. Since initially, all art and literature, whether folk or classical, was inspired by religious thought, excellence of the word came to be associated with the worship of God. Those words and expressions that questioned this were termed blasphemous and obscene. Swear words or abusive terms thus may be considered the barometer of what is considered obscene and indicate which sections of a society bear the main brunt of its censorship. Swear words like damn, what the hell, devil take you, et cetera, were once considered offensive in Christian communities. They were used in literature to take on religion or god. The making of literature is, in fact, a continuous battle between the accepted scene and the obscene.

Non-Indians often ask why Hindi (perhaps other Indian languages too) does not have equivalent swear words. It might be because the other older religions, including the various branches of the Hindu religion, prevailing here, did not possess a well-ordered set of commandments or do's and don'ts. God, in his innumerable manifestations, had so many human attributes that 'taking him on' became a highly complex matter. It could not be settled by compressing the blasphemous references to god or the devil in a succinct swear word. That is not to assert that the complex religious system of India ensured a greater freedom of expression. It did not! All that happened was that godhood became enshrined in the principle of 'Shivam Satyam Sundaram'. Very broadly, it came to mean that all literature and art was expected to sublimate the baser instinct and cast out ugly, transient and evil thoughts and desires from the minds of both the creator and the receiver of an art work. It worked well as long as no individual or community asked, what is base or ugly? And why should you decide for us? We want to do our own research, formulate our own rules, define our own moral codes and aesthetic canons.

In reality, any attempt to redefine the parameters of the omniscient three S's was considered a kind of blasphemy. What is meant in actual terms was that the less powerful sections of the society, the non-Brahmins, the poor and the women found it impossible to challenge the moral and aesthetic codes, and so could not give expression to their inner world. It is easy enough to see that their inner world would be in conflict with the three S's promulgated by an essentially inequitable power structure.

If we look at the abusive words generally used in India, this assertion gains further evidence. The majority of the *gaalis* used here denigrate women and have sexual connotations. Men fight each other, but the abuses they hurl—*'saala'*, *'bahenchot'*, *'haraami'*, son of a bitch, to quote the mildest—all question the sexual mores of the women related to them, whom the opponent has never known or seen. This is not, of course, peculiar to India. Only here, to be found wanting in sexual rectitude is a greater insult. A further irony is that these terms are forbidden to women. They are *'mardaana gaalis'*. Many a woman writer in Hindi has been pilloried for daring to use a *mardaana gaali*.

There is nothing surprising in this since religious censorship placed the main onus of maintaining the sanctity and purity of everything, including language, on women. The other power structures, when they took over from religion, kept this constraint intact.

The fact that more and more women writers these days use *mardaana gaalis* is nothing to rejoice about. It is still the women who continue to be demeaned and defined as sex objects. If, of course, a different connotation can be given to a *gaali*, and its usage in that sense comes to be accepted, it may turn the tables. As for example, if *'haraami'* is used in the sense of a *'haraamkhor'*, when referring to a man, it will mean a dastard instead of a bastard, a corrupt and dishonest profligate, condemnable for himself, and not for the sexual conduct of his mother. The other brand of *gaalis* commonly used in India denigrate the so-called lower castes of Dalits. *'Bhangi'*, *'chamar'* and *'kamjaat'* are used here as terms of abuse, in the same way as 'nigger' or 'kafir' are used in other societies.

Religious hegemony placed not only the onus of constraint on women, but also the brunt of observing its rites and rituals. If you look around you, you'll see that even today, it's the women of the family who perform the various meaningless meaningful rituals of our innumerable fasts and festivals, marriages, births and deaths. Men may opt out in the name of liberality, but women seldom do.

Since one essential characteristic of all decadent cultures is the reduction of religion to rituals, it's not surprising that the affluent women of modern India, particularly the female folk of the new rich business class, have become mired in the performance of excessive rituals. They do it with the arrogant assertion that in doing so, they are preserving our ancient culture. What exactly is this culture? It is usually defined simply as something that has been there from times immemorial. It is high time we pondered over this deadly phrase and realised how potent it has been in curbing dissent and original thinking in our country. Invoking the phrase to justify our actions is like saying it is so because it was so and, therefore, must continue to be. It eschews the need for rational rethinking and, without rethinking, there can be no freedom of expression or revamping of language as its medium. So, the sacrosanct 'times immemorial' and the three S's ensured that even after temporal power took over in India, religious dictate continued to hold sway over language.

Fascism and Censorship

The shift from religion to temporal power hegemony worked differently for different cultures, bringing in the next source of censorship. The advent of temporal power marked the beginning of a variety of political philosophies and systems of governance. Monarchies-cum-oligarchies gave way to democratic and socialist communist states. Though the underlying principle of equality and justice, with an equal share in governance for all, remained largely theoretical, universal suffrage and a modicum of social welfare and greater awareness of their rights by the weak did come into existence. But dictatorships did not come to an end. Absolute monarchies gave way to other kinds of totalitarian states—military, ideological and fascist. The difference between the ideological and fascist dictatorships was that while fascism had no political ideology other than that of the alleged superiority of a race, caste or creed, ideological dictatorships came into being as distortions of an ideal. A lot of the communist regimes fall in this category.

What was common to all dictatorships was some form of distortion of the word. All of them engineered a language which turned the phrases of approbation and disapproval into bombastic clichés. The overemphatic and melodramatic use of both the positive and the negative distorted the meanings of the words used. It made the false sound true and the unreal seem real. Language no longer remained a tool for expressing what one felt. It was meant to say what was considered correct by the party or the leader or the cultural dictate.

We must remember that all reform movements face this danger, of overemphasis on the use or non-use of certain words at a time when the movement has lost its initial zeal and has fallen into the hands of the opportunists, losing the genuine support of the people in the process. Jargon is a two-edged sword. It may lull the sensibilities and thus command the following of a half-awake people. But sooner or later, it begins to arouse resistance and denial. In the modern advertising parlance, this is known as overkill. I can't help feeling that the collapse of the communist regimes within seven decades was as much due to the reduction of language into jargon, through repetitions, overused words, as to other distortions in the political economy. I quote here from my book, *Chittacobra*, written twenty years ago:

> As long as there was a God, man sinned and put the responsibility of punishment on God. When God died, man became responsible for everything. The society continued as it was because man civilised himself. When we reach the zenith of civilisation, all our crimes will be committed in unison with proper confabulation and mutual consent, to the sound of popular approbation. Was Germany not at the peak of its civilisation in 1939? As for England, it had become civilised centuries ago.

In the so-called liberal democracies, the distortion of the word was practised mainly through the election campaigns. Hyperbole was used to sway the voters in a particular direction. The difference lay in the power that the voter could wield after the campaign was over. Where the individual voter was assured of a certain minimum standard of living and education, he had the theoretical competence to evaluate his representatives after the belligerence of the campaign was over. Whether he exercised it or not depended upon many other factors. Though the elected could not be recalled for a number of years, the people did possess the freedom to express their continuous re-evaluation during that time. Words were their only weapon to prevent the chosen ones from turning into demi-gods. So, aggressive and investigative journalism flourished in these societies, continuously reassessing the language of control. But it was left to literature to question hyperbole and hysteria, to break the taboos placed on words and to cherish and multiply their subtle nuances.

It trained people to distinguish between the multiple meanings of words, and therefore, between propaganda and the truth. By not insisting on only one version of the truth, only one meaning of a word, literature liberates the individual and helps him look for the truth on his own.

Where the individual voters were placed unequally in society, with the majority, poor and silent, the power of evaluation came to be vested in a small section of society. Language continued to be under its control. The agreement of the majority was taken for granted in the same way as in fascist states. In the equitable Indian democracy, it suited the political elite to perpetuate the bogies created by religion. It continued to be a part of the enslavement of language, which was used to the detriment of Dalits and women. Even a commonly accepted leader like Gandhiji felt the need for religion to buttress his following. To call Dalits Harijans or god's people, to make their good treatment an act of piety or godliness, was to gloss over the inherent inequity of our social and religious system. So deep-rooted is the principle of inequality in our psyche that progressive writers refer to a great Hindi novelist as 'Upanyaas Samrat'. One has never heard of any 'Emperor King of the Novel' anywhere else in the world.

The laws of aesthetics are not, we know, immutable like the laws of physics, but they are made out to be so in order to control the rebels. Even today, when so much of Dalit and woman writing is about, we are told by critics that this writing can be treated with sympathy for a while, till it refines itself enough to be judged by the accepted canons of aesthetics. What sophistry! How can people writing from a totally different realm of experience and sensibility conform to any established canons of excellence? Will not the canons themselves undergo a sea-change?

The language of a written work first expresses itself in choosing a particular area of experience. The mode of the use of words, with appropriate silences and pauses, arises out of this choice. When the area of experience is an unknown quantity for the reader, he or she can relate to it in two different ways.

He can take it to be the truth of the writer and savour it from within the parameters of the literary work. If he then finds an inner logic or sense of beauty in it, it will help him, ultimately, to empathise with the life experience or the world view freshly expressed in it. Or he can continue to search for the truth vested in his collective memory. Then, when he finds the book is plotting an entirely different course, he is bound to feel irritated. As a critic, he is required to channelise his anger. The most common way of doing it is to assert that the writer, most often a woman, is not giving spontaneous expression to her experienced world. She is consciously creating a symbolic world out of the deliberations of her mind. A mind they would rather a woman did not possess. The main problem lies in the refusal of the critic to recognise that there can be many different realms of experience, and as many ways to perceive them, cerebrally and sensually.

The more liberal of the critics have come round to admitting that new canons need to be devised to judge the new, subversive writing. The problem is that they want to apply them selectively to hitherto marginalised writing only. Such an attitude makes a mockery of the whole idea of a critique. If something so revolutionary is happening in literature that it requires new canons, does it not logically follow that they have to be applied to all new writing, whether of the privileged or the underprivileged? Better still, should not the canons be kept open-ended so that they can admit of the differences in perceptions as and when they appear in literature? And they are bound to appear continuously—that is what literature is all about.

It is no use condemning the critics as male or chauvinistic. The critics being female or Dalit will not necessarily change things. As long as writing continues to be linked to the sex, race, caste or religion of the writer, it is in danger of demanding conformity to a unilateral perception. We must remember that non-conformity and rebellion create their own prisons of political correctitude. We have seen it happen on a large scale in the US. It is now becoming rampant in India. Today, the censorship of literature comes not only from the privileged power centres, but also from 'the collectives of the unempowered margins, seeking empowerment'. I use this euphemism deliberately to highlight the insidious effect of taboos on the use of words. Otherwise, I could simply say women or Dalits or minorities without fear of being misunderstood or being politically incorrect.

It requires courage and self-introspection to recognise the danger of swinging to the other extreme—of treating all women or Dalit writers as similar, belonging to the same tribe, clan or ghetto, and subject to a unilateral realm of experience, sensibility and world view. If we want to question the censorship of words with honest intent, we have to be courageous and question ourselves first.

At the moment, when I write, as a woman, I am not only likely to be persecuted by the male Brahmin bastions of power, but also by my fellow feminists and non-Brahmins because I dare to question some of their ardent beliefs. Asking questions, probing the answers, admitting a wide variety of opinions, seeking, questioning, always seeking—that is the only way to escape the throttling censorship of hyperbole, jargon and political correctitude.

Market as a Source of Censorship

I now come to the third and most potent contemporary source of censorship of language—that is, the market. With the growth of the free market in the affluent democracies of the world, even election campaigns became subservient to the advertisement blitzkrieg. Hyperbole acquired new dimensions, with the word being given visual and audio interpretations of such subtle technical complexity that the message became largely subliminal in effect. Advertisement borrows the language from literature, but distorts it for the market in a manner that the words are divested of their meaning, as, for example, when an advertisement says, 'Better than perfect', 'perfect' ceases to mean anything.

The more affluent an economy, the more pervasive, insidious and subliminal becomes the influence of the market. The development and refinements of technology see to it.

Not surprisingly, these days, literature itself has come to depend upon advertisement and publicity campaigns. The shift in the concern of the publishing world from readers to buyers has brought about a shift in the concerns of the writers themselves. In affluent societies, it can be seen in the omnipotence of the literary agent. In India, in Hindi literature at least, of which I know, it can be seen in the proliferation of big fat novels, using local dialects, full of immense details of everyday life of little known areas and communities, with a view to capturing an assured segment of the market. Call them readers if you like. I remember Khushwant Singh had tried this experiment in the *Illustrated Weekly* with resounding success. But such literature becomes an adjunct of the information media. It does not care to probe deeper than surface descriptions and prescriptions of the social malaise being projected by the media elsewhere. It thus becomes a captive of the market. The third world is the biggest loser in this game. The affluent world sees it only in terms of a large market. The multinational marketing giants today control the media and, through it, the minds of the people everywhere. Religion has come back into its own, reduced to rituals. It has always been a characteristic of decadent culture, with the media ready to embrace, project and even generate pop religion, with its attendant cults, rites and rituals. Switch on any channel on the TV and you are sure to catch some cult figure or the other, holding forth on some esoteric form of meditation and healing to escape from the stress generated by the materialistic society we live in. A materialism whose components we are taught to know, desire and cherish by the same channel most of the day. And so language grows a little more esoteric, clichéd and meaningless, as the market and rituals combine to dominate it.

The real danger of indirect, cultural, market-centred censorship lies in the fact that though it does not impose visible curbs on the right to think and seems to allow freedom of expression, it curbs or corrodes the ability to think and, finally, the desire to think for oneself. That is the ultimate subliminal censorship. One example: We find that in the past two decades, there is an increasing and excessive use of quotations in literary and social science discourses. In the field of philosophy, social sciences and literature, anything other than a statistic is only an opinion, not a fact. Quoting other opinions to buttress our own is a symptom of the fear of taking sole responsibility for what we think. The desire to think for oneself, by oneself and to stand by it alone is diminishing in a world which considers itself free and non-conformist.

I conclude that literature also, with other visual and plastic arts, can fight the subtle forms of censorship practised today. All of them retain multilinearity of thought. Literature has always found escape routes from power polemics by giving new multiple meanings to words. It can continue to do so in the future, if it is supported in some measure by the media.

Index